ENGLISH TEACHER'S BOOK OF INSTANT WORD GAMES

RUTH RICE

ENGLISH TEACHER'S BOOK OF ◁ ▷ INSTANT WORD GAMES

THE CENTER FOR APPLIED RESEARCH IN EDUCATION
West Nyack, New York 10994

Library of Congress Cataloging-in-Publication Data

Rice, Ruth.
    English teacher's book of instant word games / Ruth Rice.
      p. cm.
    "For grades 7–12, here are over 200 reproducible games that
provide fun, practice, and review of vocabulary, word origins,
punctuation, spelling and pronunciation, grammar and usage, names,
literary devices, and more!"
    ISBN 0–87628–303–2
    1. English language–Study and teaching (Secondary) 2. Word
games. I. Title.
LB1631.R515 1992   92–3208
                                              CIP

**THE CENTER FOR APPLIED RESEARCH
IN EDUCATION**
West Nyack, NY 10994
A Simon & Schuster Company

On the World Wide Web at http://www.phdirect.com

Printed in the United States of America

ABOUT THE AUTHOR

Ruth Rice has over 20 years' experience as a teacher at the secondary level, primarily in English and social studies. She has worked as a contributing editor for Scholastic Magazines and has published more than 80 sets of instructional materials for a variety of high school subjects ranging from art to zoology.

Ms. Rice has long been fascinated by the subtle, humorous aspects of language. In her travels through 35 countries she has collected many interesting facts about the world's languages.

She has a degree in general secondary education from the University of Northern Colorado.

The ability to use language distinguishes persons from animals, and the ability to use words well distinguishes an individual from the crowd. A person's success (in any field) depends—to a large extent—on skill in using words. As an English teacher, you are in a unique position to promote students' understanding of our language and to develop their skills in wielding words. The activities in *English Teacher's Book of Instant Word Games* will assist you in your task. For example:

- Words are not merely scrawls on a piece of paper or simple uttered sounds. They are extremely powerful tools that can charm and cheer, aggravate and amuse, inspire and intrigue, terrify and titillate. In every waking moment we are constantly being bombarded by words. Even in our dreams we employ them. It is utterly impossible to escape their influence, even for a short time. Wars have been fought over words, and elections have been lost because of words. A simple *yes* or *no* can change human destiny. It has been estimated that half the cost of most manufactured articles can be attributed to spoken or written words—words at board meetings, sales conferences, and on television and radio; words in newspaper ads and letters; words on order forms and tax forms, etc. Once students realize the truth of the statement that the pen *is* mightier than the sword, they will become fascinated with the study of language. Many of the activities in this book illustrate the significance and the power of words and help students to see their fascinating aspects.
- Words are slippery, elusive creatures, difficult to capture. Finding exactly the right word to convey a thought precisely is a difficult task but never a dull one. Mark Twain said that the difference between the right word and one that is almost right is like the difference between lightning and a lightning bug. The *English Teacher's Book of Instant Word Games* will help your students in their search for the right words.
- Words should be scrutinized as closely as a jeweler examines a diamond, studying its various facets to determine how its greatest brilliance can be revealed. Certain word games in this book provide microscopic examinations of words by showing their source, illustrating the changes they have undergone, or analyzing their elements.
- Words have great psychological impact. It has been shown, for example, that a person's name can influence other people's attitudes toward him or her. Certain words that are basically synonymous can have entirely different connotations in different situations, producing different impressions. Many of the instant word games included here illustrate this dimension of words.
- Words do not merely serve to inform or to convey impressions; they also produce sound effects that are pleasing to the ear. The devices that poets employ—such as alliteration, assonance, and rhyme—create verbal music. Students will explore the musical quality of words by using some of the special activities in this book.

The material in *English Teacher's Book of Instant Word Games* will not only inform and challenge your students, it will also entertain them, for many amusing devices are used to motivate even the least motivated students. Some of the word games employ puzzles, riddles, hidden messages, and other gimmicks that act as self-correcting features. (If the puzzle does not work out right, the student knows immediately that a mistake has been made and therefore can correct it at once.) Another important feature is that even though students may not know all the required facts and information in advance, they can determine the right answers from the various clues provided.

These word games are designed to supplement the basic textbook in English and, since they are short and versatile, can be fitted into your English program at many different points. They vary widely in difficulty, and therefore can be used with students at different levels of learning. Some of the word games are best suited for individual desk work, while others are useful for small group activities, contests, or oral discussion by the class as a whole. They are particularly useful on days when your lesson plan does not quite fill the time allotted and you have a few minutes left at the end of the class period. It is recommended, however, that with activities where there are certain rules involved (such as rules of punctuation, grammar, spelling, etc.), these rules should be reviewed before students start the activity, since space on the worksheets simply does not permit a complete explanation of the specific rules involved.

The activities in *English Teacher's Book of Instant Word Games* touch on almost every aspect of the language taught in secondary English classrooms: punctuation, parts of speech, types of clauses, prefixes, spelling, pronunciation, and more. But they also go far beyond that, giving students a much greater insight into the nature of language and those wonderful, winged, iridescent things we call words.

Ruth Rice

CONTENTS

Section 2
GRAMMAR AND USAGE ■ 45

Section 3
PUNCTUATION ■ 79

Activity Title	Skill/Topic
3–1 The Importance of Punctuation	punctuation marks
3–2 Types of Punctuation Marks	punctuation marks
3–3 Punctuation Rules	punctuation rules
3–4 Which Punctuation Mark?	punctuation rules
3–5 End Punctuation	end punctuation
3–6 Punctuating a Series	using commas
3–7 Punctuating Appositives and Adjective Clauses	using commas
3–8 Punctuating Interrupters	using commas
3–9 Punctuating Quotations	quotation marks
3–10 Apostrophes in Possessive Nouns	apostrophes
3–11 Apostrophes in Contractions	apostrophes
3–12 The Importance of Periods and Apostrophes	apostrophes
3–13 Common Abbreviations	abbreviations

Section 4
SPELLING AND PRONUNCIATION ■ 93

Activity Title	Skill/Topic
4–1 Rules for Spelling Plurals	spelling rules
4–2 Irregular Plurals	irregular plurals
4–3 Silent Letters	silent letters
4–4 I Before E	*i* before *e*
4–5 The Schwa	schwa
4–6 Words with Repeated Letters	words with repeated letters
4–7 The "Eyes" Words	words containing the sound of "eyes"
4–8 The "Seed" Words	words containing the sound of "seed"
4–9 Words Containing E's	words containing E's
4–10 Words Containing the Sound of $\overline{OO}$	words containing the sound of $\overline{OO}$
4–11 Words Containing the Sounds of $\overline{A}$ and $\hat{A}R$	words containing the sounds of $\overline{A}$ and $\hat{A}R$
4–12 Words Containing the Sounds of $\overline{E}$ and $\overline{I}$	words containing the sounds of $\overline{E}$ and $\overline{I}$
4–13 Words Containing the Sound of SH	words containing the sound of SH
4–14 Unusual Vowel Combinations	words with unusual vowel combinations
4–15 Words with ABLE and IBLE	adding suffixes
4–16 Doubling Letters Before Suffixes	adding suffixes
4–17 Adding Prefixes	adding prefixes
4–18 Similar Words Often Confused	confusing words
4–19 Synonyms	synonyms
4–20 Synonyms Inside Words	synonyms
4–21 Oodles of Synonyms	synonyms
4–22 Antonyms	antonyms
4–23 Antonym Chain	antonyms

Section 5
NAMES OF PEOPLE, PLACES, AND THINGS ■ 131

Section 6
LANGUAGE AS AN ART FORM ■ 149

Activity Title		Skill/Topic
6-8	Allusions to Fables, Myths and Literature	using allusions
6-9	Symbolism	symbolism
6-10	Parallel Proverbs	proverbs
6-11	Malapropisms	malapropisms
6-12	Oxymorons	oxymorons
6-13	Connotation	connotation
6-14	Sound Effects	sound effects in words
6-15	Tautonymic Expressions	sound effects in words
6-16	Inner Rhyme	sound effects in words
6-17	Vowel Change	sound effects in words
6-18	Echoic Words (Onomatopoeia)	sound effects in words
6-19	Rhyme	poetic devices
6-20	Rhyme Schemes and Stanzas	poetic devices
6-21	Rhythm	poetic devices
6-22	Concrete Poems (Calligrams)	poetic devices

Section 7
MISCELLANEOUS WORD GAMES ■ 173

Activity Title		Skill/Topic
7-1	October Quiz	vocabulary
7-2	Thanksgiving	vocabulary
7-3	Yuletide	spelling
7-4	January Game	spelling
7-5	Be My Valentine	expressions using the word "heart"
7-6	Presidents Day	names of Presidents
7-7	March Game	spelling
7-8	Easter Eggs	spelling
7-9	Arbor Day	spelling
7-10	Mother's Day and Father's Day	spelling
7-11	Shopping for Rhymes	rhymes
7-12	Hink Pink People	rhymes
7-13	Tom Twisties	word play
7-14	Animals in Sayings	animal sayings
7-15	Terms Related to Animals	animal words
7-16	More Animal Terms	animal words
7-17	Sounds Animals Make	animal words
7-18	Dogs	animal words
7-19	Colorful Expressions	expressions involving colors
7-20	Expressions Using UP	expressions using UP
7-21	Expressions Involving a Series	expressions involving a series
7-22	Expressions Involving Food	expressions involving food
7-23	Misleading Expressions	expressions that mislead
7-24	Terms Containing Body Parts	body parts found inside words
7-25	Expressions Involving Body Parts	body parts in expressions

Activity Title	Skill/Topic
7–26 Double Meanings	expressions with double meanings
7–27 Misinterpretations	understanding misinterpretation
7–28 Money Terms	terms related to money
7–29 Postal Abbreviations	abbreviations of state names
7–30 Gobbledygook	overstated speech
7–31 Letterspeak	shorthand speech
7–32 Daffy Definitions	inaccurate definitions
7–33 Baseball and Football Terms	sports terms
7–34 Words Containing Roman Numerals	Roman numerals inside words
7–35 Numerical Prefixes	numerical prefixes
7–36 The Wicked Witch	spelling
7–37 Break-Aparts	words that can be divided
7–38 Phobias	vocabulary
7–39 Repeated Words	repeated words
7–40 Most Beautiful Words	special words
7–41 The End	words with -end

ANSWER KEY ■ 215

1

DEVELOPMENT OF THE ENGLISH LANGUAGE

FROM OBSCURE TRIBES IN THE BRITISH ISLES, THE ENGLISH LANGUAGE SPREAD AROUND THE WORLD

1-1 STAGES OF DEVELOPMENT

The statements below deal with the development of the English language. Select words from the list at the top, writing the letter of your selection in the blank space at the left. These letters, when read from the bottom up, form a word related to this quiz. Write it here with its definition:

_____

A. Latin	E. elements	I. Bible	O. speech	S. modern
C. silent	G. borrowing	L. universal	P. Vikings	X. dictionary
D. spelling	H. Norman	N. textbook	R. Standard	Y. Saxons

_____ 1. Two Germanic tribes that invaded the British Isles in the fourth century were the Anglos and the _____, whose language became the basis of Old English.

_____ 2. In the eleventh century the _____ French invaded the British Isles and brought many new words, especially words dealing with government, law, fashion, and food.

_____ 3. The Norsemen, or _____, arrived later and left fragments of their language behind.

_____ 4. Scholars and the clergy introduced _____ and Greek words. At first these words were not used by the common people.

_____ 5. There were several different dialects of Middle English. Eventually the dialect of the East Midlands became _____ English.

_____ 6. Words were added to English by _____ from neighboring languages, such as Flemish, Dutch, and German. Through trade with distant lands, other words also entered the language.

_____ 7. Gradually words already in use were being used in new ways—as different parts of _____, in different contexts, or with entirely new meanings.

_____ 8. Many of the _____ letters in words such as *light* and *knife* were originally sounded. Later, when the pronunciation was changed, the spelling was not.

_____ 9. The first translation of the _____ into English was made during the 1300s by John Wycliffe, a scholar and religious reformer.

_____ 10. During the 1700s Samuel Johnson compiled a _____ of the English language, while Noah Webster did the same in the United States.

_____ 11. Thousands of new words are created every year, many using _____ already in existence, but only a small number of them endure over a period of time.

_____ 12. At the present time English may be considered the closest thing to a _____ language that the world has ever known, since it is spoken around the globe with many dialectal variations.

Name _____ Date _____

1-2 SYNONYMS FROM ANGLO-SAXON AND LATIN

Anglo-Saxon words were largely one-syllable or two-syllable words, while Latin words for the same things were generally words of several syllables. Listed below are words of Anglo-Saxon origin along with clues to their Latin counterparts. Fill in the missing letters.

Then write the circled letters in order here: _____

Now think of each of these letters as representing an entire word or a syllable. These letters will give you the answer to the question below. Write the answer on the line next to the question.

Where is everybody? _____

_____

ANGLO-SAXON WORDS	LATIN WORDS
1. weak	f r __ ◯ __ __
2. small	d i ◯ __ __ __ __ __ __ __
3. fear	c o n __ __ __ __ __ __ __ ◯
4. bold	a u ◯ __ __ __ __ __
5. ask	i n __ __ __ __ __ __ ◯ __
6. folk	p __ ◯ __ __
7. begin	c __ __ __ __ __ ◯ __ __
8. deep	◯ r o __ __ __ __ __
9. lonely	s o __ __ ◯ __ __
10. tale	◯ __ __ __ r __
11. leave	a b ◯ __ __ __
12. young	◯ __ __ __ __ __ l
13. house	d o __ __ ◯ __

BONUS

Pick any page in a dictionary and check to determine how many of the words on that page come from Latin. Write several of them below. Do any of the words have just one syllable?

1-3 LATIN AND GREEK SYNONYMS

Many words we use every day come from Latin and Greek and are synonyms of Anglo-Saxon words. For example, the Anglo-Saxon word *teacher* has its counterparts in the Latin *tutor* and the Greek *mentor*. Fill in the missing letters in the sets of words below. Then place the circled letters in order in the answer to this question: Why didn't the cowardly dragon observe the Sabbath?

Because he only _____ on _____ _____.

ANGLO-SAXON	LATIN	GREEK
1. rim	circumference	◯_____ e r
2. witchcraft	s ◯_____	magic
3. chide	reprimand	c r _____◯
4. roving	m _ g_____◯	nomadic
5. sorrowful	doleful	m◯_____
6. problem	predicament	◯____ m a
7. ◯_____p	adore	idolize
8. bliss	rapture	◯____ s y
9. madman	l _ _◯_ _	maniac
10. y a_____◯	standard	criterion
11. c h____ l ◯_	immature	unsophisticated
12. strong	powerful	d y◯_____
13. wordbook	d◯_____	lexicon
14. riddle	conundrum	e _ _◯_ _
15. s m__◯_ _	suffocate	asphyxiate
16. tease	torment	t a _◯_____
17. funny	h_____◯	comical

BONUS

What is unusual about the reply to the question at the top? Explain on the back of this sheet.

Name _____ Date _____

1-4 LATIN PHRASES

Latin may be considered a "dead" language by some, but in a very real sense it is alive. We use many Latin prefixes and suffixes in our English words, and we also employ Latin phrases (such as those below) in many situations. In Part 1, select the meaning of each phrase from the list at the top and write it to the right of the phrase, placing the circled letter in the blank at the left. These letters will form a word made from two Greek elements—a word that represents something quite rare in the English language. Look up the word and write it and its definition on the following line:

_____

Part 1

The v(o)ice of the people is the voice of God
For the (g)ood of the public
One from (m)any
(L)et the buyer beware
P(e)ace be with you

I(n) the year of our Lord
Time flie(s)
Always fa(i)thful
Bef(o)re the war

_____ 1. Anno Domini: _____

_____ 2. Pax vobiscum: _____

_____ 3. Vox populi, vox Dei: _____

_____

_____ 4. Caveat emptor: _____

_____ 5. Ante bellum: _____

_____ 6. Pro bono publico: _____

_____ 7. Semper fidelis (Marine Corps motto): _____

_____ 8. Tempus fugit: _____

_____ 9. E pluribus unum (on the Great Seal of the U.S.):

_____

Part 2

Look up the following mottoes and write their meanings on the back of this sheet.

Annuit coeptis (on the Great Seal of the U.S.)

Sic semper tyrannus (motto of Virginia)

Nil sine numine (motto of Colorado)

Semper paratus (motto of the Coast Guard)

Name _____ Date _____

1–5 WORDS FROM EUROPEAN COUNTRIES

The words below came into English from European languages. Unscramble the name of each language. If you do it correctly, the names will be listed in alphabetical order.

ENGLISH WORDS

LANGUAGE SOURCE

1. pistol, robot   _____ (HEZCC)

2. cookie, cruise   _____ (TUDHC)

3. camouflage, chassis   _____ (CHNERF)

4. cobalt, hamburger   _____ (MERGAN)

5. tragedy, alphabet   _____ (KEREG)

6. goulash   _____ (RAGNAHINU)

7. geyser   _____ (LACECIIND)

8. notorious, brogue   _____ (SHIRI)

9. volcano, madonna   _____ (LITANIA)

10. tapioca, caste   _____ (USETUGREOP)

11. pastrami   _____ (MANINARO)

12. mammoth, vodka   _____ (SURSINA)

13. plaid, galore   _____ (CHOSSITT)

14. suede   _____ (SHEDISW)

BONUS

Scandinavian words (Old Norse) often start with *sc* or *sk,* as in *sky, scold,* and *scrub.* Look in the *sc* and *sk* sections of your dictionary and find several words of Scandinavian origin. Write them on the back of this sheet.

Name _____ Date _____

1-6 WORDS FROM THE ROMANCE LANGUAGES

French, Italian, Portuguese, and Spanish are languages that developed from Latin, the language of the Romans. For that reason they are referred to as the Romance languages. English borrows words and phrases directly from Latin as well as from these other Latin-based languages. In the four paragraphs below, fill in the missing vowels in order to form words that make sense in these short stories. Then count all the A's you supplied. There should be twenty, if you have spelled the items correctly.

FRENCH WORDS:

Pierre drove his car into the (1) g__r__g__. Then he called his (2) f___n c___ [a beautiful (3) b r__n__t t__] and suggested that they (4) r__n d__z v___s at a (5) r__s t___r__nt and then go shopping for (6) __n t__q___s.

ITALIAN WORDS

When the (7) s__p r__n__ and her husband [a (8) v___l__n player] finished making a recording at the (9) s t__d___, they went home and cooked some (10) m__c__r__n__ for their supper. They spent the rest of the evening gambling at a (11) c__s__n__.

SPANISH WORDS

José lit a (12) c__g__r and stepped outside of his small (13) __d__b__ cottage into the evening air. A (14) m__s q___t__ buzzed around his head, and he swatted it. Then he looked up and saw a bird swoop down the (15) c__n y__n and up toward the distant (16) m__s__.

PORTUGUESE WORDS

When the little boy was served a bowl of (17) t__p___c__, he said, "I want some (18) m__l__s s__s and (19) c__s h__w nuts on it." Unfortunately, his mother had none of either. The boy whined and complained until she finally commanded, "Stop that (20) p__l__v__r."

1–7 WORDS FROM ASIA, THE MIDDLE EAST, AND THE PACIFIC ISLANDS

Match each set of words with the language from which it comes. You will be able to guess some of them, but you may need to use a dictionary for others. You will know whether you have matched the words and languages correctly if you see words appear vertically and horizontally in the diagram after you transfer the letters entered on the blank lines appropriately.

```
                    ┌───┐
                    │ S │
              ┌───┬─┴───┴─┬───┐
              │ 1 │  10   │ 6 │
          ┌───┼───┼───┬───┼───┼───┐
          │11 │10 │ 8 │ 5 │ 9 │   │
      ┌───┼───┼───┼───┼───┼───┼───┬───┐
      │ 1 │10 │ 3 │10 │ 8 │ 7 │ 9 │   │
  ┌───┼───┼───┼───┼───┼───┼───┼───┼───┐
  │ S │10 │ 8 │10 │ 3 │ 7 │ 4 │10 │ 8 │
  └───┼───┼───┼───┼───┼───┼───┼───┼───┘
      │ 6 │ 5 │ 8 │ 7 │ 1 │ 9 │10 │
      └───┼───┼───┼───┼───┼───┼───┘
          │ 9 │ 7 │ 4 │ 9 │10 │
          └───┼───┼───┼───┼───┘
              │ 9 │10 │10 │
              └───┼───┼───┘
                  │ 8 │
                  └───┘
```

—— 1. tycoon, jujitsu   A. Persian

—— 2. bungalow, thug, shampoo   C. Hindi (**a major language of India**)

—— 3. kibitz, bagel, kosher   D. Arabic

—— 4. zenith, cotton, sofa   E. Chinese

—— 5. ukulele, hula, aloha   G. Japanese

—— 6. bosh, tulip   I. Hawaiian

—— 7. khaki, shawl, bazaar   L. Tagalog (**language of the Philippines**)

—— 8. boomerang, kangaroo   M. Turkish

—— 9. boondocks   N. Hebrew and Yiddish

—— 10. tea, kowtow   P. Malay

—— 11. bamboo, batik   R. Australian aborigine

BONUS

Many Arabic words start with *al.* These letters are placed before words in the same way we place *the* before words in English. Two examples are *algebra* and *alcove.* In a dictionary, find other examples of words from Arabic that start with *al.* List them on the back of this sheet

1–8 WORDS FROM NATIVE AMERICAN LANGUAGES

Native Americans have provided us with numerous words and names. In fact, twenty-six of our states have names based on Native American words. Two of these names will be revealed in the marked vertical column below if you can identify the words of Native American origin defined here.

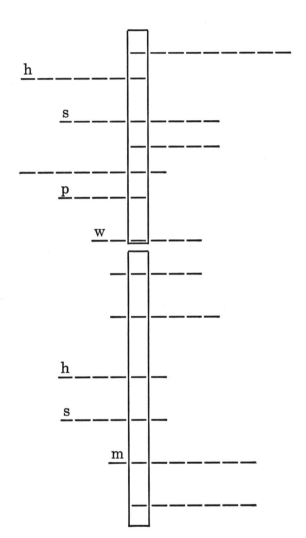

1. Another name for a groundhog

2. A hardwood tree that produces a small nut
   h _ _ _ _ _ _ _

3. A combination of beans and corn
   s _ _ _ _ _ _

4. A large member of the deer family

5. A soft leather shoe

6. A type of thin-shelled nut grown in the warmer part of the U.S.
   p _ _ _ _ _

7. A hut used by Native Americans
   w _ _ _ _ _

8. A small animal noted for its unpleasant odor

9. Slang for money (originally this referred to shells strung like beads)

10. Hulled corn with the germ removed
    h _ _ _ _ _

11. A yellow vegetable from a plant in the gourd family
    s _ _ _ _ _

12. A short coat of a heavy wool fabric (usually with a plaid design)
    m _ _ _ _ _

13. A species of cone-bearing tree that may reach a height of 300 feet

BONUS

Look up the meaning of the Native American words that formed the names of the two states revealed above. Write your answers on the back of this sheet.

1-9 WORDS FROM WILLIAM SHAKESPEARE

Scholars tell us that Shakespeare probably added about 5,000 new words to the English language. Among them are those defined below. Fill in the letters that complete the suggested words, placing the circled letters at the left. They will form the three words needed to complete this story:

A certain boy had trouble getting enough sleep because he owned a dog that barked a lot at every sound he heard during the night. The boy decided to name his dog Macbeth. Why?

Because Macbeth _____ _____ _____.

_____ 1. Jealous: g_____ - e___◯

_____ 2. Indecent, repulsive: ◯__ s_____

_____ 3. The murder of some public official: a_____◯___

_____ 4. A clue, a suggestion: ◯____

_____ 5. Dark and dismal: g____◯_

_____ 6. Thrifty: f__◯____

_____ 7. A game in which one person stoops down and another jumps over him or her:

_____◯__

_____ 8. To shrink or decrease: d w___◯___

_____ 9. Amusing, ridiculous: l a_____◯

_____ 10. To go hastily: h_◯__

_____ 11. The act of wooing a woman: c_____◯___

_____ 12. Outstanding, superior: e_____◯___

_____ 13. Solitary, depressed at being by oneself: ____◯__

_____ 14. To depend on: _◯__

_____ 15. Deliberate, planned ahead: ◯r_____

Note: Some other common words that Shakespeare was first to use are: *auspicious, barefaced, critic, exposure, suspicious, pedant, hot-blooded, acceptance,* and *eventful.*

BONUS

Look through one of Shakespeare's plays and find several expressions used in his day that are no longer in use. Write them on the back of this sheet.

Name _____ Date _____

1–10 PHRASES FROM WILLIAM SHAKESPEARE

Shakespeare's plays contain many expressions that we still use today, some of which are in the slang category, such as the phrase "He done me wrong." Fill the blanks in the phrases and sentences using the words listed below. Then, in the diagram, connect the dots in the order in which you used the words. These two sets of dots will form numbers that represent Shakespeare's age when he died in 1616.

end •   • wit   blind •   • elbow

self •   • beat   bag •   • hot

fate •   • world   there •   • light

Greek •   • idiot   fall •   • cold

1. "Brevity is the soul of _____."

2. "The beginning of the _____" (the final stages)

3. "To thine own _____ be true."

4. "_____ it." (Go away.)

5. "The _____ is my oyster."

6. "A blinking _____" (a fool)

7. "It's all _____ to me." (incomprehensible)

8. "Love is _____."

9. "_____ room" (room to move around)

10. "Not so _____" (not very good)

11. "He left, _____ and baggage." (He took everything along.)

12. "It's neither here nor _____." (not to the point)

13. "Don't _____ for it." (Don't be deceived by it.)

14. "To catch a _____" (get the sniffles)

Note: Here are additional expressions Shakespeare originated, many of which you have probably used at some time:

"A method in his madness"   "Single blessedness"
"Loved not wisely but too well"   "A sorry sight"
"The seamy side"   "Out of the question"
"Flaming youth"   "Spotless reputation"
"Star-crossed lovers"   "In my mind's eye"

Name _____ Date _____

1–11 PHRASES FROM MIGUEL DE CERVANTES

At the same time that Shakespeare was writing his plays in England, Miguel de Cervantes was producing great works, such as *Don Quixote,* in Spain. Many of our sayings come from his writings, including those listed below. Fill the blanks with words selected from the list at the top, crossing out the words as you use them. The remaining five words will form another expression originated by Cervantes. Write it here:

_____

FAIR	GIVE	YET	WISE	WORD
BOND	LIMIT	DEVIL	EGGS	FORGIVE
THE	BORN	HAVES	HIS	PUDDING
PIE	DUE	KETTLE	THROW	LEAF

1. "The pot calling the _____ black"

2. "Mum's the _____."

3. "To turn over a new _____"

4. "The sky's the _____."

5. "A finger in every _____"

6. "You haven't seen anything _____."

7. "The proof of the _____ is in the eating."

8. "The _____ sex" (**in reference to women**)

9. "_____ with a silver spoon in his mouth"

10. "Putting all your _____ in one basket"

11. "Within a stone's _____" (**not far**)

12. "The _____ and the have-nots"

13. "His word is as good as his _____."

14. "A word to the _____ is sufficient."

15. "_____ and forget."

Name _____ Date _____

1-12 PROVERBS FROM JOHN HEYWOOD

John Heywood, an English writer, lived about the same time as William Shakespeare. He is credited with popularizing many sayings we still use today. In 1546 he published a book of these sayings, some of which are listed below. One word is missing in each saying. Locate the words in the diagram, circling each as you find it. (The words are in both horizontal and vertical positions.) The letters remaining in the diagram will form another of Heywood's proverbs. Write the proverb here:

_____

```
A   P   E   N   P   A   U   L
N   Y   H   G   I   F   T   F
O   R   E   Y   T   U   R   N
O   L   A   U   C   R   T   A
H   E   D   O   H   A   Y   I
W   A   S   T   E   U   H   L
G   P   H   B   R   O   O   M
H   A   N   D   S   T   T   S
```

1. "Haste makes _____."

2. "Look before you _____."

3. "Two _____ are better than one."

4. "Little _____ have big ears."

5. "Don't look a _____ horse in the mouth."

6. "Robbing Peter to pay _____"

7. "A new _____ sweeps clean."

8. "Make _____ while the sun shines."

9. "One good _____ deserves another."

10. "Hitting the _____ on the head"

11. "Many _____ make light work."

12. "Strike while the iron is _____."

Note: Listed below are more of John Heywood's sayings:

"Half a loaf is better than none."   "Beggers can't be choosers."

"To rule the roost"   "Rome wasn't built in a day."

"A horse of another color"   "A burnt child fears fire."

Name _____ Date _____

1–13 DOUBLETS

Doublets are words slightly different in form and meaning that are really just variations of the same single word. They have come into English through the borrowing from different languages at different periods of time. The words *dignity* and *dainty* are examples of this process. *Dignity* came directly into English from the Latin word *dignitas*. The French borrowed the same Latin word and changed it to *deintie*. When the English borrowed the word *deintie* from the French, the spelling was changed to *dainty*. Identify the doublet for each word below. A definition is given for the missing word. Then, in the diagram, connect the letters corresponding to the circled letters in order to form a word that is not a doublet but that has a doubled sound. (In connecting the dots you may have to pass through another dot when you are connecting two other letters.)

```
B•   U•   Y•   E•   D•   H•

W•   F•   X•   L•   G•   O•

P•   S•   K•   T•   J•   M•

A•   V•   C•   I•   Z•   Q•
```

1. cape   _ Ⓞ _ (head covering)

2. plum   Ⓞ _____ (dried plum)

3. vote   Ⓞ ___ (solemn promise)

4. person   ___ Ⓞ ___ (minister)

5. hotel   _____ Ⓞ ___ (place where sick people are treated)

6. reason   ___ Ⓞ ___ (a fixed allowance)

7. chaplain Ⓞ _____ (a small building or room for worship)

8. imply   _____ Ⓞ (to hire)

9. frail   _____ Ⓞ _ (easily broken)

10. canker   _____ Ⓞ _ (malignant tumor)

11. canal   _ Ⓞ _____ (riverbed or body of water that joins two larger bodies)

12. jetsam   _____ Ⓞ _ (to throw goods overboard to lighten the weight)

13. ward   Ⓞ _____ (one who defends or protects)

14. twill   _____ Ⓞ (a rough woolen fabric)

Name _____ Date _____

1-14 PREFIXES

Throughout the history of the English language new words have been formed by adding prefixes and suffixes to existing words. For example, the word *television* was formed from the Greek prefix *tele* (far) and *vision,* which comes from a Latin word meaning "see." For each pair of roots below you can add the same prefix. (The definition of the prefix is given in parentheses.) After you identify all the prefixes, write the circled letters in order in the spaces below. They will form two unusual words that have something in common. Do you know what it is?

F _ _ _ _ _ _ _ _ _ _   _ _ _ _ _ _ _ _ _ _ _

1. _ _ O _ _ _ (across, through)   _____mit, _____fer

2. _ _ _ O _ _ (around)   _____navigate, _____ference

3. _ _ O (before)   _____pare, _____caution

4. _ _ O _ _ (between)   _____vene, _____sect

5. _ _ O (bird)   _____ation, _____ary

6. O _ _ _ _ (all)   _____present, _____vorous

7. _ O _ (under)   _____terranean, _____marine

8. O _ _ _ _ _ (above)   _____sede, _____intendent

9. _ _ _ O _ _ (false)   _____nym, _____science

10. _ _ O (all)   _____-American, _____orama

11. _ _ O (life)   _____logy, _____degradable

12. _ _ _ O _ (small)   _____scopic, _____biology

13. _ _ _ O (half)   _____circle, _____conscious

14. O _ (outside)   _____terior, _____clude

15. O _ _ _ (new)   _____classic, _____phyte

16. _ _ _ O _ (light)   _____graphy, _____synthesis

17. O _ _ _ _ (self)   _____biography, _____mobile

18. _ _ _ O _ _ (book)   _____graphy, _____phile

BONUS

Try to find examples of Latin and Greek prefixes that have the same meaning, such as *uni* (Latin) and *mono* (Greek), both of which refer to the number one. Write at least one example on the back of this sheet.

1-15 SUFFIXES

Throughout the history of the English language new words have been formed by adding suffixes to existing words in order to form new parts of speech. For example, we add *ly* to the adjective *rapid* to form the adverb *rapidly*. To each word below, add the letters that will form the part of speech indicated. The circled letters, when written in order, will give you the answer to this riddle:

A woman gave a beggar a dollar. The woman was the beggar's sister, but the beggar was not her brother. How is this possible?

___ _____ ___ ___ _____.

CHANGE THE...

1. verb to a noun	amuse	＿＿＿＿Ｏ
2. noun to another noun	child	Ｏ＿＿＿
3. adjective to a noun	dark	＿Ｏ＿＿
4. verb to an adjective	agree	＿Ｏ＿＿
5. verb to an adjective	differ	Ｏ＿＿
6. verb to a noun	break	＿Ｏ＿
7. noun to another noun	phrase	＿＿＿Ｏ＿
8. noun to an adjective	comic	Ｏ＿
9. noun to an adjective	element	＿Ｏ＿
10. noun to an adverb	home	Ｏ＿＿＿
11. adjective to a verb	authentic	Ｏ＿＿
12. noun to an adjective	danger	＿＿Ｏ
13. noun to another noun	friend	＿Ｏ＿＿
14. noun to an adjective	hope	＿Ｏ＿＿
15. adjective to another adjective	second	＿Ｏ＿
16. noun to an adjective	poison	＿＿Ｏ
17. verb to a noun	collect	Ｏ＿＿
18. noun to an adjective	fool	＿Ｏ＿
19. verb to an adjective	absorb	＿＿Ｏ
20. noun to an adverb	clock	＿＿＿Ｏ
21. verb to a noun	sail	＿Ｏ

Name _____ Date _____

1–16 ROOTS

Listed in the columns below are words with only their prefixes and suffixes shown and definitions of roots to be inserted. Find the correct roots, insert them, and place their corresponding numbers in the spaces at the left. Then transfer these numbers to the squares in the diagram to form a magic square in which the vertical, horizontal, and diagonal numbers all have the same total.

A	B	C	D
E	F	G	H
I	J	K	L
M	N	O	P

_____ A. dis_____ion (**twist**)

_____ B. pre_____ion (**write**)

_____ C. pro_____ile (**throw**)

_____ D. trans_____ted (**send**)

_____ E. pre_____able (**say**)

_____ F. in_____ible (**believe**)

_____ G. re____al (**live**)

_____ H. para_____ology (**mind**)

_____ I. re____ation (**new**)

_____ J. mono_____atic (**color**)

_____ K. con____tion (**come**)

_____ L. e_____ent (**see**)

_____ M. con____ential (**faith**)

_____ N. re_____or (**bend**)

_____ O. in_____ible (**hear**)

_____ P. im_____al (**death**)

1. mort
2. script
3. ject
4. fid
5. dict
6. ven
7. chrom
8. psych
9. nov
10. viv
11. cred
12. vid
13. mit
14. flect
15. aud
16. tort

BONUS

Duc is a root that we use a great deal in English words. On the back of this sheet, try to think of several different prefixes and suffixes that can be used with this root.

1–17 ORIGINS OF WORDS

Given below are descriptions of certain words and their origins. Find the words in the diagram by starting with *C* and taking every third letter until you complete a word. Write the word next to its description. To avoid confusion, circle the letters as you use them. You will go through the letters three times in order to find the ten words.

C	F	E	U	I	N	R	A	U	F	S	C	E
C	L	W	O	E	D	O	U	A	N	S	N	I
E	D	O	S	E	N	C	L	N	A	I	I	P
O	F	E	N	T	H	D	Y	O	E	U	G	S
K	W	S	U	A	E	L	S	R	E	H	T	L

_____ 1. **To get away** (made from two words meaning "out of your cloak," because in getting away your cloak might be pulled off)

_____ 2. **The center or heart of something, such as an atom** (from a word that originally referred to a nut or kernel)

_____ 3. **A yellow flower** (named for the tooth of a lion, because its petals resemble teeth)

_____ 4. **A vegetable with many layers** (related to the word *one*, since many layers form one item)

_____ 5. **Nonsense** (from swill fed to pigs)

_____ 6. **A sweet course at the end of a meal** (from a French term meaning "to clear the table")

_____ 7. **A stringed musical instrument** (from Hawaiian words meaning "jumping insect," since the fingers jump back and forth when it is played)

_____ 8. **A scheduled time for people to be off the street** (from French words meaning "cover the fire")

_____ 9. **A mistake, a failure** (from an Italian word for *flask*, since glass-blowers often failed in their attempts to make perfect flasks)

_____ 10. **A slang term for "very good" or "attractive"** (believed to have been derived from the middle portion of the word *magnificent*)

Name _____ Date _____

1–18 MORE WORD ORIGINS

In the puzzle, find the words that fit the definitions below, all of which have interesting origins. The words are either in vertical or horizontal positions in the puzzle. The remaining letters (ignore the squares) will form a phrase of nautical origin. Write it here:

_____

```
L   B   R   A   M   S   H   A   C   K   L   E
A   E   P   T   P   W   E   ■   E   N   T   ■
D   H   E   S   O   P   H   O   M   O   R   E
Y   S   T   E   L   D   E   ■   V   I   ■   L
B   U   T   T   E   R   S   C   O   T   C   H
U   R   I   A   C   R   O   W   B   A   R   N
G   L   C   D   A   S   S   A   S   S   I   N
T   Y   O   H   T   E   D   ■   E   E   P   ■
B   ■   A   F   T   E   R   M   A   T   H   L
■   U   T   E   S   D   A   I   S   Y   E   A
```

_____ 1. **An insect** (named in honor of Our Lady, the Virgin Mary)

_____ 2. **A lady's undergarment** (originally a small coat worn by men under their armor)

_____ 3. **A term for a skunk** (from a French word for a chicken, since the skunk was a chicken thief)

_____ 4. **Falling apart** (from Icelandic words meaning "very twisted")

_____ 5. **Consequences** (from words meaning "a later mowing" in reference to hay)

_____ 6. **Haughty or arrogant** (related to the words *sir* and *sire*, and originally used to describe someone who acted like a knight)

_____ 7. **A tool used as a lever** (given its name because the point of the tool resembles a bird's beak)

_____ 8. **A kind of candy** (from the name of one of its main ingredients and an old word meaning "to cut or score," since the candy was cut into pieces after it was cooled)

_____ 9. **A second-year college student** (from Greek words meaning "a wise fool")

_____ 10. **A murderer** (from Arabic words meaning "a user of hashish")

_____ 11. **A flower whose name means "eye of the day"**

1–19 COMPOUNDS

New words can be formed by combining two existing words. Usually the new word has a relationship to the original words (*bookcase*). Sometimes, however, the meaning of the new word is quite different from the original terms, as in the case of *buttercup*. Compounds may consist of more than two words, and in some instances may be hyphenated (*devil-may-care*). Some compound expressions are not joined at all (*high school*).

Part 1

Many different parts of speech can be combined to form compounds. Examples of several different types are given below. Try to think of additional examples. The person who locates the most correct examples in the allotted time is the winner.

1. Noun plus noun (**tabletop**): _____

_____

2. Noun plus adjective (**airtight**): _____

_____

3. Adjective plus noun (**blackberry**): _____

_____

4. Verb plus noun (**scarecrow**): _____

_____

5. Verb plus adverb (**touchdown**): _____

_____

6. Adverb plus verb (**income**): _____

_____

7. Adverb plus adjective (**evergreen**): _____

_____

8. Noun plus verb (**cloudburst**): _____

_____

9. Compound phrase (**know-it-all**): _____

_____

Part 2

Some surnames are compounds, such as *Shakespeare*. Look at a telephone directory and find several examples to list on the back of this sheet.

♦ ♦ ♦ ♦

Note: Some of our common words are considered to be "buried" compounds, such as the word *lord*, which was made from two words (*hlaf* and *weard*) that meant "bread giver." Similarly, *hussy* came from *hus* and *wyf*, which meant "house wife."

Name _____ Date _____

1-20 CLIPPED WORDS

New words can be formed by shortening existing words. Usually the end is clipped, as when *advertisement* was shortened to *ad*. But in some cases the front of the word is clipped, as in the case of *steroid* being shortened to form the slang term *roid*. On rare occasions a double clip occurs (*prescription* shortened to *scrip*). Write the original term from which each of the following clips was made. Then, in the diagram, shade in the circled letters to reveal the shape of a letter that when placed several times among the letters NDVSBLTY will form an unusual word. Write the word here and tell what is unusual about it: ____

A	L	C	E
F	M	I	B
G	N	Q	P
Q	R	S	W
U	V	T	Y

1. gas   _ _ _ _ _ Ⓞ _ _ _ _

2. props   _ _ _ _ _ _ Ⓞ _ _ _

3. fax   _ _ _ Ⓞ _ _ _ _

4. con   _ _ _ Ⓞ _ _ _

5. cord (**cloth**)   _ _ _ _ _ _ _ Ⓞ

6. coon   Ⓞ _ _ _ _ _ _ _

7. flu   _ Ⓞ _ _ _ _ _ _

8. seal (**animal**)   _ _ _ _ _ Ⓞ _ _ _   (**two words**)

9. math   _ _ _ _ _ _ Ⓞ _ _ _ _

10. perm   _ _ _ _ _ _ Ⓞ _ _ _

11. pol   _ _ _ _ _ _ Ⓞ _ _ _

12. perk   _ _ _ Ⓞ _ _ _ _ _ _

13. zines   Ⓞ _ _ _ _ _ _ _ _

14. hood   _ _ _ _ _ Ⓞ _

BONUS

On the back of this sheet, list other examples of clipped words. One that was developed in recent years, for example, is *temp* for *temporary worker*. Numbers 3 and 13 above are also examples of recent clips. The examples you list may be old or new.

Name _____ Date _____

1–21 BLENDS

The ain was apprehended. This sentence doesn't make sense, since *ain* is not a word. To turn it into a word you must add the same letter in four places. Discover what the letter is by following the directions that follow. Then write the word here: _____

One way to form new words is to blend two existing words by eliminating some letters from one or both. A classic example is the word *smog*, which is a blend of *smoke* and *fog*. Another good example is *mimsey*, coined by Lewis Carroll by blending *miserable* and *flimsy*. Identify the second word from which each blend below was made. Then connect the circled letters in order in the diagram to form the missing letter to insert in *ain* to make a word.

```
A   B   C   D
E   F   G   H
I   J   K   L
M   N   O   P
```

1. dumfound: dumb plus _____◯

2. brunch: breakfast plus ____◯_

3. telecast: television plus ◯_____

4. Comsat: _____◯_____ plus satellite

5. Spam (**brand name**): _____◯_ plus ham

6. stagflation: stagnation plus __◯_____

7. bit (**computer term**): binary plus __◯___

8. hazmat: ◯_____ plus material

9. chunnel: _____◯ plus tunnel

10. moped: motor plus ◯_____

11. lox: liquid plus ◯_____

12. tangelo (**fruit**): __◯_____ plus pomelo

13. cremains: ____◯_____ plus remains

BONUS

On the back of this sheet, try putting some words together to make an interesting blend of your own. For example, if you have a friend who treats you badly at times, you might refer to that friend as a *frenemy* (friendly enemy). Or you might refer to a difficult problem as a *bafflemma* (baffling dilemma). Vote on a winner from all the blends created by the members of your class.

Name _____ Date _____

1–22 ACRONYMS

Acronyms are words formed by using the initial letter or letters of several words. *NATO,* for example, is made from the first letters of *North Atlantic Treaty Organization. FBI,* on the other hand, is not considered an acronym because the letters are stated individually rather than being pronounced like a word. Occasionally, an acronym becomes so widely accepted that the letters are no longer capitalized, and we think of it as an ordinary word. The word *cop,* for example, originally came from the words "constable on patrol." Supply the missing word in each set below. The circled letters will give you the answer to this mystery:

A man who was very tired and wanted to get a long night's sleep went to bed at 8:00 and set his alarm for 9:00 the next morning. Why was he still extremely tired when the alarm went off? Write the answer here:

1. AWOL: Absent ____ _ ____ Leave
2. OPEC: Organization of __ _____ Exporting Countries
3. SAT: __ _____ Aptitude Test
4. NASA: National Aeronautics and __ _ ___ Administration
5. MADD: Mothers Against _____ Driving
6. PAC: Political Action __ _____
7. NOW: National Organization for _____ __
8. PUSH: _____ _ United to Save Humanity
9. OSHA: Occupational _____ and Health Administration
10. ASCAP: American __ _____ of Composers, Authors, and Publishers
11. CARE: Cooperative for _____ Relief Everywhere
12. AIDS: Acquired _____ Deficiency Syndrome
13. WASP: _ ___ Anglo-Saxon Protestant
14. RIF: Reduction in __ ____
15. MASH: Mobile Army __ _____ Hospital
16. RADAR: _ ____ Detection and Ranging
17. MIA: ___ _____ in Action
18. COLA: Cost of _____ Adjustment
19. PIN: Personal Identification _____ _
20. GATT: General Agreement on _____ _ and Tariffs
21. SWAT: Special ____ _____ and Tactics

BONUS

Think of at least one other common acronym. Write it on the back of this sheet, along with the words from which it was made.

Name _____ Date _____

1-23 EPONYMS

A number of words in English are derived from the names of people—people from many parts of the world, such as those mentioned below.

PART 1

Match each definition with its word from the list at the top by placing the number of the word in the space at the left. Then transfer these numbers to the math problem, forming three whole numbers and two fractions that will add up to exactly 100.

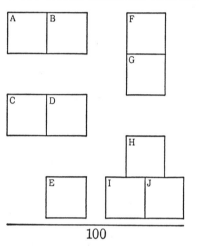

0. derrick
1. melba toast
2. praline
3. draconian
4. sideburn
5. saxophone
6. boycott
7. petrel
8. diesel
9. Machiavellian

_____ A. A type of seabird named after a saint

_____ B. A framework over an oil well, named after a seventeenth-century English hangman

_____ C. A type of candy named after a French count whose cook invented it

_____ D. A facial hair style named after a Civil War general

_____ E. A musical instrument named after a Belgian manufacturer

_____ F. A word meaning "severe" or "harsh," from the name of a Greek lawgiver

_____ G. A refusal to deal with someone, from the name of a land agent in Ireland

_____ H. A term meaning "deceitful" or "cunning," from the name of an Italian statesman and writer

_____ I. A type of crisp bread named after an Australian opera star

_____ J. A type of engine invented by a German engineer

Part 2

In each category below words made from the names of people are listed. Select several of them, look them up, and find out after whom they were named. On another sheet of paper summarize your findings.

Foods: Tootsie Roll, Baby Ruth bar, eggs Benedict
Clothes: cardigan, leotard, Levi's
Weapons: colt, Gatling gun, shrapnel
Science: ampere, volt, fahrenheit
Flowers: dahlia, poinsettia, gardenia, magnolia, fuchsia

Name _____ Date _____

1–24 WORDS FROM BRAND NAMES

Certain words that were once strictly brand names have been used so much that they have become generic words and have lost the capital letters they had originally as registered trademarks. For example, we now use *xerox* as a verb (to xerox something). Below are definitions of some such items that have become general terms or are in the process of becoming so. Place them in the spaces in the diagram as indicated. Numbers **1** and **2** will be horizontal, and the rest will fit into them vertically.

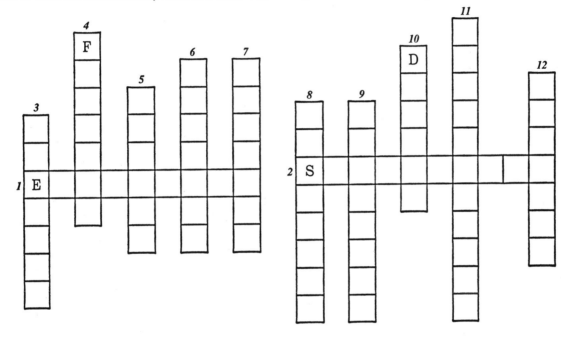

1. A power-driven set of stairs

2. Preshrunk (**cloth**)

3. A vacuum bottle

4. Laminated plastic used on kitchen counters

5. A nonstick coating used on pots and pans

6. An agent who sells homes and land

7. A small, white, pain-relieving tablet

8. A petroleum-based ointment

9. Table tennis

10. A synthetic polyester fabric

11. The process of coloring motion pictures by combining three-color photographs

12. An adhesive bandage for small wounds

Note: Several other words in this category are linoleum, Kleenex, Styrofoam, Frigidaire, and Scotch tape. (You may still see them capitalized, but they are gradually becoming generic terms and are often used without capital letters.)

1–25 GENERALIZATION AND SPECIALIZATION

Generalization is the process by which a word with a specific, restricted meaning later develops broader application, permitting its use in a variety of situations. Frequently, a word purely concrete in nature generalizes into terms with abstract significance. The color words are good examples. For instance, a Communist may have been referred to as a "red," and if he was caught committing a crime, he might have been described as "a red caught red-handed."

Part 1

All the definitions below refer to similar double uses of a single color. Write the color interpretation next to each item.

1. A healthy Communist sympathizer: _____

2. A beginner on the golf course: _____

3. A sad member of royalty: _____

4. A coward who writes for sensational tabloids: _____

5. A Caucasian purchasing a useless object at a garage sale: _____

6. Rejected by warlocks and witches: _____

7. A Nazi storm trooper frying meat: _____

8. A dismal day for members of the Confederate Army: _____

9. A lazy woman who uses her feminine charms on men: _____

10. An eloquent man with a pocketful of coins: _____

Part 2

Specialization is the opposite of generalization. Try to identify the words described here that have undergone this process:

1. _____ originally meant to die (in any manner), but now it means to die from hunger.

2. _____ originally referred to all types of food, but now it refers to products from animals, such as steaks, hams, etc.

3. _____ originally referred to any animal, but now it refers to a specific animal, the male of which has antlers.

4. _____ originally designated any grain, but now it refers just to the grain that grows in ears on tall stalks.

5. _____ originally referred to any liquid, but now it refers only to intoxicating liquids.

Name _____ Date _____

1–26 A MYSTERIOUS EXAMPLE OF GENERALIZATION

Given below are clues to a certain word. Read just one clue and try to guess the word. Then read the second clue. The person who identifies the word in the fewest clues is the winner.

1. This is a common word used every day.

2. It is a simple three-letter, one-syllable word.

3. It is of Anglo-Saxon (Old English) origin.

4. It is related to ON (Old Norse) and OHG (Old High German) words.

5. It may be used as a noun or a verb.

6. It is sometimes combined with other words to form compounds, such as "___ ___ ___way" and "home ___ ___ ___."

7. Originally it meant simply "to dash or move rapidly."

8. As a verb it has a variety of meanings, such as the following: to flee, to operate, to enter a contest, to unravel, to go back and forth, to dissolve or turn to liquid, to track down, to extend, etc.

9. As a noun it has a number of meanings as well, including the following: an enclosure for animals, the general tendency of something, a series, freedom of movement, and a score in baseball.

10. This word is often used with adverbs or prepositions following it, such as *away, around, across, along, into,* etc.

THIS WORD IS _____.

BONUS

Look up this mystery word in an unabridged dictionary and read over some of its definitions. In the space below write several sentences illustrating different uses of the word.

_____

_____

_____

_____

_____

_____

1-27 ELEVATION AND DEGENERATION

Elevation is the process by which a word with a humble beginning later gains prestige. Degeneration is the opposite process, in which a respectable word develops an unpleasant connotation. Identify the scrambled words below, for which the original and present meanings are given.

Examples of Elevation

ORIGINAL MEANING	PRESENT MEANING	
1. servant	clergyman	_ _ _ _ (TRIMSINE)
2. kneader of bread	a woman of refinement	_ _ _ (YLDA)
3. horsemanship	noble code of conduct for knights	_ _ _ _ (CRYLAVIH)
4. boy, youth	a mounted military man devoted to the service of his lord	_ _ _ (GINTKH)
5. keeper of a pigsty	a food superviser at an institution or on a train or plane	_ _ _ (WESTDRA)
6. foolish	having a liking for	_ _ (DONF)

Examples of Degeneration

ORIGINAL MEANING	PRESENT MEANING	
7. boy	a tricky, deceitful fellow	_ _ (VENAK)
8. lack of ease	illness	_ _ _ (SEESAID)
9. cheap	foul, repulsive	_ _ (LIVE)
10. soothsayer	smart aleck	_ _ _ (SACEEWIR)
11. a Christian	a person who is abnormal mentally and maybe physically	_ _ (RITENC)
12. happy, innocent	foolish	_ _ (YLILS)
13. one who works on the lord's estate	a scoundrel or a criminal	_ _ _ (LIVINAL)

© 1992 by The Center for Applied Research in Education

1-28 FUNCTIONAL SHIFT

When a word that originally was used as only one part of speech later is used as another, this constitutes functional shift. For example, the word *go* was a verb in the beginning, but now we use it in other ways, such as an adjective in this expression: Everything is in go condition. *Cocoon,* originally only a noun, in recent years has been used as a verb meaning to stay at home in a secure, warm environment. In each sentence below, underline the word that has undergone a functional shift, as indicated. Then take the first letters of the words you underlined and connect them in order in the diagram, passing through letters when necessary to make the connection. The result will be "for the birds."

R• S• T• D• G• O• F• P• Y•

L• C• A• J• M• D• V• B• U•

1. Early in the morning residents of New York City sardine themselves in the subways. (**noun changed to a verb**)

2. A crazy with a gun suddenly emerged from the crowd and started shooting. (**adjective changed to a noun**)

3. The political candidate instructed his assistants to leaflet the entire neighborhood. (**noun changed to a verb**)

4. Maybe we should give that problem a careful rethink. (**verb changed to a noun**)

5. Tube socks originated in the seventies and were very popular for a while. (**noun changed to an adjective**)

6. I think we should junk that suggestion at once, since it is totally lacking in merit. (**noun changed to a verb**)

7. The advertisement said, "Gift her with mink." (**noun changed to a verb**)

8. Otters sometimes den beneath fallen trees. (**noun changed to a verb**)

9. He ordered a hamburger, fries, and a cup of coffee. (**verb changed to a noun**)

10. He was driving around in a prowl car when he saw the store being robbed. (**verb changed to an adjective**)

11. The trend in education seems to be to eliminate the frills and to get back to the basics. (**adjective changed to a noun**)

12. The insurance agent suggested that I buy an umbrella policy for protection in case of liability. (**noun changed to an adjective**)

BONUS

Look through newspapers and find other examples, such as *spin control, to parent, to warden,* etc.

1-29 BACK FORMATION AND FOLK ETYMOLOGY

Read the following paragraphs, which explain the two word processes of back formation and folk etymology. From the clues given you should be able to fill in the blanks very quickly. The first person to complete the exercise is the winner.

Words formed through back formation are the result of a mistake—a false analogy. Since the plurals of most English words end in *s*, people assumed that *pease* was plural, and therefore started using (1) _____ as the singular. Similarly, the word *staves* was turned into the singular (2) _____, though originally the singular for *staves* was *staff*. By the same process, *cherise* (a singular form assumed to be plural) was shortened to (3) _____ (a fruit used in pies), and *statistics*, a word used only in plural form originally, now has the singular form (4) _____. One word that escaped this process is *measles*, which has never been mistaken for a plural and changed to *measle*.

The second type of false reasoning involves the creation of false verb forms from nouns that end in *ar*. The Teutonic ending *ar*, as in *beggar*, sounds like the *er* or *or* ending we use in words such as *teacher* and *sailor*, which were made from the verbs *teach* and *sail*. As a result, people mistakenly made the verb (5) _____ from *beggar* and the verb (6) _____ from *burglar*.

Folk etymology, like back formation, depends on a mistake—substituting a meaningful term for one not understood. Children frequently do this. Example: A child who lived in Hollywood once recited the opening of the Lord's Prayer this way: "Our Father, who art in Heaven, Hollywood be thy name." By this process letters may be dropped or rearranged, as when *a napron* became (7) *an* _____, and *an ekename* became (8) *a* _____. The incomprehensible Dutch word *pijjeker* was changed to (9) _____ _____ (a short jacket worn by sailors), and the Dutch *wys saeger* became *wiseacre*, because these words held meaning for English speakers whereas the originals did not. Similarly, the Native American word *wujack* (the term for a certain small animal) became (10) _____. In World War I American soldiers referred to the French street *Rue Pigalle* as (11) _____ Alley, and in World War II, Livorno (an Italian city) became *Leghorn*. What word will be next to undergo a transformation?

Name _____ Date _____

1–30 SLANG

Slang is a delightful form of informal speech that has added many new words to the English language. Complete the paragraphs below by selecting words from the list at the top. (Ignore the circled letters until you have completed the paragraphs.) Then take the circled letters from the first six words on the list and rearrange them to form a metaphorical slang term for a pretty girl. The circled letters from the four other words will form another such term when rearranged.

Write the two terms here: _____   _____

jarg(o)n   c(o)lor
p(o)etry   sh(o)ck
convenien(t)   stan(d)ard
appropria(t)e   (f)leeting
per(m)anent
h(a)bitual

Slang serves four main purposes. First, it has a definite (1) _____ value, for its uniqueness startles the uninitiated listener. Second, slang makes secrecy possible, for with a (2) _____ of its own, a subgroup of society can exclude outsiders. Third, slang adds (3) _____ to language, for slang terms are often more expressive than the words they replace. (S. I. Hayakawa has referred to slang as "the (4) _____ of everyday life.") And finally, in certain situations slang terms are often the best, shortest, and most (5) _____ terms to use.

Slang terms often have a (6) _____ quality. A term that is all the rage for now may hardly be remembered several years later. But some slang terms—even some that were originally considered crude and vulgar, such as the word *mob*—later gain respectability and become a (7) _____ part of our language.

Slang is a desirable ingredient in language, but it should be used sparingly. When it ceases to facilitate thought and becomes a substitute for it, it is no longer effective. The (8) _____ overuse of slang identifies the user as a person who is unaware of the richness and subtle qualities of (9) _____ English and unaware of its effective use. But the use of just the right slang term at the (10) _____ occasion can add sparkle to one's speech and delight the listener.

Name _____ Date _____

1–31 OBSOLESCENT AND OBSOLETE WORDS

Several thousand new words enter the language each year, and at the same time others are lost through lack of use. At one time, for example, people referred to eyeglasses as "spectacles," and food as "victuals." Today we seldom hear these terms, since they are obsolescent (going out of use), and eventually they may be completely obsolete (dead). The sentences below contain sixteen obsolescent or obsolete terms. From the clues provided in the sentences, try to determine their meanings. Write your guesses in the spaces at the bottom, placing definitions for the first word at the left and for the second word at the right.

1. He *bangled* away his inheritance through too much *jollification.*

2. *Dabbly* weather over a long period makes the ground *sposhy.*

3. The sound of that *yaffle* banging his beak on the tree trunk is *janglesome.*

4. The judge, in his white *peruke,* looked solemn as he sentenced the criminal, who squirmed and looked very *carked.*

5. As I *soodled* through the forest, I saw several *pillygrubs* crawling up a tree trunk.

6. When I looked up toward the *fell* after the rain, I saw some lovely *glints* through the trees.

7. He is a *gormless fibster,* and I don't want him as a friend.

8. He didn't need to go to the *ordinary* to get a drink, since he had a bottle stored in his *settle.*

1. _____ | _____

2. _____ | _____

3. _____ | _____

4. _____ | _____

5. _____ | _____

6. _____ | _____

7. _____ | _____

8. _____ | _____

Note: Check with your teacher to see how many you got right. If you particularly like any of these words, you might want to start using them. If a trend such as this gets started, words could be revived!

Name _____ Date _____

1-32 NEOLOGISMS AND NONCE WORDS

A nonce word is a word that is coined to fit a single situation, is used on that one occasion, and may never be heard again. Victor Neuburg, for example, once referred to another man's remarks as "ostrobogolous piffle." You will find *piffle* in the dictionary but not *ostrobogolous,* a word Mr. Neuburg made up to insult the other man.

A true neologism is a word that is completely new—not formed from any existing prefixes, roots, or suffixes and not related to any existing word. Neologisms are pure inventions. We have very few such words. The five paragraphs below describe several of them, though even a couple of these are doubtful. Try to identify them.

1. An Irishman in Dublin made a bet that he could get a word accepted into the dictionary. He made up a four-letter, meaningless word and wrote it on walls and fences all over the region where he lived. People started questioning its meaning, so the term came to be associated with questions, and now it means "a short test." This word is _____.

2. A manufacturer of an early camera wanted a unique word to identify it. He thought the letter *K* was a forceful letter, so he tried several combinations of letters with it, coming up with the brand name of _____.

3. The young nephew of mathematician Edward Kasner was asked what he would call a huge number consisting of the number *1* followed by 100 zeros. He suggested a word that in a way resembles the number, since it contains several *O*'s. This word is _____.

4. Another word that is believed to be a neologism is _____, though no one knows about its origin for certain. It starts with *sk*, consists of nine letters, and means "to run away." Sometimes it is used as a command.

5. Texas Congressman Maury Maverick coined a word to designate complex language that is hard to understand (such as the language often used in legal documents and government directives). One example of this type of language is the term "tension-supported frame structure" to refer to a tent, or "vertical personnel distributor" for elevator. Mr. Maverick's term for such language is _____. (It might not be a pure neologism, since part of the word resembles a preexisting word, the sound made by a turkey.)

Note: Three other words considered to be pure inventions are *gizmo, gimmick,* and *gadget.* All three start with the letter *g* and are synonyms for "whatchamacallit." It seems whenever people come across any item for which no name exists, they hastily invent one.

BONUS

Try to invent a word of your own to fit a particular situation.

1–33 NEW WORDS IN POLITICS AND GOVERNMENT

Robert Louis Stevenson said, "Politics is perhaps the only profession for which $\frac{}{12}\ \frac{}{7}$

$\frac{}{10}\ \frac{}{6}\ \frac{}{9}\ \frac{}{10}\ \frac{}{1}\ \frac{}{6}\ \frac{}{1}\ \frac{}{8}\ \frac{}{11}\ \frac{}{7}\ \frac{}{12}$ $\frac{}{11}\ \frac{}{2}$ $\frac{}{8}\ \frac{}{5}\ \frac{}{7}\ \frac{}{3}\ \frac{}{4}\ \frac{}{5}\ \frac{}{8}$ $\frac{}{12}\ \frac{}{9}$ $\frac{C}{}\ \frac{}{9}\ \frac{}{2}\ \frac{}{2}\ \frac{}{1}\ \frac{Y}{6}$."

To complete this statement, first complete the sentences below with words selected from the list, placing the circled letters in the blanks at the left. Then transfer the circled letters to the corresponding numbered spaces above.

linkage   humint   gag   detente
quota   fairness   floater   shuttle
sinophobia   disinformation third   polemologist
hegemony   Miranda

____ 1. The _____ warning is a statement of legal rights that must be read to a suspect at the time of an arrest.

____ 2. _____ consists of distorted facts deliberately given out by government officials.

____ 3. Under a _____ system, an employer must hire a specified percentage of minority members.

____ 4. A _____ order prohibits the news media from reporting on matters under consideration by the court.

____ 5. The underdeveloped nations of the world constitute the _____ world.

____ 6. The policy of giving political parties equal time on TV is known as the _____ doctrine.

____ 7. An undecided voter is referred to as a _____.

____ 8. _____ diplomacy involves much traveling back and forth by officials who conduct negotiations.

____ 9. _____ refers to the method of bargaining by which one point cannot be resolved unless other issues are considered along with it.

____ 10. A _____ is an expert in the study of war, while an irenologist studies peace.

____ 11. The gathering of information (spying) through human intelligence is _____, while the use of electronic mechanisms is elint.

____ 12. The influence of a strong nation over the others in a group is referred to as _____.

1–34 NEW WORDS IN BUSINESS AND INDUSTRY

Among the many new terms that have entered the English language in recent years are those listed below. Match each term with its definition by placing the word in the blank at the end of the definition. Also place the circled letter from the term in the space at the left. These letters will spell another new word. Write it here and explain its meaning in your own words:

_____

(f)lextime   gen(t)rification   ba(n)kable
middle (m)anager   (j)ob action   de(s)killing
(p)roduct liability   garb(o)logy   gi(v)e-back
dem(a)n   ki(l)obyte   (t)urnaround time
man-mon(h)   har(d) copy   wastep(l)ex

_____ 1. Simplifying a process so that a worker need not be highly skilled to perform it:

_____

_____ 2. A business that takes a variety of waste materials from other industries and recycles them: _____

_____ 3. The length of time required to complete a certain process: _____

_____ 4. An executive who supervises daily operations but does not participate in establishing company policy: _____

_____ 5. A company's responsibility for any harm its products may cause:

_____

_____ 6. A system that allows employees to select their own work schedules to suit their needs: _____

_____ 7. A 1,000-symbol unit of computer memory capacity: _____

_____ 8. To reduce the work force: _____

_____ 9. The conversion of an area of deteriorating housing in a city into one of higher property value in order to encourage middle-class people to return:

_____

_____ 10. The surrendering of benefits gained by a union during an earlier contract negotiation with management: _____

_____ 11. The study of trash in order to get clues to a society's culture, buying habits, etc.:

_____

_____ 12. Capable of producing a profit: _____

Name _____ Date _____

1–35 NEW TERMS IN SCIENCE AND MEDICINE

Hundreds of new terms dealing with science and medicine have entered our language in recent years. A few are listed below. Place them in the sentences, putting their item letters in the space at the left of each sentence. Then transfer these letters to the corresponding spaces in the square at the top in order to form words horizontally and vertically.

2	9	4	8	3
9	9	8	5	9
4	8	1	7	9
8	5	7	9	6
3	9	9	6	7

A. ecodoom

E. astration

G. echocardiogram

H. autotransfusion

I. zootoxins

L. controlled substance

N. seed bank

O. biomaterial

R. ozone shield

S. exobiology

T. cryopreservation

V. infrasonics

_____ 1. _____ is any substance that can be used to construct artificial organs or replace body tissues or parts.

_____ 2. When a doctor transfers a patient's own blood back into his body during surgery, it is known as _____ .

_____ 3. _____ refers to the freezing of living tissues, such as corneas, for reuse.

_____ 4. Extensive destruction of the environment resulting in an upset of the balance of nature is known as _____ .

_____ 5. _____ are poisons, such as snake venom, that are produced by animals.

_____ 6. A facility where seeds of endangered plant species are stored, studied, and propagated is a _____ .

_____ 7. The study of possible life on other planets in our solar system is _____ .

_____ 8. The _____ is a layer of gas above the earth that filters out some of the sun's ultraviolet rays.

_____ 9. The process by which new stars are formed is _____ .

BONUS

Find the three terms on the list above that were not defined. On the back of this sheet, write the words and their definitions. (You may need to do a little research, if you don't already know these terms.)

Name _____ Date _____

A certain artist drew the following picture of a dog and named it $\overline{}\ \overline{}\ \overline{}$
                                                                    1 2 10

$\overline{12}\ \overline{10}\ \overline{5}\ \overline{7}\ \overline{9}\ \overline{8}\ \overline{10}\ \ \overline{12}\ \overline{4}\ \overline{11}\ \overline{11}\ \overline{6}\ \overline{3}$,

To discover the title, match each item below with its definition, and then transfer the letters to the spaces above.

A. earthworks   L. kinetic art

C. bluegrass   M. crossover

E. salsa   N. soft sculpture

G. heavy metal   O. new wave

H. wrapping   R. rocker

I. hard edge   T. op art

K. sound sculpture   W. overdub

_____ 1. Art that tricks the eye by creating an optical illusion

_____ 2. Art that involves draping cloth or plastic over a building, mountain, or other structure

_____ 3. A three-dimensional structure of various textures of stuffed cloth

_____ 4. Outdoor art involving changes in the landscape, such as digging out areas, building mounds, etc.

_____ 5. Art that includes moving parts

_____ 6. Art involving definite geometric shapes

_____ 7. A type of country music

_____ 8. Music that combines elements of two or more different styles in order to attract a wider audience

_____ 9. A sophisticated form of punk rock

_____ 10. A type of Caribbean dance music

_____ 11. Loud rock music with a heavy beat

_____ 12. To blend several layers of sound in a recording

BONUS

Write the two words that were not defined above on the back of this sheet. Write definitions for them by guessing their meanings. You will probably be right, since the names give clues to their meanings.

1–37 NEW TERMS IN SPORTS

Among the many new sports terms are those listed below. Match each with its definition by placing the number of the item next to the definition. Then, in the diagram, shade in the spaces with the numbers you used. The unshaded portion will form a shape that suggests a sport.

1. dunemobile	10. desi
2. heliskiing	11. parasailing
3. superfecta	12. yokozuna
4. paralympics	13. duck hook
5. sailoff	14. Zamboni
6. crackback	15. enforcer
7. snurfing	16. spearing
8. Fosbury flop	17. slamdunk
9. rallycross	18. kickturn

_____ A. Soaring in a parachute towed by a vehicle or boat

_____ B. A basketball shot made by jumping high and slamming the ball into the basket

_____ C. A type of auto racing on a short course

_____ D. The highest rank in sumo wrestling

_____ E. Skiing on high mountains reached by helicopter

_____ F. A sideward movement on a skateboard executed by pivoting on the back wheel

_____ G. Riding over snow on a board resembling a surfboard

_____ H. A vehicle designed to drive over sand

_____ I. An aggressive ice hocky player who intimidates opponents

_____ J. In football, illegal ramming of an opponent with a helmet

_____ K. A vehicle used to smooth surfaces on ice rinks

_____ L. A tenth player in a baseball lineup who is the designated hitter

_____ M. A race of sailing vessels

_____ N. A golf shot in which the ball curves erratically

_____ O. Sports competition for people in wheelchairs

BONUS

On the back of this sheet, try to define the three words on the list that are not defined above.

1–38 NEW TERMS FOR TYPES OF PEOPLE

In recent years a number of new "types" of people have appeared in the English language, such as *hotliners* (people who host radio call-in talk shows). A number of others are listed below. Place the number of each one next to the proper definition. Then shade in the blocks containing the numbers you used. The shaded portion will form the oldest letter of the alphabet, according to the *Guinness Book of World Records.*

1	2	3
4	5	6
7	8	9
10	11	12
13	14	15

1. ecofreak
2. workaholic
3. roadie
4. second lady
5. aerophobe
6. mission controller
7. Archie Bunker
8. right-to-lifer
9. Trekkie
10. oval officer
11. TMer
12. steel magnolia
13. ghost
14. godfather
15. denturist

_____ A. A person who works constantly and cannot relax (also known as a "type A personality")

_____ B. A fan of the TV show *Star Trek*

_____ C. A dental technician who fits false teeth

_____ D. A person hired to help actors or singers on tour

_____ E. A member of the President's staff

_____ F. A Mafia leader

_____ G. A person who is overly enthusiastic about protecting the environment

_____ H. A bigoted, self-righteous member of the blue-collar class

_____ I. An influential and powerful southern woman

_____ J. Wife of the Vice President of the U.S.

_____ K. An absentee who is counted as present

_____ L. A person who directs space flights from a command center

BONUS

On the back of this sheet, list the three words not defined above and write definitions for them. You can probably guess their meanings.

Name _____ Date _____

1–39 NEW WORDS FOR FOODS AND FASHIONS

Many new food products have been developed in the last thirty or forty years, as have a number of new fashions. All of the foods and fashions described below consist of two words, such as *coolie coat* or *TV dinner*. Identify the two-word terms defined below. Then rearrange the circled letters to form a popular brand name for food, and rearrange the boxed letters to form a well-known brand name for clothing. Write them here:

_____   _____

FOODS

1. A frankfurter with chili con carne on it: c _ _ _ _ _ _ ▯ _ _

2. A cookielike breakfast bar usually made with oatmeal, raisins, and nuts:
   g _ ▯ _ _ _ _ _   _ _ _ _

3. Food high in calories but low in nutrition: _ _ _ _ _ _   _ _ _ _▯

4. Corned beef, Swiss cheese, and sauerkraut on rye bread:
   R _ _ _ _ _ _   ◯ _ _ _ _ _ _ _

5. A high-nutrition, canned drink for people on a diet:
   l _ _ _ _ _ _ _   p _ _ _ ◯ _ _

6. An alcoholic drink made of pineapple juice, coconut milk, and rum: p _ _ _ _
   c _ _ _ _ ◯

FASHIONS

7. A tight-fitting shirt or blouse that is snapped between the legs: b _ _ _ _
   s _ _ ◯ _

8. A cord or leather necktie with a clasp: b _ _ _ _   _ ▯ _

9. A knitted covering for the legs that extends from the ankle to the upper leg: ◯ _ _
   w _ _ _ _ _ _

10. Socks with no heels: t _ _ ◯ _ _ _ _ _ _

11. A look produced by several garments of various types and lengths worn over one
    another: l▯_ _ _ _ _ _   _ _ _ _ _

12. A type of hat resembling those worn by hunters in Africa: s◯_ _ _ _ _   h _ _ _

13. A suit for informal wear that has an open collar, shirtlike jacket, and casual look:
    l _ _ ▯ _ _ _   s _ _ _ _

Name _____ Date _____

1-40 NEW NAMES FOR NEW PRODUCTS

If Rip Van Winkle had gone to sleep about twenty-five or thirty years ago and awakened recently, he would be astounded at the number of unfamiliar terms we have for items that did not exist at the time he fell asleep. Identify the new products described below, placing their names in the vertical spaces as indicated. The letters in the shaded boxes will spell the names of two more new products.

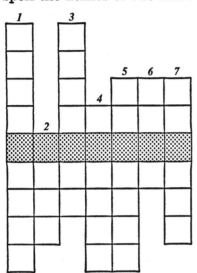
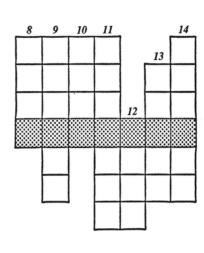

1. _____ is the trademark of an artificial grass used on playing fields.

2. A _____ tab is a metal tab used to open cans of soda.

3. A _____ bullet is made of PVC and used in riot control.

4. A _____ is a device for killing insects by attracting them to light and using electricity or microwaves to destroy them.

5. _____ is the brand name of a device that swirls water in a bathtub.

6. A hand-held hair dryer that directs warm air for styling hair is a _____ dryer.

7. Weapons that consist of two nontoxic chemicals that become deadly when combined are _____ weapons.

8. A _____ is a pipe for smoking marijuana or hashish.

9. A long, narrow, upward-curving bicycle seat is called a _____ seat.

10. The _____ of life is a hydraulic mechanism shaped like a pair of scissors that is used in rescue work to get people out of crushed automobiles, etc.

11. A device that automatically copies a person's signature is an _____.

12. A _____ restraint is a device attached to the top of a car seat to prevent injury to the neck in a crash.

13. Sun _____ is a cream that protects the skin from sunburn better than a sunscreen does.

14. _____ is the trademark for a strong but lightweight fiber used in making bulletproof vests.

Name _____ Date _____

1–41 BRITISH ENGLISH

It has been estimated that approximately ten percent of British words differ from ours in spelling, meaning, or grammatical use. In Britain, for example, the spellings *theatre, colour,* and *cheque* are used rather than our spellings of *theater, color,* and *check.* Many words have different pronunciations as well, such as *lieutenant,* which is pronounced as if it were spelled *leftenant.* Americans, it seems, started changing the language immediately after disembarking from the *Mayflower.* From the list below, select the American counterparts for the British terms, all of which deal with food and transportation—terms a tourist might need to know. Write the American term beside the British term, and place the circled letter from the word you select at the left. These letters will complete the following British message:

Give ___ ___ _ _____ ___ ____ _____.

What does this mean? Write the American version here:

_____

fru(i)t pie	pea(n)ut	ov(e)rpass	t(r)unk	(m)uffler
mo(l)asses	de(s)sert	link (s)ausage	h(o)od	gaso(l)ine
oatm(e)al	p(o)tato chip	biscui(t)	(h)orn	traffic circl(e)
crac(k)er	ham(b)urger	(w)indshield	fe(n)der	(t)ruck

_____ 1. silencer (**on a car**): _____

_____ 2. a sweet: _____

_____ 3. banger: _____

_____ 4. crumpet: _____

_____ 5. tart: _____

_____ 6. wing (**on a car**): _____

_____ 7. biscuit: _____

_____ 8. petrol: _____

_____ 9. roundabout: _____

_____ 10. crisp: _____

_____ 11. groundnut: _____

_____ 12. lorry: _____

_____ 13. hooter: _____

_____ 14. porridge, gruel: _____

_____ 15. wimpie: _____

_____ 16. treacle: _____

_____ 17. bonnet (**on a car**): _____

_____ 18. windscreen: _____

_____ 19. flyover: _____

_____ 20. boot (**on a car**): _____

1–42 AUSTRALIAN ENGISH

English developed in quite a different way in Australia. For one thing, Australians pronounce long *a*'s like long *i*'s. (A bison is a plice where Austrilians wash their fice.) They also have a number of colorful terms we don't use. Often the meanings can be guessed by using a little imagination. For instance, you can see why a mongrel dog is called a *bitzer*. (He's a bit of this and a bit of that.) Match each "Strine" (Australian) term at the left with its American version at the right by placing the letter of your choice in the space at the left. Then, in the diagram, connect the letters with three separate lines—one line for items 1 through 5, another for 6 through 10, and a third for items 11 through 17. These lines, along with the others in the diagram, will form three letters that make up a slang Australian term for an Englishman.

```
A  B      C  D      E  F  G
                |
H—I      J  K      L  M  N
                |
O  P      Q  R      S  T  U
```

_____ 1. bloke

_____ 2. jackeroo

_____ 3. sheila

_____ 4. a roly-poly

_____ 5. boomer

_____ 6. real dinkum

_____ 7. shivoo

_____ 8. mob

_____ 9. muster

_____ 10. tinny

_____ 11. jumbuck

_____ 12. outback

_____ 13. tucker

_____ 14. donk

_____ 15. to mizzle

_____ 16. smoodger

_____ 17. station

A. a young girl

B. tumbleweed

C. truth

D. party, spree

E. food

F. kettle

G. to complain

H. cowboy

I. big kangaroo

J. chicken

K. herd

L. remote bush region

M. fool

N. flatterer

O. man

P. water hole

Q. can of beer

R. roundup

S. sheep

T. wild dog

U. ranch

GRAMMAR AND USAGE

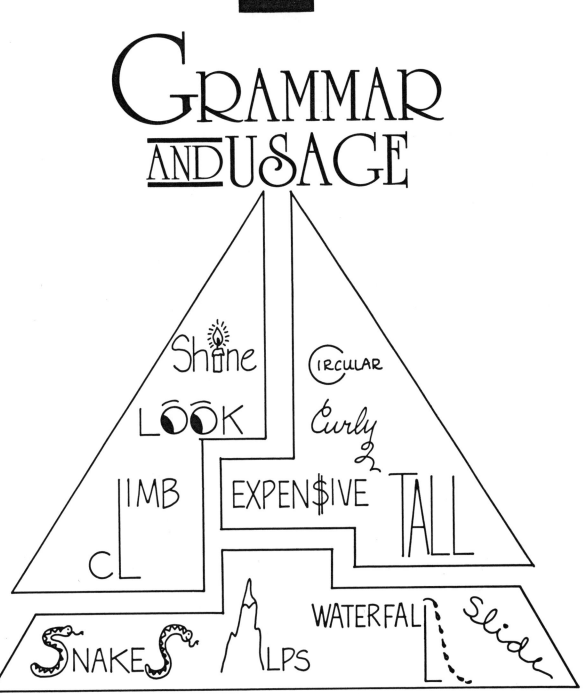

Name _____ Date _____

2-1 PARTS OF SPEECH

Identify the part of speech of each underlined word and write the name of that part of speech in the proper vertical column, starting at the top and leaving blank whatever spaces you don't need at the bottom. If you do it correctly, a word will magically appear in the shaded boxes. What is unusual about the beginning and ending of this word?

Write your answer here: _____

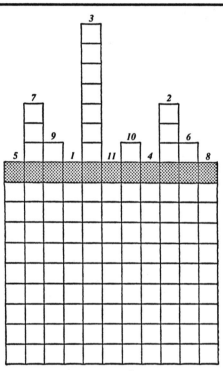

1. From this hill on a <u>clear</u> day you can see for miles.
2. <u>Clear</u> the snow off the walk as soon as possible.
3. <u>Wow</u>, what a performance he gave!
4. Our club meets <u>monthly</u>.
5. Our last <u>monthly</u> meeting accomplished little.
6. The cat climbed <u>up</u> the ladder right behind me.
7. That dealer may <u>up</u> the price on new cars next week.
8. The <u>up</u> side of this situation is that the robber stole very little.
9. Though I like Melvin, I won't vote for <u>him</u>.
10. Tie the horse <u>fast</u> to the post.
11. The label on this cloth says the color is <u>fast</u>.

BONUS

Two parts of speech were not included in the exercise above. The word *but* in the following sentences illustrates these two parts of speech. Write the part of speech next to each sentence in the blank provided.

_____ *But* is a three-letter word.

_____ JoAnn went to the play, *but* I stayed home.

2-2 TYPES OF NOUNS

Identify the types of nouns described below and then transfer the circled letters to the following quotation from R. Buckminster Fuller:

"$\overline{1}\ \overline{12}\ \overline{10}$, $\overline{6}\ \overline{12}$ $\overline{5}\ \overline{13}$ $\overline{4}\ \overline{6}$ $\overline{7}\ \overline{13}\ \overline{13}\ \overline{5}\ \overline{7}$, $\overline{4}\ \overline{7}$ $\overline{14}$ $\overset{V}{\underline{13}}\ \overline{11}\ \overline{3}$, $\overline{8}\ \overline{12}\ \overline{6}$ $\overline{14}$

$\overline{8}\ \overline{12}\ \overline{2}\ \overline{8}$, $\overline{9}\ \overline{11}\ \overline{12}\ \overline{9}\ \overline{13}\ \overline{11}$ $\overline{12}\ \overline{11}$ $\overline{4}\ \overline{5}\ \overline{9}\ \overline{11}\ \overline{12}\ \overline{9}\ \overline{13}\ \overline{11}$."

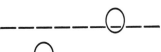

1. A noun that refers to just one person or thing (**box, mouse**)

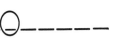

2. A noun that refers to several persons or things (**boxes, mice**)

3. A noun made from a verb that still retains some qualities of a verb, such as gerunds (**swimming**) and infinitives (**to fight**)

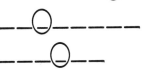

4. A noun that refers to a male (**father, boy**)

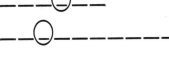

5. A noun that refers to a female (**lady, girl**)

6 A noun that refers to sexless objects (**cup, book**)

7. A noun that shows ownership and contains an apostrophe (**Andy's, Rover's**)

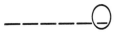

8. A noun that is not capitalized and that refers to a class of persons, places, or things rather than a specific object (**mountain, city**)

9. A noun that is capitalized and refers to a specific person, place, or thing (**Mt. Rushmore, Cleveland**)

10. A noun that is made up of two words (**Englishman, houseboat**)

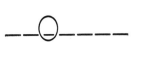

11. A noun that consists of several words (**Fourth of July, Duchess of Kent**)

12. A noun that refers to a group and may be considered singular in some instances and plural in others (**committee, class**)

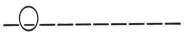

13. A noun that names a physical object that can be seen and touched (**cheese, candle**)

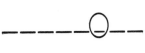

14. A noun that names a quality or idea—something that cannot be seen or touched (**patriotism, love**)

2–3 TYPES OF OBJECTS

Direct objects receive the action of the verb. Indirect objects tell to whom or for whom something is done. Objects of a preposition come in phrases with a preposition preceding them. Each of the sentences below contains all three types of objects. Place each type of object in the chart. If you do it correctly, you should see a pattern developing in the first two columns.

What is this pattern? _____

1. The zookeeper gave the zebra an apple from the bag.

2. Did you show Yolanda that book about Houdini?

3. Take Theresa this bowl of fruit.

4. When Mr. Phelps died, he left his son a house in Florida.

5. He sold me his old kit of carpenter tools.

6. I taught her the basic rules of tennis.

7. After school, why don't you show Debbie that trick?

8. Last summer Grandpa told Carrie a variety of ghost stories.

9. Did you lend Bob this volleyball for the tournament?

10. This sauce with lemon juice gives baked apples real zest.

INDIRECT OBJECT	DIRECT OBJECT	OBJECT OF PREPOSITION
1. _____	_____	_____
2. _____	_____	_____
3. _____	_____	_____
4. _____	_____	_____
5. _____	_____	_____
6. _____	_____	_____
7. _____	_____	_____
8. _____	_____	_____
9. _____	_____	_____
10. _____	_____	_____

BONUS

On the back of this sheet, list all the prepositions you can think of. The person with the longest list is the winner.

Name _____ Date _____

2-4 DIRECT OBJECTS

Samuel Taylor Coleridge defined _ _ _ _ _ _ _ as "words in their best order" and
_ _ _ _ _ _ _ _ as "the _ _ _ _ _ _ words in the best order." To discover the three words
needed to complete the quotation, underline the direct object in each sentence below and
place the first letter of the word you underlined in the space at the left. These letters will
spell out the three words.

_____ 1. On the seashore I found a pebble that is perfectly round.

_____ 2. Dad gave me a shortwave radio for my birthday.

_____ 3. When the waves are high, I fear the ocean.

_____ 4. Mother always keeps the good silverware in a box lined with velvet.

_____ 5. The clerk sold Alice a ceramic eagle holding a flag in its talons.

_____ 6. Please slice these pears for the salad.

_____ 7. Becky plays the organ for Sunday services at the Episcopal Church.

_____ 8. Shall I dye these eggs with red beet juice and onion skins?

_____ 9. I value truthfulness above all other qualities in my close friends.

_____ 10. Mr. Babson owns a cattle ranch in the outback of Australia.

_____ 11. Indian women wear yards of lightweight cloth draped around them.

_____ 12. Eagerly we picked the berries in anticipation of pie for supper.

_____ 13. Did you know that he has a first edition of a book by Mark Twain?

_____ 14. The company sent samples of various kinds of tea from India and China.

_____ 15. Have you selected a title for your poem yet?

BONUS

What do you think of Coleridge's statement? Write your opinion on the back of this sheet.

Name _____ Date _____

2-5 RECOGNIZING VERBS

In each sentence, underline the verb (simple predicate). Then place all the verbs in the puzzle. Since each verb is a different length, each will fit in only one spot in the puzzle. Some of the verbs consist of more than one word; in the puzzle, just run the words together.

1. Some valuable objects can be found at flea markets and garage sales.

2. There are only two authenticated copies of this manuscript.

3. Jack and Jim don't want to enter the spelling contest.

4. Across the meadow scampered a frightened rabbit with a yapping dog not far behind.

5. Manufacturers are constantly devising new products for world markets.

6. Could a car like this be purchased for less than $18,000?

7. Will dinner be served after the meeting or before?

8. Unemployed airline workers must seek new jobs in other areas.

9. Why didn't Mary do the dishes after supper?

10. Have Steve and Alice really been to Paris three times?

11. Seeing the Statue of Liberty for the first time is a truly awe-inspiring experience.

12. Hose off the car before soaping it.

Name _____ Date _____

2-6 PRINCIPAL PARTS OF VERBS

A group of Shriners attending a convention encountered traffic problems. One man noticed that cars with placards on them bearing titles such as "Potentate" or "Past Potentate" got through to the convention hall more rapidly, so he decided to place a placard on his car that read __ __ __ __ __ __ __ __ __ __ __ __ __ __ __ __, and he got right through.
$\overline{13}\ \overline{4}\ \overline{2}\ \overline{5}\ \overline{14}\ \overline{9}\ \overline{6}$ $\overline{17}\ \overline{1}\ \overline{8}\ \overline{3}\ \overline{7}\ \overline{11}\ \overline{10}\ \overline{12}\ \overline{15}\ \overline{16}$

To learn what words he used, fill in the principal parts missing below and transfer the circled letters to the spaces above.

PRESENT	PAST	PAST PARTICIPLE	PRESENT PARTICIPLE
1. give	_ Ⓞ _ _	given	giving
2. eat	ate	_ _ _ Ⓞ _	eating
3. go	_ _ _ Ⓞ	gone	going
4. bear	bore	_ _ Ⓞ _ _ or _ _ _ _	bearing
5. _ _ Ⓞ _	lost	lost	losing
6. fight	fought	_ _ _ _ _ Ⓞ	fighting
7. ski	skied	skied	_ _ _ Ⓞ _ _
8. burst	_ _ Ⓞ _ _	burst	bursting
9. freeze	froze	_ _ _ _ _ Ⓞ	freezing
10. _ Ⓞ _	lay	lain	lying
11. catch	caught	caught	_ _ _ Ⓞ _ _ _ _
12. hop	_ _ _ Ⓞ _ _	hopped	hopping
13. speed	_ Ⓞ _ _	sped	speeding
14. see	saw	seen	_ _ Ⓞ _ _
15. fall	fell	_ _ _ Ⓞ _ _	falling
16. rise	rose	_ _ _ Ⓞ _	rising
17. _ _ Ⓞ _	hoped	hoped	hoping

2-7 TRANSITIVE, INTRANSITIVE, ACTIVE, AND PASSIVE VERBS

When a verb is transitive, some other word in the sentence receives the action. If the direct object receives the action, the verb is in the active voice; if the subject receives the action, the verb is in the passive voice. Intransitive verbs do not show action, and therefore no word receives action. Intransitive verbs may be complete in themselves or may be classified as linking verbs if they are followed by a predicate noun or predicate adjective. Underline the verb in each sentence and place the number of that verb in the proper category. If you do it correctly, the total in all four columns will be the same.

TRANSITIVE ACTIVE	TRANSITIVE PASSIVE	INTRANSITIVE COMPLETE	INTRANSITIVE LINKING
_____	_____	_____	_____
_____	_____	_____	_____
_____	_____	_____	_____
_____	_____	_____	_____

1. Rhonda sang two songs at her audition.

2. The rocket will be launched at 2:00.

3. That frail old man seems very unhappy.

4. I am the youngest member of my class.

5. The fish are swimming upstream to spawn.

6. The eagle soared gracefully over the peak.

7. Down the stairs came Johnny with the dog right behind.

8. You have only two choices.

9. These bushes were planted too close to the fence.

10. At Christmas, wreaths are hung on all the doors in the house.

11. Pennies contain copper, zinc, and tin.

12. How good that apple pie smells!

13. Was the message written in code?

14. Everyone should obey traffic signals.

15. He has been ill for a long time.

16. Look carefully at these diagrams.

2–8 *LIE* AND *LAY*

Why did Mary name her twin kittens _____ and _____? First you must find their names by doing the exercises below. Then see whether you can answer the question. Start by reading the explanation of *lie* and *lay* in your English book. Then circle the correct verb forms in the sentences below. In the string of letters preceding each set of sentences, cross out the letters in the words you selected. The remaining letters will spell the two names.

A A A D E E G I I I I I I L L L L L L L N N S W Y Y

1. The mountain range (lays, lies) south of the main highway.

2. If you are feeling ill, why don't you (lay, lie) down?

3. Every time he (laid, lay) down his glasses, he forgot where they were.

4. All the time I was trying to type, the cat (lay, laid) on my lap.

5. Has the dog been (lying, laying) here on this cushion?

6. That locket has (laid, lain) in this jewel box for over half a century.

A A A A D E E G H I I I I I L L L L L L L N N S S Y Y

7. Joshua has (lain, laid) on the hammock all afternoon.

8. Did you see the book (laying, lying) on the table?

9. The last time I saw it, the book (laid, lay) on the top shelf.

10. With a serious look, he (layed, laid) the briefcase down.

11. Don't (lay, lie) on the couch with your shoes on.

12. His farm (lays, lies) on the other side of the river.

BONUS

On the back of this page, try to give a reason why Mary might give her kittens the names indicated above.

Name _____ Date _____

2-9 VERB TENSE

Fill the blanks with the form of the verb specified. Then place the words in the puzzle. Each will fit into only one spot in the puzzle, since all the words are of different lengths.

1. Sally _____ a music box for her sister's birthday. (**past tense of** *buy*)

2. Considering her lack of experience, Barbara _____ well. (**present tense of** *do*)

3. _____ Harry and Arthur _____ about the picnic? (**present perfect tense of** *forget*)

4. On our trip we _____ Mt. Rushmore. (**future tense of** *see*)

5. _____ now and you may still catch her. (**present tense of** *go*)

6. Luke _____ an essay that may be a winner. (**present perfect tense of** *write*)

7. After Dad washed the car and mowed the lawn, he _____ down on the hammock. (**past tense of** *lie*)

8. If he _____ about the sale last week, he could have bought the stereo at a lower price. (**past perfect tense of** *know*)

9. Will Rogers _____ the lariat expertly and told jokes at the same time. (**past tense of** *swing*)

10. Mr. Hamilton _____ at numerous graduation exercises. (**present perfect tense of** *speak*)

11. If they _____ the plans as scheduled, there would not have been a cash-flow problem. (**past perfect tense of** *execute*)

12. I _____ him with the evidence first thing in the morning. (**future tense of** *confront*)

Name _____ Date _____

2-10 SUBJUNCTIVES

A certain artist drew the picture below and gave it this title:

$\overline{5}$ $\quad$ $\overline{2}$ $\overline{1}$ $\overline{7}$ $\overline{8}$ $\quad$ $\overline{17}$ $\overline{11}$ $\quad$ $\overline{4}$ $\overline{12}$ $\overline{3}$ $\quad$ $\overline{9}$ $\overline{15}$ $\overline{5}$ $\overline{2}$ $\overline{14}$ $\quad$ $\overline{18}$ $\overline{7}$ $\overline{1}$ $\overline{3}$ $\overline{16}$ $\overline{4}$ $\quad$ $\overline{5}$ $\overline{4}$

$\overline{6}$ $\overline{17}$ $\overline{13}$ $\overline{11}$ $\overline{17}$ $\overline{10}$ $\overline{12}$ $\overline{4}$

To discover the title, study the rules about subjunctives in your English book. Then read the sentences below and select the correct forms of the verbs, placing the circled letter from your choice at the left. Transfer these letters to the spaces above as your last step in discovering the answer.

_____ 1. If George Washington (was, were) here today, I wonder what he would think of the city named after him.

_____ 2. If Grandma (had come, came) on the early plane, she could have had supper with us.

_____ 3. I wish that my birthday (was, were) tomorrow.

_____ 4. If Patty (expected, had expected) to finish by noon, she should have started earlier.

_____ 5. If I (wait, waited) for you every day, I would never get there on time.

_____ 6. We could have tied the score if Jack (had made, made) that hit in the last inning.

_____ 7. If Mrs. Jones (had told, told) the truth at the trial, she failed to convince the jury.

_____ 8. I wish I (was, were) a beautiful yellow monarch butterfly.

_____ 9. If Mom (had been, were) here, Joey would not have got by with that.

_____ 10. Suppose I (went, had gone) to London with them; then I could have seen Queen Elizabeth!

_____ 11. Could you have finished in time if she (gave, had given) you some help?

_____ 12. Would you have made that remark yesterday if you (knew, had known) that Betty could hear you?

_____ 13. I wish I (met, had met) you long ago.

_____ 14. If Sally (had known, knew) where the necklace was, why didn't she tell us?

_____ 15. If a flying saucer (landed, would land) in our backyard tomorrow, I'd rush out to speak to the aliens.

_____ 16. If he (was, were) here, I certainly didn't see him.

_____ 17. If Will (studied, had studied) German, his trip to Berlin would have been more interesting.

_____ 18. I wish I (found, had found) out about this sooner.

2–11 NOUNS OR VERBS?

The same word may be a noun in one sentence and a verb in another. In each instance below, determine whether the underlined word is used as a noun or a verb and place the circled letter in the appropriate column. The letters in the two columns, when read from the bottom up will give the more common names for the following items:

A hand-held, portable communications inscriber is a _____.

A manually operated, fastener-driving impact device is a _____.

NOUN   VERB

1. In both pl**a**ys she had been cast in the role of an attorney.

2. I am going to pape**r** the wall in the bedroom myself.

3. The t**i**me for action has arrived.

4. According to the recipe, you bon**e** the chicken before baking it.

5. Who is going to ti**m**e the contest?

6. Because of my sprained ankle, I can't cli**m**b on the roof to fix the antenna.

7. The **c**limb up Walton Mountain took us two hours.

8. A fish b**o**ne, if swallowed, may require surgical removal.

9. He pl**a**ys chess like an expert.

10. The deserted hous**e** on the hill will soon be demolished.

11. This apartment complex can **h**ouse up to a thousand people.

12. Did you hand in your **p**aper on time?

© 1992 by The Center for Applied Research in Education

BONUS

Think of a long-winded definition for some simple object (such as the two at the top of the page). Write it on the back of this sheet and let your classmates guess what you are defining.

2-12 AGREEMENT OF SUBJECTS AND VERBS

Verbs must agree with their subjects in number. If one is singular, the other must be singular, too. In each sentence below, underline the correct form of the verb. If you select a singular verb, then circle the word in the Singular column at the left. If you select a plural verb, circle the word in the Plural column. Then transfer these words to the corresponding spaces in this nonsense poem:

6	2	8	10
4	9	1	
3	7	5	

SINGULAR PLURAL

SINGULAR	PLURAL
problems	person
house	in
dealing	caught
men	have
plurals	cheese
squirrels	dancing
William	with
discover	the
running	singular
chased	Urals

1. Nobody in our club (s., has; pl., have) volunteered for this project.

2. This is one of those apples that (s., comes; pl., come) from Oregon.

3. One problem with all these books (s., is; pl., are) that the print is so small.

4. Either Sheldon or his two assistants (s., is; pl., are) working on the problem.

5. Every summer either Mom or Dad (s., drives; pl., drive) us to camp.

6. Neither the Johnsons nor Mr. Johnson's sister (s., was; pl., were) home when I called.

7. Inside the abandoned mine (s., was; pl., were) found parts of a human skeleton.

8. Either Betty or her sisters (s., takes; pl., take) Sally to school each day.

9. This is one of those homeless cats that (s., lives; pl., live) in that old barn on the hill.

10. For each person who enters the contest there (s., is; pl., are) paper and pencils provided.

2-13 PRONOUNS

A pronoun takes the place of a noun. Some of the most common pronouns are *I, my, me, mine, we, us, our, you, your, he, him, his, she, her, hers, they, them, their, theirs, this, that, these, those, who, whom,* and *whose.*

Part 1

Listed below are definitions of words that contain pronouns. (Some contain more than one.) Write the defined word and circle the letters that form a pronoun.

1. Entire, complete   _ _ _ _ _ _

2. To cry in a low, whining voice   _ _ _ _ _ _ _

3. The opposite of *sweet*   _ _ _ _ _

4. A short written composition   _ _ _ _ _

5. A roof covered with straw or leaves   _ _ _ _ _ _ _

6. What you wash after cooking a meal   _ _ _ _ _ _

7. An important organ in your chest   _ _ _ _ _

8. Any instrument of war   _ _ _ _ _ _

9. A buyer   _ _ _ _ _ _ _

10. A type of prickly plant   _ _ _ _ _ _

11. A marshy body of water   _ _ _ _ _

12. A weasel-like animal with a coat of white fur   _ _ _ _ _

13. A metal tool used in shaping wood or stone   _ _ _ _ _

14. Surgery to remove the appendix   _ _ _ _ _ _ _ _

15. A winged child in painting and in sculpture   _ _ _ _ _

Part 2

1. Can you think of four letters that can be added to each of the following pronouns to create new pronouns?

   my _____ your _____ him _____ her _____

2. Add six letters to the following pronouns to form new ones:

   our _____ your _____ them _____

3. Add four letters to each of the following to form new pronouns:

   who _____ whom _____

Name _____ Date _____

2–14 TYPES OF PRONOUNS

Select the pronouns that match the descriptions given at the ends of the sentences, placing the letter of your choice at the left. Then, in the diagram, connect the letters, using three separate lines (one each for items 1 through 5, 6 through 9, and 10 through 13). These lines will form another pronoun that can also be a verb and a noun.

```
F   H   D   K   N   M   B        A. they    F. him      K. us
•   •   •   •   •   •   •        B. them    G. herself  L. we
            |           —        C. me      H. who      M. she
•   •   •   |   •   •   •        D. whom    I. you      N. your
I   A   L   G   C   J   E        E. each    J. its
```

_____ 1. Are _____ and she twins? (**second person, singular, nominative**)

_____ 2. At the banquet I sat between Barry and _____. (**third person, singular, masculine, objective**)

_____ 3. _____ didn't tell us about that. (**third person, plural, nominative**)

_____ 4. To _____ was Brent speaking on the phone? (**interrogative, singular, objective**)

_____ 5. May _____ girls join you for lunch? (**first person, plural, nominative**)

_____ 6. Give this information to _____ sister. (**second person, singular, possessive**)

_____ 7. Mom handed Beth and _____ aprons and said, "Get busy." (**first person, singular, objective**)

_____ 8. Frieda sold _____ boys some T-shirts. (**first person, plural, objective**)

_____ 9. Joyce prefers to work by _____. (**third person, singular, feminine, reflexive, compound**)

_____ 10. Later _____ of the members will have a chance to express an opinion. (**indefinite, singular**)

_____ 11 The bird has broken _____ wing. (**third person, singular, neuter, possessive**)

_____ 12. I can sing just as well as _____. (**third person, singular, feminine, nominative**)

_____ 13. The teacher sent _____ both to the office. (**third person, plural, objective**)

2–15 RECOGNIZING ADJECTIVES

The teacher refused to let her class study *Ivanhoe* because she said it contained too much $\overline{8}\ \overline{5}\ \overline{13}\ \overline{3}\ \overline{12}\ \ \overline{10}\ \overline{6}\ \overline{2}\ \overline{9}\ \overline{4}\ \overline{7}\ \overline{11}\ \overline{1}$.

To find out the teacher's reason, select the underlined word in each sentence that is an adjective, writing the first letter of that word in the space at the left. Transfer these letters to the corresponding spaces above. (Remember that adjectives answer the questions "which," "what kind of," and "how many.")

_____ 1. Grandpa <u>always</u> told us <u>exciting</u> tales about his <u>boyhood</u> in the "old country."

_____ 2. He will <u>probably</u> be reelected, since his <u>performance</u> during his term in office has been <u>outstanding</u>.

_____ 3. Among <u>older</u> workers <u>there</u> is less absenteeism and greater <u>productivity</u>.

_____ 4. This painting appears to be an <u>exact</u> copy of an earlier <u>work</u>.

_____ 5. Visiting the site of the <u>ancient</u> city of Troy was an <u>experience</u> I will never <u>forget</u>.

_____ 6. Bud's <u>reply</u> to the teacher's <u>question</u> was <u>instantaneous</u>.

_____ 7. The salesman said he was <u>nervous</u> because it <u>was</u> his first <u>day</u> on the job.

_____ 8. Helen is the <u>most</u> <u>sensible</u> girl in this <u>group</u>.

_____ 9. I wonder how Vivian can <u>afford</u> to wear the <u>very</u> <u>latest</u> styles.

_____ 10. <u>Vigorous</u> exercise several times a week is recommended for keeping <u>muscles</u> in good <u>condition</u>.

_____ 11. As he stared at the <u>trophy</u>, he pictured <u>himself</u> making the <u>crucial</u> hit that won the game.

_____ 12. <u>Neglected</u> children <u>often</u> have serious psychological problems that get <u>them</u> into trouble.

_____ 13. Water <u>shortages</u> in parts of the United States have prompted the <u>growing</u> of <u>xeric</u> plants (those requiring less water).

BONUS

On the back of this sheet, list several suffixes that are often found on adjectives, making them easy to recognize in some instances.

Name _____ Date _____

2–16 RECOGNIZING ADVERBS

"When is your dental appointment?" asked Mother.

Jean replied, "__ __   __ __ __ __ __   __ __ __ __ __!"
            3 1   8 9 7 4 10   5 11 6 12 2

To learn what Jean said, select the adverb from each set of three underlined words, placing the first letter of your choice in the space at the left. Then transfer the letters to the spaces above. (Remember that adverbs answer the questions "how," "when," "where," "why," "how much," and "how often.")

_____ 1. Set the <u>plant</u> <u>there</u> on that table right in the <u>center</u>.

_____ 2. Agatha called <u>yesterday</u> and said her dog had been <u>located</u> through the <u>newspaper</u> ad.

_____ 3. He wandered <u>about</u> for several hours <u>on</u> the mountain before he <u>was</u> found by the searchers.

_____ 4. I don't <u>know</u> how to tell her <u>tactfully</u> that she is not <u>invited</u>.

_____ 5. I always work <u>harder</u> early in the day because I am <u>tired</u> by <u>afternoon</u>.

_____ 6. A <u>really</u> <u>beautiful</u> sunset can inspire <u>one</u> to write poetry.

_____ 7. The coach is <u>often</u> <u>nervous</u> just <u>before</u> a game.

_____ 8. Call Alice and tell her that it is <u>too</u> cold and <u>icy</u> to <u>go</u> out today.

_____ 9. She chattered <u>on</u> all evening <u>and</u> bored <u>everyone</u>.

_____ 10. Come <u>here</u> and tell me all <u>about</u> your <u>recent</u> trip to your cousin's farm.

_____ 11. <u>Ultimately</u> we will have to pull out <u>some</u> of those bushes because they are becoming <u>crowded</u>.

_____ 12. The front page of the <u>daily</u> newspaper had an article about <u>seven</u> people who died <u>tragically</u>.

BONUS

What three kinds of words do adverbs describe? Write their names on the back of this sheet.

2-17 ADJECTIVES OR ADVERBS?

Most words that end in *ly* are adverbs, but some adjectives end in *ly* as well. Adjectives describe nouns and answer the questions "which," "what kind of," and "how many." Adverbs describe verbs, adjectives, and other adverbs and answer the questions "how," "when," "where," "why," "how much," and "how often." Determine whether each under-lined word below is an adjective or an adverb and place the circled letter in the appropriate column. The letters in the two columns, when read from the bottom up will form the name of a president who, when his spelling was criticized, remarked that it was a very poor mind that couldn't think of more than one way to spell a word.

Write his name here: _____

ADJECTIVE   ADVERB

1. The w̲o̲o̲l̲l̲y̲ mammoth is believed to be the ancestor of the modern elephant.

2. She jumped up s̲u̲d̲d̲e̲n̲l̲y̲ and left the room.

3. This recipe calls for c̲o̲a̲r̲s̲e̲l̲y̲ ground nuts.

4. The e̲a̲r̲l̲y̲ bird gets the worm.

5. She speaks so s̲o̲f̲t̲l̲y̲ that I can hardly hear her.

6. She has c̲u̲r̲l̲y̲ blond hair and blue eyes.

7. "Come here q̲u̲i̲c̲k̲l̲y̲," she said, "and help me get this curtain hung."

8. At the pet shop a c̲u̲d̲d̲l̲y̲ little kitten snuggled up to me, and I almost bought it.

9. A n̲i̲c̲e̲l̲y̲ trimmed hedge is an asset to a yard.

10. His k̲i̲n̲g̲l̲y̲ bearing makes him a perfect choice for the role of the pharaoh in our play.

11. That oil painting is a̲b̲s̲o̲l̲u̲t̲e̲l̲y̲ magnificent!

12. Toothpaste ads on television always feature models with gleaming, p̲e̲a̲r̲l̲y̲ teeth.

13. "I'm the greatest," he said j̲o̲k̲i̲n̲g̲l̲y̲, as he flexed his almost nonexistent muscles.

2-18 RECOGNIZING PREPOSITIONS

In the sentences below, place parentheses around the prepositional phrases. (There is just one such phrase in each sentence.) Then place the preposition from each phrase in the diagram, starting at the numeral 1 and writing the preposition vertically. The preposition from sentence 2 will fit horizontally into the preposition from sentence 1. Number 3 will fit into number 2 vertically, number 4 into number 3 horizontally, etc. The first two are given to help you get started. **Note:** Some of the prepositions are two-word items. Check the list of prepositions in your English book.

(crossword grid with the word SINCE across the top row starting at cell 1, and SINCE reading down from the I in the first column)

1. Inside the haunted house we found some old newspapers and an empty trunk.

2. Since January 1 we have had two severe storms.

3. All the puppies are totally black except this one.

4. Beyond the river lies a lovely meadow.

5. Please go across the street and mail this letter.

6. Around noon Mr. Sampson's chauffeur arrived.

7. Let's put this vase next to the mantel clock.

8. The witness said he saw the defendant walk toward the car.

9. Either Mike or his brother is behind this, you can be sure.

10. Aboard the plane were two congressmen, a senator, and also a reporter.

11. After dinner the hostess served chocolate-covered mints and coffee.

12. Dad went through the roof when he learned I had wrecked the family car.

13. Santa Claus climbed out of the chimney and called his reindeer.

14. As the parade moved along Third Avenue, we all stood up and saluted the flag.

2-19 CONJUNCTIONS

Coordinate conjunctions connect words, phrases, or clauses of equal value, while subordinate conjunctions connect items of unequal value, such as a main clause and an adverb or adjective clause. Adverbial conjunctions connect adverb clauses, and relative pronouns are used to connect adjective clauses. Most conjunctions are one-word items, but some come in pairs and are called correlative conjunctions. In the sentences below, underline the conjunctions and decide into which category each one fits. Place the number of the sentence in the proper category. The totals in the three columns will be the same when you complete the exercise.

COORDINATE	SUBORDINATE	CORRELATIVE
——	——	——
——	——	——
——	——	——
——	——	——
[ ]	[ ]	[ ]

1. I like to stroll through the park early in the morning and listen to the birds.

2. Tomorrow is color day; consequently, classes will not be held in the afternoon.

3. Either the bulb is burned out or the connection is loose.

4. Unless his health improves, he will not be able to come.

5. Will Rogers said, "My ancestors didn't come over on the *Mayflower,* but they met the boat."

6. Not only Bill but also Ron submitted a resignation.

7. Sharon spends most of her spare time either reading or playing the violin.

8. He was late again, and I left without him.

9. I will do what you say.

10. The witness said he saw neither Alicia nor her sister at the party.

11. People with degrees in physics and those with degrees in geology are in short supply.

12. When he held the paper over the hot bulb, a message appeared.

13. A book which contains lots of adventure is usually popular with junior high boys.

14. At the convention I met both the president and the vice president of the union.

15. Take this note to the principal or his asistant.

Name _____ Date _____

2–20 PREFIXES AND SUFFIXES

Clifton Fadiman described adjectives as the "_____ _____

of the _____ of _____."

To find the words to fit into the blanks, first change the words below into the parts of speech indicated by adding either a prefix or suffix from the list given. In some instances you may have to change a letter or two of the original word when you make the combination. You will use each prefix and suffix just once. Then take the circled letters in order and write them in the spaces above.

PREFIXES: a-, be-, co-, de-, re-

SUFFIXES: -able, -an, -ance, -ant, -ful, -ish, -ism, -ist, -ize, -less, -ly, -ment, -ous, -ship, -tion, -ward

1. laugh (**v. or n.**) plus _____ = _____Ⓞ__ (adjective)

2. way (**n.**) plus _____ = Ⓞ____ (adverb)

3. defy (**v.**) plus _____ = _____Ⓞ_ (adjective)

4. decorate (**v.**) plus _____ = ____Ⓞ____ (noun)

5. move (**v.**) plus _____ = _____Ⓞ_ (noun)

6. endure (**v.**) plus _____ = ____Ⓞ____ (noun)

7. Europe (**n.**) plus _____ = ____Ⓞ___ (adjective)

8. sun (**n.**) plus _____ = ____Ⓞ__ (adjective)

9. memory (**n.**) plus _____ = _____Ⓞ (verb)

10. swift (**adj.**) plus _____ = ____Ⓞ_ (adverb)

11. peace (**n.**) plus _____ = Ⓞ_____ (adjective)

12. back (**n.**) plus _____ = ____Ⓞ__ (adverb)

13. view (**n. or v.**) plus _____ = Ⓞ_____ (noun or verb)

14. type (**n. or v.**) plus _____ = _____Ⓞ (noun)

15. Catholic (**adj.**) plus _____ = _____Ⓞ_ (noun)

16. glory (**n.**) plus _____ = _____Ⓞ (adjective)

17. friend (**n.**) plus _____ = _____Ⓞ (noun)

18. friend (**n.**) plus _____ = _Ⓞ_____ (verb)

19. scribe (**n.**) plus _____ = _Ⓞ_____ (verb)

20. exist (**v.**) plus _____ = Ⓞ_____ (verb)

21. child (**n.**) plus _____ = _____Ⓞ_ (adjective)

Note: The words above may also be used as other parts of speech, but the most common uses are indicated here.

Name _____ Date _____

2–21 DEPENDENT CLAUSES

Each of the sentences below contains one dependent clause used as a noun, adverb, or adjective. Underline the entire dependent clause. Then circle the subject of each dependent clause. In the string of letters preceding each set of five sentences, cross out the letters contained in the subjects. The remaining letters in each set will form a word, and the two words formed will answer this question: Why are mushrooms so popular?

Because they are _____ _____.

A A B C E E E H H I J N N O S S T T T U W Y

1. When Annie did not turn in her report, she received a failing grade.

2. Because Betsy left the gate open, our dog escaped.

3. Foods that are high in protein help build body cells.

4. Is that the same girl we played tennis with at camp?

5. What Joe said amused young and old alike.

C E E E E F H H H H H G I I N O O R S T U V W W W W Y

6. Pass out these brochures to whoever attends.

7. The Pentagon, which has sixteen miles of corridors, covers a million square feet.

8. The new shopping center will be built where we are now standing.

9. When they are lost, people tend to walk in circles.

10. Mr. Wilson is the salesman who represents our company in the Southwest.

BONUS

Now go back and determine how each dependent clause is used. Write the number of each sentence in the proper category below. If you do it correctly, you should get the totals indicated.

	NOUNS	ADJECTIVES	ADVERBS
TOTALS	11	24	20

Name _____ Date _____

2–22 SUBORDINATE CLAUSES

A clause that acts as a noun, adjective, or adverb is called a subordinate or dependent clause because it cannot stand alone. In each sentence below, underline the entire dependent clause and determine how it is used in the sentence. Circle the letter in the column that fits your choice. These circled letters will provide the names of two other clauses. (It may seem confusing at first, but just write the letters in order and then figure out how to divide them into words.) Write them here:

_____

ADJECTIVE	ADVERB	NOUN	
M	A	P	1. This is the style I like.
C	O	R	2. A man's health depends on what he eats.
M	Y	A	3. My main regret is that I didn't apologize.
I	N	B	4. The kitten arched its back because it was frightened by the big dog.
F	D	U	5. Whenever I visit my grandparents, they always take me to the beach.
M	E	S	6. Show me the gun with which he was killed.
H	G	R	7. I couldn't believe what she told me.
S	A	K	8. I found an old dime that is worth more than a hundred dollars.
S	L	O	9. Anyone who thoroughly enjoys reading will never be lonesome.
P	A	M	10. He ran so fast that he almost collapsed.
W	E	N	11. Whatever is worth doing is worth doing well.
S	T	U	12. Since snakes can't hear airborne sounds, you can't call to them by name.
A	J	L	13. Rover barks at anything that moves.

BONUS

On the back of this sheet, try to write a sentence that contains all three types of subordinate clauses.

2-23 SIMPLE, COMPOUND, AND COMPLEX SENTENCES

A simple sentence expresses one complete thought, though some of its elements may be compound. A compound sentence has two or more main thoughts. A complex sentence has one main thought plus a subordinate thought—a clause that contains its own subject and verb. It may be a noun clause, an adjective clause, or an adverb clause. Classify each sentence below by placing its number in the appropriate column. If you do it correctly, the totals of the three columns will be the same.

SIMPLE   COMPOUND   COMPLEX

1. The ducks were swimming in the pond, and the cows were grazing peacefully.

2. Sally does excellent work and will surely win the trophy.

3. He wasn't there when I arrived.

4. Both Bob and his brother play the guitar and sing.

5. The daffodils bloom first, but the tulips are not far behind.

6. The boy who won the race is my cousin.

7. Whoever wins tonight will receive a medal.

8. The fog cleared, and we set out.

9. For Christmas I got a bicycle, a camera, and a box of stationery.

10. If you are late, you can't go with us.

11. The door burst open, he strutted in, and everyone stared.

12. Over the noise of the battle came the shrill notes of a bugle.

13. Who spilled this flour on the kitchen floor?

14. I know Mary will come.

15. Lorrie will drop off the report today, or her sister will bring it in the morning.

TOTALS

© 1992 by The Center for Applied Research in Education

2–24 SENTENCE FRAGMENTS

A sentence fragment is a group of words that lacks some elements necessary to form a complete sentence and express a complete thought. Listed below are song titles, some of which are fragments and others of which are complete sentences. Classify them by placing the number of each sentence in the appropriate column. If you do it correctly, the total in both columns will be the same.

FRAGMENT   SENTENCE

FRAGMENT	SENTENCE

1. "I Want to Hold Your Hand"

2. "April in Paris"

3. "Don't Fence Me In"

4. "Let Me Call You Sweetheart"

5. "Where Have All the Flowers Gone"

6. "When Irish Eyes Are Smiling"

7. "Home on the Range"

8. "In the Still of the Night"

9. "Don't Be Cruel"

10. "The Waltz You Saved for Me"

11. "Meet Me in St. Louis, Louis"

12. "I'll Take You Home Again, Kathleen"

13. "When the Moon Comes Over the Mountain"

14. "Deep in the Heart of Texas"

15. "It Came Upon the Midnight Clear"

TOTALS

BONUS

On the back of this sheet, list several song titles that you think are complete sentences. See whether your classmates agree.

2–25 MISPLACED MODIFIERS

Misplaced modifiers produce sentences that sound ridiculous because they don't say what was intended. Each sentence below contains an underlined misplaced modifier (adjective, participial phrase, prepositional phrase, adjective clause, infinitive, etc.). Circle the word that the phrase now modifies incorrectly and put a box around the noun it should modify. Place the boxed words in the puzzle starting at the numeral 1, writing the first correct noun vertically. The noun from sentence 2 will fit horizontally into the noun from sentence 1. Number 3 will fit into number 2 vertically, etc. The first two words are given to help you get started.

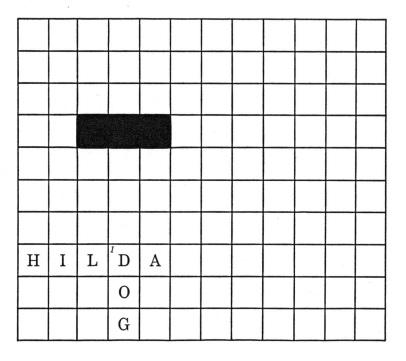

1. Jim could hardly restrain his dog in the tub <u>splashing wildly</u>.

2. <u>Although a good student</u>, no scholarship was awarded to Hilda.

3. <u>Rolled up in a cardboard tube</u>, I mailed my drawing to the judges in Alabama.

4. <u>To grow properly</u>, nourishing food must be eaten by babies.

5. <u>To enter this country</u>, a visa must be presented by each tourist.

6. <u>Hot and tired</u>, the iced tea tasted good to Deborah.

7. <u>Not working properly</u>, I returned my calculator to the company for repairs.

8. The body of the missing woman was found by the police <u>stuffed into the freezer</u>.

9. Give all the boys these blue ribbons <u>that placed first in each division</u>.

10. <u>Flying around the ceiling</u>, Jill was terrified by the bat.

2–26 THE IMPORTANCE OF CAPITAL LETTERS

A spy was ordered to somehow smuggle a large sum of money to the revolutionaries, and the government was aware of it. He was stopped and searched at the border. His bag was found to contain only his clothes, shaving equipment, and several letters. The authorities, fearing he might have concealed diamonds or other valuables by swallowing them, x-rayed him but found nothing. He was released and managed to complete his mission. How did he do it? Answer: He had $\overline{10}\,\overline{1}\,\overline{2}\,\overline{11}$ $\overline{6}\,\overline{5}\,\overline{1}\,\overline{4}\,\overline{3}\,\overline{6}$ $\overline{8}\,\overline{12}$ $\overline{5}\,\overline{7}\,\overline{11}$ $\overline{11}\,\overline{12}\,\overline{13}\,\overline{11}\,\overline{9}\,\overline{8}\,\overline{3}\,\overline{11}\,\overline{6}$.

To find the answer, identify the words defined below, each of which has a different meaning when capitalized. Then transfer the circled letters to the corresponding numbered spaces above.

Meanings When Capitalized	Meanings Uncapitalized	
1. a large country in Asia	porcelain tableware	_ _ _ _ Ⓞ
2. member of a Denver ball team	an untamed horse	_ Ⓞ _ _ _ _
3. Slavic language	a substance used to make surfaces shine	Ⓞ _ _ _ _
4. a planet	silvery metallic element	Ⓞ _ _ _ _ _ _
5. city in Iowa	a couch	_ _ _ _ _ _ _ _ Ⓞ
6. type of expensive car	small portions of bread baked in a variety of shapes	_ _ _ _ Ⓞ
7. citizen of an Asiatic country	woolen blanket or shawl	_ _ _ _ Ⓞ _
8. a popular soft drink	slang for *cocaine*	_ Ⓞ _ _
9. language spoken in Wales	to avoid payment on a debt	_ _ Ⓞ _ _
10. a month	steady movement in a rhythmic step	_ _ Ⓞ _
11. a Greek epic poet	a way to score in baseball	_ _ _ Ⓞ _
12. Greek god of shepherds and fields	utensil for frying foods	_ _ Ⓞ _
13. type of credit card	a stamp on a passport allowing one to enter a country	Ⓞ _ _ _

2–27 CAPITALIZATION

The detective investigating the murder of Hal Brooks questioned family members and neighbors about the shooting. One neighbor said, "When I heard the shot, I walked to Hal's house and knocked on the door. Getting no response, I walked to the kitchen window, wiped off the frost, and looked in. Hal was lying on the floor, face down with a bullet wound in his back." How did the detective know the neighbor was lying? To find out, circle all the letters in the following sentences that should be capitalized and also those that are capitalized but should not be. These circled letters, in order, will form the answer. You must decide where to divide the string of letters into words. Write the eight words here:

_____ _____ _____ _____

_____ _____ _____ _____

1. In november olga went to florida to visit her aunt and uncle.

2. "The republican Party is holding its convention in New orleans," Said the Teacher.

3. On friday the American Society for the Prevention Of Cruelty to Animals will hold its Regional Meeting.

4. People in the south grow a lot of Okra, which they use in making gumbo—something seldom eaten in the Northern part of the United States.

5. terry is studying hungarian and working at an Embassy as an assistant to one of the Officials.

6. My uncle Ben, who is a portrait photographer, wrote a book entitled *the Art of sitting Pretty,* which is to be published by an indiana company.

7. What other Denominations follow practices similar to those of the episcopalians?

8. He said, "often I think about the *firebird,* my boat that I spent so much time on one Winter."

9. Just a short distance off interstate 87 is the headquarters of the nevins Company.

10. dependents of servicemen who are now Overseas and Widows of those who lost their lives in the war organized a Support group to discuss their problems.

BONUS

Which school subjects are capitalized and which ones are not? Explain on the back of this sheet.

© 1992 by The Center for Applied Research in Education

Name _____ Date _____

2-28 PARALLEL CONSTRUCTION

Thoughts that are similar and are included in the same sentence should be constructed similarly. For example, if one item in a series is a prepositional phrase, the others should be too. Likewise, if one clause of a compound sentence is in the active voice, the other clause should be also. Select the endings below that will give the sentences parallel construction, writing the numbers of your choices at the left. Their total has a connection with a couple of sentences in the quiz. Do you know what it is?

Explain here: _____

_____

_____ A. Melanie says she likes swimming and skiing better than (12) playing volleyball. (25) a game of volleyball.

_____ B. Either look up the names of the constellations in advance or (18) a chart can be used. (6) use a chart.

_____ C. There is hate in his heart and (9) he has revenge on his mind. (4) revenge on his mind.

_____ D. I promised Mom and Dad that I would study my piano lessons well, practice diligently, and (14) make them proud of me. (20) that they would be proud of me.

_____ E. She participated in three events and (16) was awarded a prize in each one. (8) won a prize in each one.

_____ F. The answer is not to lose your temper but (11) you should talk to Brent calmly. (7) to talk to Brent calmly.

_____ G. The performer walked onto the stage, smiling at the orchestra and (1) with a bow to the audience. (5) bowing to the audience.

_____ H. He wanted to know where I had been and (10) why I was late. (29) the reason I was late.

_____ I. The walls of the kitchen had been painted green by the previous tenants, and (13) the ceiling had been painted yellow. (18) they had painted the ceiling yellow.

_____ J. Jackson is bright, creative, and (17) works hard. (9) hard-working.

_____ TOTAL

2–29 UNNECESSARY WORDS

Each of the sentences below contains an unnecessary word or phrase. Cross out the words that aren't needed, but don't change any of the other words in the sentence. You may eliminate one, two, or three words. At the left indicate the number of words you crossed out. Then take the total and multiply it by 5 to get a nice round number that will answer this question: How many squares and rectangles are there in this figure?

Write the answer here: _____

_____ A. After a long disagreement, the leaders of the two nations reached a mutual agreement between them.

_____ B. Our country has made some serious mistakes in its past history. (**Cross out the unnecessary adjective.**)

_____ C. Have you read the story about the prince who exchanged places with a look-alike penniless pauper?

_____ D. I received a free gift for opening an account at the bank on Tennyson Avenue.

_____ E. Two of the three triplets look exactly alike, but the third has a dimple in her chin.

_____ F. Isn't that the most beautiful bouquet of flowers you have ever seen?

_____ G. The foreign competition from abroad is hurting American industries. (**Cross out the larger number of words.**)

_____ H. The parts of this model plane are joined together with a special glue.

_____ I. Please continue on with what you were saying when we were interrupted.

_____ J. It is refreshing to see a TV show with a lady heroine.

_____ K. I would hate to be all alone in solitary confinement in prison. (**Cross out the shorter set of words.**)

_____ L. This old clock, with its intricate carvings and marble base, is very unique.

_____ M. Thomas Edison was a diligent worker and quite a brilliant genius.

_____ N. Manually he lifted the heavy piece of equipment with his hands. (**Cross out the larger number of words rather than the smaller number.**)

Name _____ Date _____

2–30 USAGE

Noah Webster published the first American dictionary, *An American Dictionary of the English Language*, in the year _____. To discover the answer, look at the sentences below, each of which contains an error in usage. The incorrect word in each sentence is underlined. Write the correct word at the left. Count the number of letters in the word you supplied and cross out that number in the string of numbers at the top. The four numbers that remain, when rearranged, will form the answer. (**Clue:** The second and fourth numbers in the date are the same.)

1 2 2 3 3 3 4 4 4 4 5 5 5 5 5 6 8 8 8

_____ A. We haven't got <u>no</u> more paper cups for the picnic.

_____ B. Neither Fred nor Ben <u>find</u> French an interesting subject.

_____ C. At the moment a large <u>amount</u> of dogs are being held at the pound.

_____ D. I could <u>of</u> won if I had tried a little harder.

_____ E. The reason he was late was <u>because</u> he ran out of gasoline.

_____ F. Why didn't you mix the ingredients <u>like</u> the home economics teacher showed us?

_____ G. There have been <u>less</u> complaints by the students since the menus in the lunchroom have been changed.

_____ H. The gangster broke the window, climbed in, and <u>robbed</u> all the money on my desk.

_____ I. His cruel remarks made her feel <u>badly</u>.

_____ J. In Rome many tourists who visit Trevi Fountain throw coins <u>in</u> it.

_____ K. Divide the watermelon <u>between</u> the four boys.

_____ L. Can't you <u>convince</u> him to run for the student council in the upcoming election?

_____ M. This design is surely different <u>than</u> the one Mike presented.

_____ N. He has been in this country only a few months and doesn't speak English very <u>good</u>.

_____ O. How did you like <u>them</u> cookies Alma made?

_____ P. Mom wouldn't <u>leave</u> me go.

2–31 PREFERRED USAGE

Are you _____? In other words, do you have blond hair? The word in question is an interesting one, and one you probably have never heard. To discover it, select the right forms to use in the blanks below. (In several instances both forms are in use, though one is considered better than the other. Select the form that is more acceptable.) Place the letter of your choice at the left. These letters, in order, will form the word that means "having blond hair."

_____ 1. Loud noises can _____ your hearing. **(B) effect; (X) affect**

_____ 2. Is it _____ for me to spend the night at Susie's house? **(C) alright; (A) all right**

_____ 3. Have the guests come _____? **(N) already; (P) all ready**

_____ 4. There's not _____ left in the box. **(E) a one; (T) one**

_____ 5. Brenda is _____ pretty. **(S) awfully; (H) very**

_____ 6. The statements in this article are simply not _____. **(O) credible; (D) credulous**

_____ 7. I am not _____ at all about this idea. **(T) enthusiastic; (L) enthused**

_____ 8. I don't intend to pursue this matter any _____. **(K) farther; (R) further**

_____ 9. She certainly looks _____ in that outfit. **(I) good; (F) well**

_____ 10. I _____ to notify him before noon. **(A) have got; (C) have**

_____ 11. Did you get an _____ to Beverly's party? **(V) invite; (H) invitation**

_____ 12. I think we're _____ to lose the contest. **(C) liable; (O) likely**

_____ 13. I gave _____ all the candy to Joey and his brother. **(U) almost; (G) most**

_____ 14. She walked a short _____ with us. **(S) way; (L) ways**

2-32 PARAGRAPHING

Listed below are facts about Mark Twain. They are not in logical order, and they are all written in short, choppy sentences. Rearrange the facts into logical paragraphs (probably three). Use adverb and adjective clauses, participial phrases, inverted sentences, and whatever other devices will give you variety and make your writing interesting. You may combine two or more sentences into one. Be sure to include all the facts, but condense the material wherever possible. Your teacher will pick the five best compositions, and the class will select a winner from the five.

Mark Twain died in 1910 when Halley's comet appeared.

He wrote *Tom Sawyer* and *Huckleberry Finn.* These are based on his boyhood in Hannibal, Missouri, along the Mississippi River.

His real name was Samuel Langhorne Clemens.

He was born in 1835 when Halley's comet appeared.

He became famous as a humorist.

Roughing It is based on his trip to the Nevada silver mines.

For a while he was a pilot on a Mississippi steamboat.

His pen name came from a call the river pilots used to indicate the depth of the water.

He was a newspaperman and traveled to other parts of the world.

Innocents Abroad is based on his travels in Europe.

He went on many lecture tours.

Two other books he wrote are *A Connecticut Yankee in King Arthur's Court* and *The Prince and the Pauper.*

He came from the heart of America but made his permanent home in the East.

His stories are still read by many people today.

People still quote things he said.

3

PUNCTUATION

PUNCTUATION MARKS ARE THE TRAFFIC SIGNS ON THE ROAD OF LANGUAGE.

3-1 THE IMPORTANCE OF PUNCTUATION

"Punctuation isn't very important. The words are more important." Right? Wrong! Sometimes punctuation marks can totally change the meaning of the words. Each of the sentences below can be made to have another meaning by simply inserting or removing punctuation marks. Rewrite each sentence, punctuating it differently. (You may have to capitalize letters, but don't change any of the words.) Can you think of more than one way to change some of the sentences?

1. Don't do anything stupid.

   _____

2. The committee consists of Mary Jane, Sue Ann, and Louise.

   _____

3. The team said the coach is great.

   _____

4. Let's talk turkey.

   _____

5. Well, leave it alone.

   _____

6. The ladies have cast off clothing at the garage sale.

   _____

7. Bring four gallon jugs.

   _____

8. Go fetch Fido.

   _____

9. Listen, to me that doesn't make sense.

   _____

10. Don't eat fast.

   _____

Note: If the above sentences haven't convinced you of the importance of punctuation, read the following true story:

In Russia a period once actually saved a man's life. The czar had condemned the man to death and sent this note to the jailer, who had been instructed to wait for orders: "PARDON IMPOSSIBLE. TO BE EXECUTED." The czarina, who felt sympathetic toward the prisoner, intercepted the note and changed the punctuation as follows: "PARDON. IMPOSSIBLE TO BE EXECUTED." The jailer thereupon released the prisoner, who escaped from the country before the czar discovered what had happened.

3-2 TYPES OF PUNCTUATION MARKS

Each of the following sentences requires a single additional punctuation mark—or, in the case of marks that come in pairs, a pair of marks. Fill in the missing punctuation and at the left write the number that represents the name of the punctuation mark you used. Then, in the diagram, connect the numbers in the order you used them. This line will form the shape of something related to this quiz.

1. semicolon
2. double quotation marks
3. single quotation marks
4. dash
5. virgule
6. exclamation point
7. hyphen

8. period
9. ellipsis
10. colon
11. comma
12. brackets
13. apostrophe
14. parentheses

8   11   13
•   •   •
2•   •1
6•   9   •10
            •
14•   •3
7•   •5
4•   •12
•

_____ A. Mr Anderson called and said he'd come later today.

_____ B. When she learned her apartment had been burglarized she sat down and cried.

_____ C. Im sure we are on the wrong road.

_____ D. Drinking while driving is illegal furthermore, it can be deadly.

_____ E. This recipe has just three ingredients lime gelatin, cottage cheese, and pineapple.

_____ F. You may be right, but

_____ G. How lovely this garden is in the moonlight

_____ H. The FDA Food and Drug Administration is setting new standards for food labels.

_____ I. He received a two thirds majority of the vote.

_____ J. She plans to make a profit something that seems impossible at this point.

BONUS

On the back of this sheet, write sentences that illustrate the punctuation marks on the list above that were not used in the quiz.

3–3 PUNCTUATION RULES

Listed below are several punctuation rules. Match each one with the sentence at the bottom to which the rule applies and place the circled letter from the sentence in the space at the left. These letters will spell the name of a man in colonial times who wrote a book without a single punctuation mark. At the end he included a page full of punctuation marks, with the instruction to readers to "pepper and salt it as you please."

Write the man's name here: _____.

Then punctuate the sentences at the bottom of the page.

RULES

_____ 1. Use a period at the end of an indirect question.

_____ 2. When an abbreviation comes at the end of a sentence, only one period is required.

_____ 3. Introductory words (*yes, no,* etc.) that are not part of the main thought are followed by a comma.

_____ 4. In an address all items after the first are set off by commas. (The house number and street are considered a single item, as are the state and ZIP Code.)

_____ 5. Separate items in a series with commas and, for clarity, use a comma before the *and* in the series.

_____ 6. In numbers commas are used to separate hundreds, thousands, millions, etc.

_____ 7. When two items, such as two phrases or two adjectives, are used without a conjunction between them, a comma is needed.

_____ 8. To form the plural of a number, letter, or symbol, use an apostrophe.

_____ 9. Use a comma after an adverb clause at the beginning of a sentence.

SENTENCES

Oh I didn't know (M)ac was here.

Woodchucks goph(e)rs and prairie dogs are related to squirrels.

Well-groomed courteous applican(t)s make the best impression.

The mailman asked where the Car(t)ers live

While I was taking a bath the telephone (r)ang.

Mail this to Miss June Hill 1221 Sixth Avenue (D)enver Colorado 80202.

You must writ(e) your As and Os more clearly.

The tra(i)n is scheduled to arrive at 7:30 p m

Mr. Ba(x)ter said over 50000 varieties of plants can be found in the jungles of the world.

BONUS

On the back of this sheet write one other punctuation rule not listed above.

3-4 WHICH PUNCTUATION MARK?

In the space at the left of each item indicate the punctuation mark required. Then, in the diagram, connect the items in the order you used them. The result will be a number of similar geometric shapes.

• SEMICOLON

PERIOD •   • APOSTROPHE

COMMA •   • COLON

• QUOTATION MARKS

_____ 1. After the closing of a letter

_____ 2. After initials

_____ 3. After the greeting of a business letter

_____ 4. To replace omitted letters in contractions

_____ 5. At the end of a politely worded question

_____ 6. Between independent clauses when no conjunction is used

_____ 7. To show possession in proper nouns

_____ 8. To set off the name of the person spoken to

_____ 9. To separate the minutes and hours when writing time

_____ 10. To enclose titles of poems, articles, and chapters of books

_____ 11. After the salutation of a friendly letter

Name _____ Date _____

3–5 END PUNCTUATION

A certain artist drew the picture shown below and named it _____
_____. To find the two-word name, place the proper end punctuation on each sentence below and label each sentence as *declarative* (making a statement), *interrogative* (asking a question), *imperative* (giving a command), or *exclamatory* (showing strong feeling). Write the first few letters of each answer in the short spaces and place the rest of the word on the line. The title of the artist's drawing will be revealed in the marked vertical column.

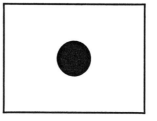

1. Don't eat foods high in cholesterol

2. The largest bird in North America is the California condor

3. Have you practiced your music lesson today

4. Cut some flowers for Grandma

5. How cold it is outside today

6. Iron filings group themselves around the ends of magnets

7. Pick up your clothes, hang them in the closet, and come down to dinner

8. He is a riveter in an airplane factory

9. Did you participate in the school spelldown last year

10. What a lovely antique vase you have

11. Can you touch your nose with your tongue

3-6 PUNCTUATING A SERIES

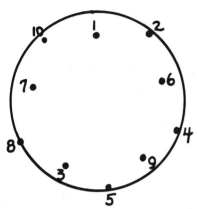

The sentences below all contain a series of some type. (Ordinarily there are three or more items in a series, but two items, such as two adjectives, are also separated by commas if the first does not modify the second and there is no conjunction between them.) Punctuate the sentences below, using a comma before the *and* in the series for clarity. Then, at the left under the ONE and TWO columns, place a check to show how many commas you used. In the diagram, connect in order the numbers of the sentences containing one comma and close off the figure by connecting the first to the last. Also connect in order the numbers of the sentences with two commas, closing the figure by connecting the last with the first. You should end up with two familiar shapes.

ONE   TWO

1. In our musical family Mom plays the piano Dad sings and my sister and I play the violin.

2. How can a totally uneducated illiterate person function in today's complex world?

3. Smallpox bubonic plague and cholera have practically been eliminated.

4. In the lineup he identified a hulking tough-looking hoodlum as the mugger.

5. Would you rather have some of this fine Belgian lace or this hand-painted imported pottery?

6. I mowed the lawn trimmed the hedge and picked flowers.

7. She's in the pep club in the school choir and on the student council—and an officer in all three.

8. This exciting suspense-filled story would make a great movie.

9. On the beaches in the mountains and at all the other resort areas there seem to be large numbers of people.

10. This excellent simple-to-prepare recipe contains just four basic ingredients.

BONUS

Go back and identify what items are in the series in each sentence—adjectives, nouns, prepositional phrases, etc.

3-7 PUNCTUATING APPOSITIVES
AND ADJECTIVE CLAUSES

Scarface, a notorious crook (but one who knows how to punctuate appositives and nonrestrictive adjective clauses), devised a plan to foil the warden and get a message to his friends regarding the time of his planned jailbreak. He wrote the sentences below and left out all the commas. Punctuate each sentence and, in the blank at the left, write the number of commas you used. Total each set of commas to form the number of the month, day, and hour of the escape. When did Scarface plan to escape?

Write it here: _____

Hint: Each sentence may require from zero to four commas, and the total of all the sentences is 20.

_____ A. I wonder if Bill Burton the new boy in our class is related to Richard Burton the actor.

_____ B. Men who work in coal mines can develop respiratory problems.

_____ C. Milk contains calcium which helps develop strong bones.

_____ D. Johnson's Garage the sponsor of the local baseball team furnished uniforms for all the players.

♦ ♦ ♦ ♦

_____ E. Does your cousin Joe still play the violin in the orchestra?

_____ F. Buttons my meandering cat has disappeared again.

_____ G. I'm here to see Dr. Carrington my orthodontist.

_____ H. Did you know that Lewis Carroll who wrote *Alice in Wonderland* also wrote books on mathematics?

♦ ♦ ♦ ♦

_____ I. Julius Squeezer the big boa constrictor and King Tusk the huge elephant are both big attractions at the zoo.

_____ J. People who can't pay attention to detail should not attempt to become accountants.

_____ K. Eileen my neighbor and best friend didn't get a chance to meet Matt my cousin from Florida.

_____ L. Carl Wilburn who once worked for the Chandler Corporation is now the local chief of police.

20 = TOTAL

Name _____ Date _____

3-8 PUNCTUATING INTERRUPTERS

What do you get when you cross James Bond and a big jet? Why, 00747, of course. And what do you get when you cross a baseball player and grain? To find out, place commas in the sentences below wherever they are needed to punctuate interrupting elements, such as nouns of address, parenthetic expressions, participial phrases, etc. Only one additional comma is needed in each sentence. In the space beside each sentence, place the *first* letter of the word immediately *following* the comma you inserted. These letters will spell the answer.

Write it here: _____

_____

_____ 1. Owls contrary to popular opinion, are not very wise.

_____ 2. The recession will not last long according to an economist I saw on TV.

_____ 3. Will you teach me how to pitch Tom?

_____ 4. These two books covering about the same period of history, are both suitable for book reports.

_____ 5. This company, if it does not find a buyer by Friday has to go out of business.

_____ 6. Judy, regardless of what her parents say expects to find a way to go to college.

_____ 7. Barbecuing Rachel said, was the chef's specialty.

_____ 8. This television show in my opinion, is the best new show of the season.

_____ 9. The Secretary of State feels nevertheless, that one more effort at negotiation should be attempted.

_____ 10. The telephone call the witness insists, came at 9:30.

_____ 11. Tell me Hannah, have you discussed this with your mother?

_____ 12. Mail a copy of this report to each officer Evelyn.

_____ 13. This movie Rosemary warned me, is very scary.

_____ 14. Every day this week yesterday especially, the food in the lunchroom has been unusually good.

_____ 15. Of course every interrupter at the beginning of a sentence requires one comma.

3-9 PUNCTUATING QUOTATIONS

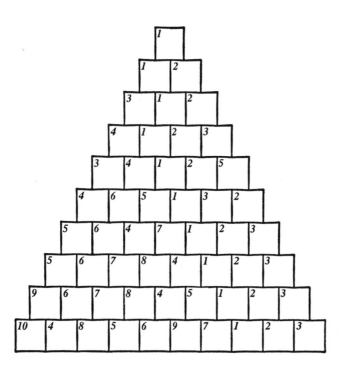

You will be able to build a pyramid much faster than the pharaohs did simply by supplying the missing punctuation marks in the sentences below. Circle the letter that represents the correct set of marks for each sentence. Then transfer these letters to the appropriate spots in the diagram. (Place the letter for number 1 in all the spaces marked *1*, the letter for number 2 in all the spaces marked *2*, etc.) You will see a new word formed on each horizontal line as an additional letter is added to each line.

© 1992 by The Center for Applied Research in Education

1. Didn't John give you my message asked Bill
   I. " ? " .   A. " , " ?

2. Mark exclaimed You've got to be kidding
   S. , " " !   N. , " ! "

3. Take this note to Mr. Andrews said the teacher
   G. " , " .   T. " . " .

4. Mary said she didn't have the right change to give me
   E. , " " .   R. .

5. Come here said Gerald to his dog and bring the ball
   L. " , " . " . "   S. " , " , " . "

6. How strangely that movie ended exclaimed Peggy
   E. " ! " .   C. " , " !

7. I'm hungry Billy said Let's eat now
   V. " , " . " . "   O. " , " , " " .

8. My mom said Ben loves to cook She is always trying new recipes
   E. " , " , " . . "   F. " , " , " . " . "

9. Who said I have not yet begun to fight
   U. , " ? "   R. , " " ?

10. The general in Operation Desert Storm was known as Stormin' Norman
    D. , " . "   P. " . "

3-10 APOSTROPHES IN POSSESSIVE NOUNS

A certain lady had twin sons and wanted to give them names that had something in common with each other as well as with their last name. To discover the names she chose, read each phrase below and, if the possessive form is correct, circle the letter of that item. If the possessive is incorrect, rewrite it. Then on the lines provided, print the boys' first and last names in *capital* letters.

Boys' names: _____ _____ _____
                First   First   Last

A. Bens' sneakers
B. The principal's office
C. A bullets' speed
O. All dogs' noses
E. The teacher's lounge
B. Billy's and Johnny's bikes

♦ ♦ ♦ ♦

R. The worlds' deserts
D. The church's steeple
O. Floridas' climate
I. Three months' time
C. Life's problems
Y. All the student's records
K. The two women's sons

♦ ♦ ♦ ♦

J. John Waynes' movies
H. India's population
I. The little bird's wing
O. This citys' problems
C. All the members' votes
N. Mens' suits
K. The senator's speech
E. Ladie's purses
O. Ten sheep's pens
X. This lady's son
G. The thieve's hideout
S. These book's covers

BONUS

What do the boys' names have in common? Turn the sheet over and upside down and hold it to the light to find out. Explain here:

3-11 APOSTROPHES IN CONTRACTIONS

Unlike possessive nouns, which use apostrophes, possessive pronouns do not. When a pronoun is used in a contraction, however, an apostrophe is needed to indicate where one or more letters have been omitted. From the choices given below in Part 1, select the right words for the blanks. If the choice is a contraction, indicate at the left how many letters were omitted in forming the contraction. Your total should be 20, including items in Part 2.

Part 1

_____ 1. "_____ my turn," said Susan. (Its, It's)

_____ 2. _____ wallet is missing? (Whose, Who's)

_____ 3. He says _____ his best friend. (your, you're)

_____ 4. _____ roof was damaged by hail. (They're, Their)

_____ 5. _____ the book I lost. (There's, Theirs)

_____ 6. _____ that man in the brown jacket? (Who's, Whose)

_____ 7. As soon as _____ friend gets here, we can go. (your, you're)

_____ 8. The cat got _____ tail caught in the door (its, it's)

_____ 9. _____ going with us. (Their, They're, There)

Part 2

Place apostrophes wherever needed in the following sentences and, as above, indicate the number of letters omitted in each contraction.

_____ 10. I cant understand this at all.

_____ 11. Hed go if he could.

_____ 12. Lets dig up some worms and go fishing.

_____ 13. Youll be glad you came.

_____ 14. Weve come a long way.

_____ 15. Do you think hell win the election?

_____ 16. He wasnt here when the earthquake struck.

_____ 17. You mustnt mention this to anyone.

BONUS

In the contractions *ma'am* and *o'clock,* what letters have been omitted? Indicate below.

3–12 THE IMPORTANCE OF PERIODS AND APOSTROPHES

Groups of letters with a period after them can mean something quite different from those same letters without a period. There is quite a difference, for example, between *ill* (sick) and *ill.* (illustrated). In Part 1, the same letters will fit the definitions in both columns. Write these letters at the left. Then take the circled letters and rearrange them, along with the letter *s,* to form a very unusual word. (**Hint:** Not all the words in this exercise contain circled letters.)

S _ _ _ _ _ _ _ _ _

Part 1

		WORD	ABBREVIATION
_ _ _		1. girl	four quarts
_ _ _ Ⓞ		2. a boy's name	a country in Asia
_ _ _		3. a girl's name	a month
Ⓞ _ _		4. Dad	the number of people living in an area
_ Ⓞ _		5. an insect	a word opposite in meaning to another
Ⓞ _ _ _		6. lengthy	distance from the prime meridian
_ Ⓞ _ _		7. a penny	system for measuring temperature
_ _ Ⓞ		8. a vehicle	industry, commerce
Ⓞ _ _ _		9. to make musical sounds with the voice	referring to just one
_ _ _ _ _		10. a fellow	a major section of a book

Part 2

Similarly, the addition of an apostrophe can change the meaning of a group of letters. For example, there is considerable difference between *cant* (singsong speech) and *can't* (cannot). Identify the words defined below, write them at the left, and indicate where the apostrophe would go to change their meaning.

_ Ⓞ _	11. to marry
_ Ⓞ _ _	12. Hades
_ Ⓞ _ _	13. a pit from which water or oil is drawn
Ⓞ _ _ _	14. the hard covering of an egg
Ⓞ _ _ _	15. a small building used for storing equipment

Name _____ Date _____

3–13 COMMON ABBREVIATIONS

Americans are people in a hurry; consequently, we use lots of shortened terms in conversation and lots of abbreviations in writing. Fill in the missing words that each abbreviation below represents. (**Hint:** Some of these abbreviations are ordinarily capitalized, while others are written in small letters. Some use periods, while others don't.) Write the words at the right.

1. D.A.: District _____

2. B.A.: _____ of Arts

3. Blvd.:

4. P.S.:

5. RIP: _____ in peace

6. rpm: _____ per minute

7. cu. mm.: _____ millimeter

8. Co.:

9. MSG: monosodium _____

10. lat.:

11. kwh.: kilowatt _____

12. oz.:

13. bu.:

A	___ ___ ___ ___
B	___ ___ ___ ___ ___
B	___ ___ ___ ___ ___ ___
R	___ ___
E	___
V	___ ___ ___ ___ ___
I	___ ___
A	___ ___ ___
T	___
I	___ ___ ___
O	___ ___
N	___ ___
S	___ ___ ___

BONUS

In the space below, list at least ten abbreviations you might find used in a dictionary to explain an entry—such as *vi.* (verb intransitive), *Fr.* (French), etc. Be sure to include the necessary periods.

_____

_____

_____

_____

_____

_____

4

SPELLING AND PRONUNCIATION

Name _____ Date _____

4-1 RULES FOR SPELLING PLURALS

A string entered a cafe, and the waiter said, "We don't serve strings here." So the string went outside, tied itself into a knot, and fluffed out both ends. When it reentered the cafe, the waiter asked, "Aren't you the same string that was in here before?" The string replied,

" __ __ , __ __ __ __ __ __ __ __ __ __ __ __ K __ __ __ ."
$\overline{3\ 4}$ $\overline{11}$ $\overline{10\ 5}$ $\overline{10}$ $\overline{7\ 1\ 8\ 12\ 2\ 9}$ $\overline{3\ 4\ 6}$

To discover the answer, fill the blanks in the spelling rules below and transfer the circled letters to the appropriate spaces above.

1. Most nouns form their plurals by simply adding *s* to the __ __ __ __ __ __ __ ◯ .

2. Nouns that end in *s, sh, ch, x,* or *z* form their plurals by adding ◯ __ .

3. Nouns ending in *y* preceded by a __ __ ◯ __ __ __ __ __ __ __ change the *y* to *i* and add *es.*

4. Nouns ending in *y* preceded by a __ ◯ __ __ __ simply add *s.*

5. Most nouns ending in *man* (salesman, etc.) form their plurals by changing *man* to ◯ __ __ .

6. Most nouns ending in *o* form their plurals by adding *s,* but a few use *es.* Several such nouns may be spelled __ __ ◯ __ ways.

7. Some nouns ending in *f* or *fe* change the ◯ to *v* and add *es,* while others merely add *s.*

8. Nouns ending in *ful* form their __ __ __ __ __ ◯ __ __ by adding *s.*

9. In __ __ __ __ __ __ __ ◯ words, such as *son-in-law,* the main term in the compound is made plural.

10. Some nouns have the __ ◯ __ __ form in both the singular and plural. (Example: sheep)

11. Some plurals are ◯ __ __ __ __ __ __ __ __ __ __ and follow no set of rules. (Examples: mouse, ox)

12. When in doubt about plural forms, always consult the __ __ __ __ __ __ __ __ __ __ __ ◯ .

4–2 IRREGULAR PLURALS

Most nouns form their plurals by adding *s* or *es*. A number of them, however, form their plurals in other ways. Complete the columns below by filling in either the singular or plural form, as indicated. The circled letters, in order, will form the words to complete this conversation:

Teacher: Give an example of a singular noun and a plural noun.

Student: I know one that is singular at the top and plural at the bottom. It is _ _ _ _ _ _ _ _ _ _ _ _'_ _ _ _ _ _ _ .

SINGULAR	PLURAL
1. _ _ O _	beaux
2. hypothesis	_ _ O _ _ _ _ _ _
3. stratum	_ _ _ _ _ O _
4. alumnus	_ _ _ _ _ O _
5. _ _ _ O _ _	cherubim
6. _ _ _ _ _ _ _ O _	phenomena
7. _ _ _ O _	wolves
8. _ _ _ _ O _	data
9. crisis	_ _ _ _ O _
10. _ _ _ _ _ _ _ O	criteria
11. species	_ _ _ _ _ _ O
12. sheep	_ _ _ _ O _
13. insigne	_ _ _ _ _ _ O _
14. salmon	_ _ _ _ _ O
15. _ _ _ O _ _ _ _	bacteria
16. son-in-law	_ _ _ _ O _ _ _ - _ _ _

BONUS

Two archaic (out of fashion) plurals are *kine* and *brethren*. What is the singular form of each of these words? Write them below.

Name _____   Date _____

4–3 SILENT LETTERS

    In the diagram, circle all the words of five letters or more that contain silent letters. There are sixteen of them, all placed vertically or horizontally in the diagram. Write the words under the diagram and circle the silent letters in each one. The letters remaining in the diagram, when taken in order, will form a humorous definition for the word *microscope*.

Write it here: _____

```
L  E  A  G  U  E  R  A  M  G
O  U  C  A  U  G  H  T  K  N
P  S  A  L  M  T  Y  H  N  A
W  C  H  P  L  U  M  B  E  R
W  R  E  S  T  L  E  A  A  L
R  U  I  K  N  I  F  E  D  E
E  M  G  H  A  S  T  L  Y  D
A  B  H  S  H  T  I  G  H  T
T  F  T  O  R  E  M  I  D  G
H  E  T  T  O  N  G  U  E  S
```

1. _____   9. _____

2. _____   10. _____

3. _____   11. _____

4. _____   12. _____

5. _____   13. _____

6. _____   14. _____

7. _____   15. _____

8. _____   16. _____

BONUS

On the back of this sheet, write definitions for several words that contain silent letters. Let your classmates guess the words and then spell them.

Name _____ Date _____

4-4 I BEFORE E

Remember the old rule about *i* before *e* except after *c* or when sounded like *a* as in *neighbor* and *weigh*? Unfortunately, there are many exceptions to this rule, some of which are included in the list below. If a word is incorrect, rewrite it. If a word is correct, circle its number. Then, in the diagram, shade in the squares that contain the numbers you circled. These shaded numbers will form a shape that suggests another word that contains *i* and *e*.

Write it here: _____

1	2	3	4
5	6	7	8
9	10	11	12
13	14	15	16
17	18	19	20
21	22	23	24
25	26	27	28

1. sheild
2. brief
3. leisure
4. counterfiet
5. weird
6. weild
7. retreive
8. siege
9. seize
10. protien
11. kercheif
12. kaleidoscope
13. cieling
14. perceive

15. thief
16. releive
17. heifer
18. shiek
19. shreik
20. mischievous
21. receipt
22. weiner
23. greif
24. species
25. conciet
26. financier
27. forfeit
28. foriegn

4–5 THE SCHWA

Each of the words below contains a schwa (an indistinct vowel sound that resembles the sound of *uh,* as does the *i* in *pencil*). Fill in the vowel that is the schwa in each word. Then transfer these vowels to the corresponding spaces in the following unusual set of sentences. Can you figure out what is unusual about this set? Write your idea here:

_____

D __ C, N __ T __ __ D __ SS __ NT. __ F __ ST N __ V __ R PR __ V __ NTS __
  13   19 6 11   3   12   1   9   2   16   18 8   7

F __ TN __ SS. __ D __ T __ N C __ D.
  14   10   15   3 20   17   4

  1. sep __ rate   11. priv __ lege

  2. ben __ fit   12. exist __ nce

  3. defin __ tely   13. impost __ r

  4. glam __ rous   14. begg __ r

  5. irresist __ ble   15. sens __ ble

  6. cem __ tery   16. persist __ nce

  7. gramm __ r   17. hum __ rous

  8. skel __ ton   18. occurr __ nce

  9. resist __ nce   19. profess __ r

 10. juv __ nile   20. d __ cision

BONUS

None of the examples above contain the letter *u* as a schwa. It can be a schwa, as in the case of the second *u* in *ukulele*; however, some dictionaries show it just as a short *u.* Another group of words that have the schwa sound are those with no-vowel syllables, such as *rhythm,* in which the schwa sound precedes the *m.* Glance through your dictionary and find examples of words with schwa sounds. Write them on the back of this sheet, circling the letter that constitutes the schwa.

Name _____ Date _____

4–6 WORDS WITH REPEATED LETTERS

Each of the first fifteen words below contains the same letter in three different positions; numbers 16 to 20 contain three sets of double letters. Fill in the missing letters. Some of the words contain circled letters. Take these circled letters and rearrange them to form the two rhyming words that complete this statement:

When you propose to a girl, you are making a _____ _____.

1. An anteater
   a a _ _ _ a _ _

2. Commotion
   _ _ b b _ b _

3. Stretched out of shape
   d _ _ _ _ _ _ d _ d

4. Honorable, well-bred males
   _ e _ Ⓞ _ e _ e _

5. A silly laugh
   g _ g g _ _ _

6. To cast a bright light upon in order to make something stand out
   h _ _ _ h _ _ _ _ h _

7. A merry-go-round
   _ Ⓞ i _ _ i _ i _

8. A song sung to a baby
   l _ l l _ _ _

9. An ancient relative of the elephant
   m _ _ m m _ _ Ⓞ

10. The act of naming a candidate
    n _ _ Ⓞ n _ _ _ _ n

11. A dentist who straightens teeth
    o _ _ _ o _ o _ _ _ _ Ⓞ

12. Seasoned too much with a certain spice
    p _ p p _ _ _ _

13. To place in different positions
    r _ _ r r _ _ _ _

14. Good fortune, favorable results for one's efforts
    s _ Ⓞ _ _ s s

15. Lying, false
    u _ _ _ u _ Ⓞ _ u _

16. Glumness, sadness
    _ _ l l _ n n _ s s

17. A group of people appointed by a chairman to perform a certain function
    Ⓞ _ m m _ t t e e

18. The state of being ordinary
    _ _ m m _ n n _ s s

19. One who keeps records of business transactions
    _ o o k k e e Ⓞ _ _

20. Self-assertiveness, boldness
    _ g g _ _ s s Ⓞ _ _ _ _ s s

BONUS

Can you think of any other words containing several sets of double letters or letters used three or more times within the words? If so, write them on the back of this sheet.

Name _____ Date _____

4-7 THE "EYES" WORDS

What kind of eyes might a hypnotist have? How about hynot*ize* or mesmer*ize*? Verbs that end with the sound of "*eyes*" may use the following spellings: *-ize, -ise,* or *yze*. Try to think of an *"eyes"* word related to each of the professions below and check to see whether your spelling is correct.

Part 1

WHAT KIND OF "EYES" WOULD EACH OF THE FOLLOWING HAVE?

1. Arctic explorer: _____

2. Twins: _____

3. Movie star: _____

4. Musician: _____

5. P.E. teacher: _____

6. Attorney: _____

7. Inventor: _____

8. Manager: _____

9. Writer: _____

10. Minister: _____

11. Nurse or doctor: _____

12. Prison warden: _____

13. Army officer: _____

14. Battery manufacturer: _____

15. Scientist: _____

16. Manufacturer of stun guns: _____

Part 2

Other spellings for the *"eyes"* sound are listed below, together with examples of words that use these spellings. Can you think of any other spellings? Write them below.

-ies: supplies _____

-uys: buys _____

-ighs: sighs _____

-yes: dyes _____

Name _____ Date _____

4–8 THE "SEED" WORDS

The sound "seed" can be spelled -cede, -sede, or -ceed. In each sentence below, combine one of these spellings with one of the following prefixes: ac-, ante-, con-, ex-, inter-, pre-, pro-, re-, se-, suc-, and super-. Definitions are given for the words you will supply. Then transfer the circled letters to the corresponding spaces in the following sentence:

H̲ H̲_ _ T̲ H̲_ _ _ _ _ L̲ L̲ _ G̲_ _ _ G̲_ _ _ _ BUT _ _ _
7   10 6   8 4 11   5 1   7   11   6 7   8 4 11 9   6 3 6

_ T̲ L̲ T̲ H̲_ _ _ U̲ _ T̲_ _ _ G̲_ T̲_ H̲_ _ H̲_ _ _ .
2 1   4   3 9   7 6   5 10   3 1 2   1   1   3 9   11 10 6

1. The parade will __◯_____ from here to Main Street. **(go)**

2. I will not __◯_____ on that point. **(give in)**

3. We may have to get an outsider to ◯_____ between the union and management. **(mediate)**

4. Did Jefferson _____◯___ Madison? **(come before)**

5. Which state was first to __◯____ from the Union? **(break away)**

6. Do you think this plan will _____◯? **(work out well)**

7. Try not to _____◯_ the speed limit. **(go beyond)**

8. Your hairline may ◯_____ as you grow older. **(draw back)**

9. This new law will _____◯___ all previous laws. **(replace)**

10. Will your country ◯_____ to the U.N. proposal? **(agree to)**

11. What is the _____◯_____ of this pronoun? **(the word to which the pronoun refers)** Hint: For this word you must add a suffix as well as a prefix.

BONUS

Think of other suffixes (besides the one in item 11) that can be used with the "seed" words. Write them on the back of this sheet.

4–9 WORDS CONTAINING *E*'S

Part 1

Each word below begins and ends with *e* but contains no other *e*'s. Identify the words.

1. To increase or lengthen   e __ e
2. Freedom from pain   e ___ e
3. A bird of prey   e ____ e
4. A large area under one ruler   e _____ e
5. Obscuring of one heavenly body by another   e _____ e
6. Qualified to be chosen   e _____ e
7. Fancy, intricate   e _____ e
8. To set free   e _____ e
9. To grant the right to vote   e _____ e
10. To drain of blood (Look this one up in the *ex*
    section of your dictionary.)   e _____ e

Part 2

Each of the following words has *e*'s in the positions indicated. Fill in the missing letters.

11. To hold in high regard   e ___ e e __
12. An insect   __ e e __ e
13. To decide   e __ e ____ e
14. To count out   e ___ e __ e
15. A particular order or series   __ e __ e __ e
16. To kill with an electric charge   e __ e _____ e
17. To come out   e __ e __ e
18. A souvenir   __ e e ___ e
19. To go before   __ e __ e __ e
20. To decrease in value   __ e __ e ___ e

BONUS

Can you spell a word for a horsewoman that contains four *e*'s?

e ___ e _____ e __ e

Do you know any other words with four *e*'s? If so, write them on the back of this sheet.

4–10 WORDS CONTAINING THE SOUND OF $\overline{oo}$

Because many different combinations of letters can produce the same sounds, and because in most instances there are no rules that apply, English spellings are very difficult. All of the words below, for example, contain the sound of $\overline{oo}$, but in each word the sound is produced by a different letter or set of letters. The letters that produce the sound are circled. As you fill in the missing letters, try not to confuse the sound of $\overline{oo}$ (as in *fool*) with the sound of $\bar{u}$ (as in *fuel*).

1. One who does

2. An exact copy

3. A broth that may contain meat and vegetables

4. A low number

5. Inflammation and pain in the joints and muscles

6. A small, narrow boat

7. To chase

8. Retreated, went away

9. A treelike grass that grows in Asia

10. Something annoying or unpleasant

11. A meeting or a spot where a meeting is held

12. A thick stew of meat and vegetables

13. Finished, completed

14. A Native American tribe from the Dakotas

BONUS

Can you think of any combination of letters other than those listed above that can form the sound of $\overline{oo}$? If so, write words containing those combinations on the back of this sheet.

4–11 WORDS CONTAINING THE SOUNDS OF Ā AND ÂR

At Mozart's grave they played his music backward because he was
_____. To find the answer, look at the words below that contain
the sound of long $\bar{a}$ (items 1 to 13) and fill in the missing letters. Do the same for the words
containing the sound of $\hat{a}r$ (items 14 to 23). The letters that form these sounds are given to
you, and each word has a different set of letters producing the sound. Then take the circled
letters, rearrange them, and form a word that will fit the blank.

LONG Ā

1. How old you are   a _ _ _

2. To wander away   ◯ _ _ a y

3. A characteristic   _ _ a i _

4. A cut of beef   _ _ e a _

5. A device for measuring something,
   such as rain   _ a u ◯ _

6. A blood vessel   _ e i _

7. What Santa Claus rides in   _ _ e i g h

8. Third person plural pronoun   _ _ e y

9. A thick liquid consisting of crushed,
   cooked fruit or vegetables   ◯ _ _ e e

10. An expert on food and drink   _ _ _ _ ◯ e t

11. A dish containing egg yolks and
    stiffly beaten egg whites   _ ◯ _ _ _ e

12. The British spelling of *jail*   _ a o _

13. A game played with mallets, balls,
    and wickets   _ _ ◯ _ u e t

ÂR

14. Loss of hope   ◯ _ _ _ _ a i r

15. To point out similarities   ◯ _ _ _ a r e

16. A large wild animal   _ e a r

17. Some other place   _ _ _ _ _ e r e

18. Card game played by one person   _ _ ◯ _ a i r e

19. Contraction for *never*   ◯ e ' e r

20. A message spoken to God   _ _ a y e r

21. Third person plural possessive pronoun   _ _ e i r

22. A French boy's name   _ _ e r r e

23. French medal awarded for military
    bravery   _ _ _ _ _ _ ◯ _ u e r r e

4-12 WORDS CONTAINING THE SOUNDS OF $\bar{E}$ AND $\bar{I}$

The first eight answers below contain the sound of $\bar{e}$, and in each word the sound is formed by different letters. Similarly, the answers in items 9 to 17 contain the sound of $\bar{i}$, all formed by different letters, as indicated. Supply the missing letters. Then take the circled letters (from the words that have circled letters) and transfer them to the spaces here that answer this question: What came after the Iron Age?

$\overline{3}\ \overline{14}\ \overline{5}\ \ \overline{7}\ \overline{15}\ \overline{17}\ \overline{6}\ \overline{10}\ \overline{12}\quad \overline{2}\ \overline{9}\ \overline{1}\ \overline{13}\ \overline{4}$

$\bar{E}$

1. Someone not present
    _ _ _ ◯ _ _ e e

2. To beg
    ◯ _ e a _

3. What cattle do when frightened
    _ _ _ _ _ ◯ e _ _ _

4. To grab
    ◯ e i _ _ _

5. To scream
    _ _ ◯ i e _

6. A musical instrument resembling a small drum with metal disks around the edge
    _ _ _ _ _ _ _ _ _ i _ ◯

7. A type of primate
    ◯ _ _ _ e y

8. The study of plants
    _ _ _ _ _ _ y

$\bar{I}$

9. A type of grain
    ◯ y e

10. A country in Asia
    _ _ _ a i _ _ ◯ _

11. A friend
    _ _ _ _ y

12. Upper part of the leg
    ◯ _ i g h

13. A small, white flower associated with Switzerland
    _ _ _ _ _ _ e i ◯ _

14. An affirmative vote (Hint: The entire word has the sound of $\bar{i}$.)
    _ _ ◯

15. Opposite of an acid
    ◯ _ _ _ _ i

16. Altitude
    _ e i g h _

17. To unfasten
    _ ◯ _ i e

Name _____ Date _____

4–13 WORDS CONTAINING THE SOUND OF *SH*

The sound of *sh* can be produced in a variety of ways. Listed below are definitions for words that contain this sound. In each word the sound is spelled in a different way, as indicated. Take the circled letters and rearrange them to form an interesting word that denotes a female but contains two male words plus another feminine word. Write it here:

_ _ _ _ _ _ _

1. To become smaller or more compact

   s h ◯ _ _ _ _

2. The seasonal movement of animals, such as birds, to new regions

   _ _ _ _ _ _ t i _ _

3. A major body of water

   ◯ c e _ _ _

4. Certain, definite

   s _ _ _ _

5. A sum paid to an individual by an employer after retirement

   _ ◯ _ s i _ _ _

6. A person sent by a church to preach in another region

   _ ◯ s s i _ _ _ _ _ _

7. Leather leggings worn over trousers by cowboys

   c h _ _ _ _

8. A type of small, German-named dog with a wiry coat, heavy eyebrows, and a beard

   s c h _ _ _ _ _ ◯ _

9. The act of assuming something is wrong without having proof

   _ _ _ _ _ _ c i ◯

10. Alert, awake

    _ _ _ _ s c i _ _

11. A reddish-violet color, a species of bush bearing reddish-violet flowers

    _ _ _ _ c h s _ _

12. An exclamation expressing disapproval or disbelief

    p s h _ _ _

BONUS

Write the two masculine words and the feminine word found in the word formed by the circled letters above.

Name _____ Date _____

4–14 UNUSUAL VOWEL COMBINATIONS

Most words of any length have a couple of vowels, but few have the unusual arrangements of vowels in this exercise. Follow the directions for each set of words below. Then transfer the circled letters to the following spaces to form a word with six consecutive consonants:

$$\overline{}\ \overline{}\ \overline{}\ \overline{}\ \overline{}\ \overline{}\ \overline{}\ \overline{}\ \overline{}\ \overline{}\ \overline{}$$
$$2\ \ 3\ \ 7\ \ 10\ 11\ \ 8\ \ 4\ 17\ \ 9\ 20\ \ 5$$

The following words have three vowels in a row:

1. Compress, push together   _ _ _ u e e _ _

2. An outline drawing   _ Ⓞ _ o u e _ _ _

3. A tableland   _ Ⓞ _ e a u _

4. Moral, righteous   _ _ _ Ⓞ u o u _

5. Brave   _ _ _ _ _ Ⓞ e o u _

6. Running away   _ _ _ e e i _

7. Strange, odd   _ u a i _ Ⓞ

8. A sharp, shrill sound   Ⓞ _ u e a _

9. Savage, fierce   _ Ⓞ _ i o u _

10. Paddling in a small, narrow boat   Ⓞ _ _ o e i _ _

The following words have four consecutive vowels:

11. A person from the fiftieth state   Ⓞ _ _ a i i a _

12. The use of words having sounds that suggest their meaning   _ _ _ _ _ _ _ o e i a _

13. A type of large tree in California   _ _ _ _ u o i a

The next word has five consecutive vowels:

14. Lining up in a row   _ _ u e u e i _ _

The following words contain only one vowel:

15. Power   _ _ _ e _ _ _ _

16. An irregular spot   _ _ _ o _ _ _

Some words contain a vowel sound formed without the use of any of the five regular vowels. Usually the sound is produced by *y* representing the sound of short *i*, as in the following words:

17. The regular rise and fall of sounds and accents   Ⓞ _ y _ _ _

18. A gift brought by one of the Three Wise Men   _ y _ _ _

19. An underground vault   _ _ y _ _

20. A mythical maiden living in the mountains, forests, or water   Ⓞ y _ _ _ _

4–15 WORDS WITH *-ABLE* AND *-IBLE*

Study the rules in your English book for adding the suffixes *-able* and *-ible* to root words. Then fill in the missing letters in the words below, placing the letters in the words and also in the spaces at the left. In some instances you will supply two letters and, in others, only one. Place all the letters in order into the string of letters below. After that, divide the string of letters into words and write the sentence here:

_____

_____

__B__S__N__S__PL__CEWHER___USTR__L___NSW__SHTHE__RF__C__.

— 1. break__ble

— 2. perish__ble

— 3. sens__ble

— 4. irresist__ble

— 5. mov__ble

— 6. us__ble

— 7. manag___ble

— 8. blam__ble

— 9. defens__ble

— 10. laugh__ble

— 11. dispens__ble

— 12. collect__ble

— 13. peace__ble

— 14. knowledg__able

Try saying aloud the sentence above and substituting the sound of long *i* for all the long *a*'s. By doing this you will sound like a native of Australia.

BONUS

Think of at least two other words that end in *-able* and two words that end in *-ible*. Write them below.

Name _____   Date _____

4–16 DOUBLING LETTERS BEFORE SUFFIXES

One-syllable words ending in a single consonant preceded by a single vowel usually double the final consonant before adding suffixes that begin with a vowel, such as *-ed, -ing, -er,* etc. Two-syllable words that end in a single consonant generally double the consonant only if they are accented on the second syllable. In each instance below, spell the word called for by using as many of the spaces at the right as needed. The circled letters, when transferred, will fit into this piece of advice:

W _ _ _ _ _ _ _ _ _ _   F _ _ _   S _ _ S _ _ _   C _ _ _ S _ _
  3 2 14 4 3 16 4 7 1 3   9 9 11   4 7 13 6 4 5   9 6 13 1 9

Y _ U _ _ _ _ _ _ , _ _ _ _ _ _ _ _ _ _ _ _ _ _ _ _ .
 9   8 11 9 9 8   15 9 4 3 13 4 11 4 14 11 10 12 1 4 6 12 14

_____ 1. admit (ed)   _ _ _ _ _ Ⓞ _ _ _ _

_____ 2. bar (ed)   _ _ _ _ Ⓞ _ _ _ _

_____ 3. man (ish)   _ _ _ _ _ _ Ⓞ _ _ _

_____ 4. profit (able)   _ _ _ _ _ _ Ⓞ _ _ _

_____ 5. open (ing)   _ _ _ _ _ Ⓞ _ _ _ _

_____ 6. drum (er)   _ _ _ _ Ⓞ _ _ _ _

_____ 7. control (ed)   _ _ _ _ _ _ _ Ⓞ _ _

_____ 8. occur (ence)   _ _ _ _ _ Ⓞ _ _ _

_____ 9. marvel (ous)   _ _ _ _ _ _ Ⓞ _ _

_____ 10. rev (ed)   _ _ _ Ⓞ _ _ _ _ _

_____ 11. rid (ance)   _ _ _ Ⓞ _ _ _ _ _

_____ 12. ride (ing)   _ _ _ Ⓞ _ _ _ _ _

_____ 13. label (ed)   _ _ _ _ _ Ⓞ _ _ _

_____ 14. begin (ing)   _ _ _ _ _ Ⓞ _ _ _

_____ 15. shine (ing)   _ _ _ _ _ _ Ⓞ _ _ _

_____ 16. travel (er)   _ _ _ _ _ _ Ⓞ _ _

4–17 ADDING PREFIXES

When adding prefixes such as *mis-*, *dis-*, and *un-* to words, don't add any extra letters. For example, when adding *un-* to *affected,* simply join the two items: *unaffected.* If the root starts with *n,* follow the same rule—simply place the prefix before *needed* to form *unneeded.* (In this case you end up with two *n*'s, since both the prefix and the word had an *n* to start with.) Fill in the proper number of letters below and indicate the number of letters at the left. Total up the sets indicated and place the first three totals at the top to form a three-digit number. Do the same with the second set of three totals. Then reverse each of the numbers and subtract. If you do it correctly, you should get the same result from both sets of numbers.

THREE-DIGIT NUMBER _____
REVERSED   – _____

_____ A. I __ ATURE (M)
_____ B. MI __ TAKE (S)
_____ C. OVE __ IDE (R)
_____ D. MI __ PELL (S)
_____ E. U __ OCCUPIED (N)
☐ **TOTAL**

_____ F. I __ ORAL (M)
_____ G. U __ ECESSARY (N)
_____ H. MI __ UNDERSTOOD (S)
_____ I. I __ ESPONSIBLE (R)
☐ **TOTAL**

_____ J. DI __ IMILAR (S)
_____ K. I __ PERFECT (M)
_____ L. MI __ TATEMENT (S)
_____ M. DI __ APPOINT (S)
☐ **TOTAL**

THREE-DIGIT NUMBER _____
REVERSED   – _____

_____ N. OVE __ HEARD (R)
_____ O. UNDE __ ATED (R)
_____ P. I __ EFFECTIVE (N)
☐ **TOTAL**

_____ Q. DI __ TRUST (S)
_____ R. U __ DECIDED (N)
_____ S. UNDE __ COOKED (R)
☐ **TOTAL**

_____ T. I __ egal (L)
☐ **TOTAL**

4–18 SIMILAR WORDS OFTEN CONFUSED

In the exercise below are a number of words that are often confused with other words. Select the correct spelling to place in each blank and write the number of your choice in the corresponding space in the multiplication problem at the top. If you make the right choices and then multiply, you will know you are right because the result will be amazing.

G F C A D J H B

— — — — — — — —

x __ __ (I E)

ANSWER:

A. The _____ of Alaska is Juneau. (4) capital (1) capitol

B. Were you at the last meeting of the student _____? (6) counsel (9) council

C. He proved to be a _____ witness for the defendant, and the jury found him

innocent. (3) credible (7) credulous

D. The _____ of Pike's Peak proved less difficult than we had expected.

(2) assent (5) ascent

E. The criminal _____ the police. (9) alluded (8) eluded

F. He gave her a nice _____ about her new dress. (2) compliment

(5) complement

G. The tourists left the bus and _____ to the various hotels in the area.

(7) disbursed (1) dispersed

H. He is honest as the day is long. His _____ has never been questioned.

(7) veracity (5) voracity

I. That is nothing but an optical _____. (3) allusion (1) illusion

J. The money involved doesn't matter; it's the _____ of the thing. (6) principle

(4) principal

Name ———————————————— Date ——————————

4–19 SYNONYMS

Whenever you write illegibly, you can be said to be performing a ————————
————————. To find out what you're doing, write synonyms (words corresponding in
meaning) for the items listed below, placing the answers on the lines at the left. Then place
the words in the vertical positions indicated in the diagram. The shaded boxes will give
you the answer. Notice that all the synonyms start with the letter *a.*

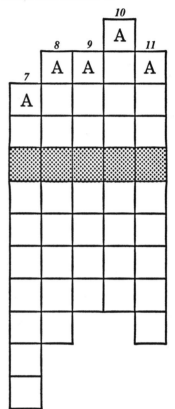

————————— 1. ridiculous, stupid (**adjective**)

————————— 2. bold, daring (**adjective**)

————————— 3. arrest, seize (**verb**)

————————— 4. treaty, union (**noun**)

————————— 5. clothing, raiment (**noun**)

————————— 6. real, genuine (**adjective**)

————————— 7. tempting, charming (**adjective**)

————————— 8. enemy, rival (**noun**)

————————— 9. obvious, conspicuous (**adjective**)

————————— 10. helper, associate (**noun**)

————————— 11. relieve, lessen (**verb**)

Name _____ Date _____

4–20 SYNONYMS INSIDE WORDS

Some words contain their own synonyms. For example, the word *within* contains *in* which is its synonym. Sometimes the letters are not right together, as in the case of *clue* and *cue*, but they are in correct order within the word.

Part 1

Find the hidden synonym in each word below and write it where indicated.

1. equivalent   _ _ _ _ _ _

2. deceased   _ _ _ _ _

3. latest   _ _ _ _ _

4. slithered   _ _ _ _ _

5. blossom   _ _ _ _ _ _

6. indolent   _ _ _ _ _

7. encourage   _ _ _ _ _

8. joviality   _ _ _ _

9. fallacies   _ _ _ _ _

10. appropriate   _ _ _ _

Part 2

Now try it the other way. Provide the additional letters that will form a synonym for the shorter word inside.

11. g i __ a n t __ __

12. __ __ i s __ __ __

13. __ t __ u g __ __ __

14. f r a __ i l __

15. c u __ t __ __ __ __

16. __ __ s e __ e

17. m a __ __ __ l __ e

18. h a t __ e __

19. c a v e __ __

20. __ __ p a r __ t __

4-21 OODLES OF SYNONYMS

Synonyms are words that are approximately the same in meaning, though there are usually slight differences. For example, synonyms for *white* include *snowy* and *milky* but may also include such words as *spotless, colorless, pure, unblemished,* etc. The word *cool* has synonyms such as *frosty, icy,* and *chilly,* which display different levels of coolness.

Part 1

For each of the three words below, try to think of as many synonyms as you can in the time provided by your teacher. You may use slang items as well as standard terms. The winner is the person with the most items listed and spelled correctly.

1. green: _____

_____

_____

_____

2. happy: _____

_____

_____

_____

3. crazy: _____

_____

_____

_____

Part 2

Look at the words below. For each set, think of a more general term that could be synonymous with them.

4. gale, breeze, zephyr, chinook, sirocco, hurricane: w _ _ _ _

5. valor, mettle, pluck, grit, intrepidity, courage: b _ _ _ _ _ _ _

6. sauntered, strolled, trudged, tramped, hiked, strode: w _ _ _ _ _ _

7 hodgepodge, miscellany, conglomeration, medley, blend, alloy: m _ _ _ _ _ _ _

4–22 ANTONYMS

When their English teacher was sick, the members of the class sent her a letter. The greeting of the letter was as follows:

Dear _____ _____

To discover the salutation find an antonym starting with the letter *p* for each pair of words below. (Antonyms are words opposite in meaning.) Write the antonyms in the spaces at the left and also place them in vertical positions in the diagram, as indicated. The letters on the shaded horizontal line will then give you the answer.

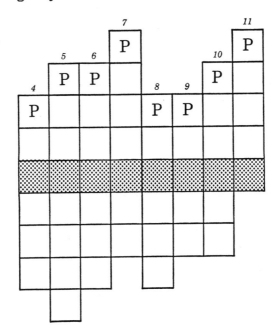

_____ 1. modern, newfangled (**adjective**)

_____ 2. ordinary, common (**adjective**)

_____ 3. safe, secure (**adjective**)

_____ 4. rude, discourteous (**adjective**)

_____ 5. negative, dubious (**adjective**)

_____ 6. total, universal (**adjective**)

_____ 7. faulty, defective (**adjective**)

_____ 8. condemn, punish (**verb**)

_____ 9. war, hostility (**noun**)

_____ 10. ugly, unsightly (**adjective**)

_____ 11. continue, persevere (**verb**)

4–23 ANTONYM CHAIN

Antonyms are words that are opposite in meaning. For each word below, supply an antonym that will fit into the chain as indicated, with the last letter of the first word forming the first letter of the next word. (To make it easier to see the entire word, the last letter on each line is repeated as the first letter on the next line.)

1. shorten

2. wide

3. valuable

4. crooked

5. false

6. contract

7. easy

8. defeat

9. arrogant

10. full

11. no

12. deep

13. ignorance

14. few

15. aged

16. dark

17. fearlessness

18. give

19. tiny

20. dull

21. loss

22. thick

23. disregard

24. indifference

25. feminine

26. insufficient

27. light

28. resists

4-24 HOMONYMS

Homonyms have the same pronunciation but different spellings and meanings. Usually they come in pairs, but sometimes they are in sets of three or even four (as in the case of *write, right, rite,* and *wright*). The items below deal with sets of three, all of which are defined. You are to supply the spelling of the third homonym in each set. Then transfer the circled letters into the following story. The answer will contain additional homonyms.

A man said to his psychiatrist, "Doc, sometimes I think I'm a wigwam, and other times I think I'm a tepee. What's wrong with me?"

"Why," said the doctor, "___ ___ ___ ___ ___ ___ $\overset{j}{—}$___ ___ ___ ___ ___ ___ ___ ___ ___ ___."
    1 8 9   3 15 6   11 12 10   13 14 5   10 2 7 12 4

1. idle (**unemployed**), idol (**image**), __ _(_)_ __ (**a type of narrative poem**)

2. liar (**one who tells lies**), lier (**one who lies down**), __ __ __ _(_)_ (**a musical instrument**)

3. pair (**two of a kind**), pear (**a fruit**), _(_)_ __ __ (**to peel**)

4. bowl (**a dish**), boll (**pod of a cotton plant**), __ __ __ _(_)_ (**the trunk of a tree**)

5. so (**therefore**), sew (**to stitch**), __ _(_)_ __ (**to plant seed**)

6. carrot (**vegetable**), carat (**unit of weight for precious stones**), __ __ __ _(_)_ (**a wedge-shaped mark on written work that indicates where something should be inserted**)

7. vein (**blood vessel**), vain (**conceited**), __ __ _(_)_ (**a device that shows wind direction**)

8. cord (**a string**), cored (**having the center removed**), __ __ _(_)_ __ (**a combination of harmonious tones**)

9. peak (**mountain**), peek (**to glance**), __ __ __ _(_)_ (**to excite or provoke**)

10. cents (**pennies**), sense (**vision, hearing, touch, etc.**), __ __ __ __ _(_)_ (**odors**)

11. Hugh (**boy's name**), hew (**to cut**), __ _(_)_ __ (**color**)

12. sees (**looks**), seas (**oceans**), _(_)_ __ __ __ __ __ (**to grab**)

13. sight (**vision**), cite (**to refer to**), __ __ _(_)_ __ (**location**)

14. road (**route**), rode (**did ride**), __ _(_)_ __ __ __ (**paddled a canoe**)

15. rain (**precipitation**), rein (**bridle**), _(_)_ __ __ __ __ __ (**to rule**)

Name _____ Date _____

4-25 ANIMAL HOMONYMS

Some animals have names that are homonyms. For each definition below, write the word defined to the right and place its animal homonym in the mini-crossword puzzles as shown. Several of the animal names may be unfamiliar to you; do the ones you know, and their letters will give you clues to the others.

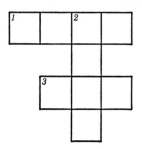
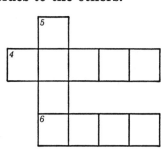
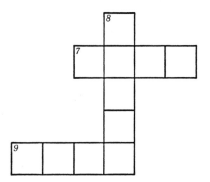

1. To whimper; to make crying sounds: _____

2. Sections of a chain: _____

3. Not old: _____

4. Having a rough voice: _____

5. Pulled: _____

6. Very expensive, beloved: _____

7. What grows out of the scalp: _____

8. A thin candle: _____

9. Uncovered, naked: _____

10. Atmospheric conditions: _____

11. Second person pronoun: _____

12. Bread batter: _____

13. A chilled dessert made with whipped cream and gelatin: _____

14. To make a hole: _____

15. The blood-pumping organ of the body: _____

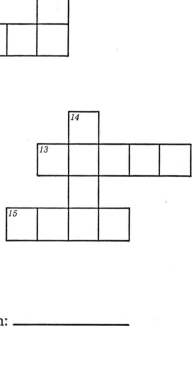

Name _____ Date _____

4-26 HETERONYMS

Heteronyms are words with the same spelling but different pronunciations and meanings, such as *sewer* (an underground pipe for waste water) and *sewer* (one who sews). Each sentence below has two blanks, which you are to fill with the same word. Definitions are given for some of the words to help you. Read the sentences aloud to hear the differing pronunciations of the two words. Then, in the diagram, connect the circled letters from items 1 and 7 with a single line and those from items 8 to 14 with another. These two lines will give you the answer to this question: What might a well-dressed cow wear?

A _____

```
 M   A   T   R       D   C   L   K
 •   •   •   •       •   •   •   •

 •   •   •   •       •   •   •   •
 S   W   B   U       P   O   V   E
```

1. The _____◯ fiddle player went fishing and caught a _____.

2. In a ◯_____, after I adjust this microscope, we will be able to study these _____ (tiny) particles.

3. The strong ◯_____ caused the sheet to _____ (twist) around the clothesline.

4. She made a grand ___◯_____, which she hoped would _____ (charm) the audience.

5. When he went back out on the stage to take a ◯____, his _____ tie fell off.

6. The doctor ___◯____ the bandage around her arm where the _____ (injury) was.

7. When she got a _____◯ (rip) in her new dress, I saw a _____ in her eye.

8. For goodness ___◯__, don't drink all that _____ (Japanese wine).

9. Please don't __◯_____ (leave) me here in this _____ without at least a canteen of water.

10. The ___◯_____ (disabled person) learned that his claim to his uncle's fortune was _____.

11. This company took the ◯_____ in removing _____ (a metal) from its paint products.

12. A __◯__ (disturbance) broke out in the last _____ in the theater.

13. Those two ◯_____ (female deer) seem in good health but the buck _____ not.

14. He ___◯___ (sulked) around in his room because he didn't get a _____ for Christmas.

4–27 ANAGRAMS

Part 1

In each sentence below is a word which, when its letters are rearranged, will form the word needed in the blank. You must decide which word to select, underline it, and then place its anagram in the blank. For example, in the following sentence you would underline *East* and then write *teas* in the blank:

Most of our fancy _____ come from the far East.

1. I may use a _____ instead of a sweet potato in this new recipe.
2. Part of the problem with this rabbit _____ is that it can cause serious injury to the rabbit.
3. He _____ the state contest and will now enter the regional competition.
4. Among the _____ the robber took was a tool that Allen uses in his work.
5. It took _____ men to pull in the net with the fish.
6. After you put away all the pots and pans, you can _____ for the day.
7. The diet of the men on these athletic _____ includes lots of whole-grain cereals, vegetables, and meats.
8. Don't _____ at that girl over there, as she is already in tears.

Part 2

In the sentences below, rearrange the letters in the two italicized words to form the single word that will fit into the blank.

9. The _____ sold a number of properties but was unable to sell the *rear lot.*
10. When Rod entered, the other _____ in the office laughed at *Rod's tie.*
11. The _____ was a *great help* to people in the 1900s, since it enabled them to communicate long distances through the use of Morse Code.
12. I found my shoes but was in a state of _____ because I couldn't find *Ed's pair.*
13. The natives are going to *help Nate* capture the _____ and ship it to the zoo.
14. A *real pall* settled over the members of the city council when they learned that the new highway would run _____ to the main street instead of intersecting it.

Name _____ Date _____

4-28 MORE ANAGRAMS

In each set of sentences below, try to figure out the word that fits into the first sentence, writing it in the blank in the sentence and also in the spaces at the left. Then, using the same letters in new arrangements, form the words for the other sentences. The circled letters in each set represent the same letter of the alphabet. When these four letters from the four sets are rearranged, two anagrams of the original word can be formed. Write the three words here:

_____ _____ _____

1. _____ to that wind howl!

2. When in doubt, don't speak. Just keep _____.

3. When did Gregory _____ in the army?

4. Put this _____ on the Christmas tree.

5. Fishermen catch lots of salmon along these _____.

6. Mother used to tell us lots of fairy _____.

7. Thou shalt not _____.

8. We've all heard those jokes before. They're _____.

9. That is the _____ of my problems.

10. Years ago children did their math on _____ boards.

11. The papers were held together by a _____.

12. I don't like _____ colors. They are too pale to suit me.

13. How many _____ does a dandelion have?

14. Set the table with five _____ and glasses.

15. This skirt has six _____.

16. The horses are all in the _____.

17. We will need two _____ for the picnic.

18. Which of these boys is the _____ drummer?

19. That goat _____ all day long.

BONUS

Take these letters and form five words from them: ISTREP

_____ _____ _____ _____

_____

4–29 PALINDROMES

Palindromes are words that are spelled the same forward and backward. In each sentence below, supply the palindromes that are defined.

1. _____, _____, and _____ all came to my gradua-
   (mother)   (father)   (female sibling)
   tion.

2. The baby bird opened one _____ and made a _____.
   (organ of vision)   (small sound)

3. As the two Eskimos sailed along in their _____, they related
   (type of canoe)
   _____ to each other.
   (epic narratives)

4. The _____ of Iran have almost been _____.
   (rulers)   (worshiped as gods)

5. One _____ of a democracy is that it is a _____ duty to vote.
   (principle)   (of a citizen)

6. When you _____, be sure to stand on a ladder that is _____.
   (put wallpaper on again)   (even, flat on top)

7. He drank a bottle of _____ as he tied the _____ around the
   (soda)   (protective cloth or plastic)
   neck of the _____.
   (small child)

8. _____ he _____ to the _____ demonstration to be
   (past tense of *do*) (make reference)   (detection system
                                               using radio waves)
   given at _____?
   (middle of the day)

9. "_____!" he said. "Now I understand how this _____ works."
   (exclamation)   (a device that revolves)

10. If that _____ doesn't stop barking, I may have to _____ him.
    (young dog)   (put something
                                                    in his mouth)

BONUS

Try to think of some palindromic names, such as *Otto, Bob,* and *Anna* and write them on the back of this sheet.

Name _____ Date _____

4–30 SPELLING DEMONS

A certain child was given twenty-eight words to spell and spelled them all just as they sound, as shown below. Place the corrected spellings in the vertical columns, as indicated. One of the longest English words will appear in the shaded horizontal line.

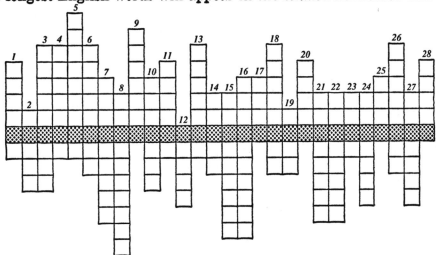

1. simbl (**musical instrument**)

2. nole (**small hill**)

3. kumity (**group of people**)

4. biskit

5. sooperseed

6. likerish

7. kunsensus

8. lootenent

9. shamee (**a type of soft leather cloth**)

10. kaptin

11. skweek

12. bayzh (**a tan color**)

13. resl

14. seez (**to grab**)

15. fasinate

16. diptherea

17. com (peaceful, quiet)

18. sematary

19. nat (**insect**)

20. deepoe

21. gardeun

22. sarjnt

23. air (**one who inherits**)

24. jelus

25. him (**song sung in church**)

26. safire (**a gem**)

27. obseen

28. som (**a sacred poem**)

BONUS

Is there a certain word that always gives you trouble when you try to spell it? If so, write it below and see how many of your classmates can spell it correctly.

4–31 SPELLING HEXAGON

Spell as many words as you can by starting anywhere in the diagram and moving along the connecting lines. Do not skip letters. For example, you cannot form the word *snore*, since to get to the *e*, you would have to skip *n*. You may come back and use the same letter again, as when you form the word *noun*, but you cannot use the letter twice in succession. You cannot, for example, form the word *sell*. Proper nouns, contractions, and abbreviations do not count. Words must have four letters or more. Count one point for each four-letter word, two points for five-letter words, and three points for words of six letters or more. The person with the most points in the given time is the winner.

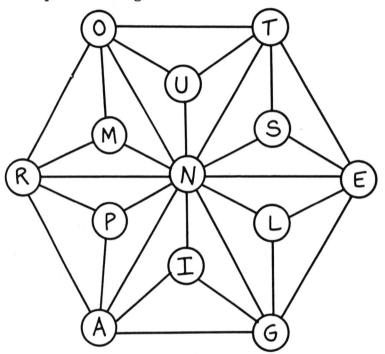

Four-letter words	Five-letter words	Longer words

4–32 SPELLING MAZE

You are captured by a spelling fanatic and trapped in a maze at the point where the circle is. You can only reach the exit by determining which words are spelled correctly and following their route. Starting at the circle, draw a line to the center of the adjacent square containing a correct word, then to the center of the next adjacent square with a correct word, etc. You will know whether you are right because the line you are drawing will indicate what you might say when you reach the exit. Then rewrite the incorrect words in the spaces indicated, spelling them correctly. (There are thirteen incorrectly spelled words.)

exaggerate	liquefy	antique	digestible	surgeon
occasion	dietition	fude	nickle	millionaire
secretary	calander	complection	chaufer	omision
rebelled	paralel	beggar	solemn	separate
burglar	schedual	●	judgement	wrestle
squeak	sincerly	truely	aironautiks	reign
panicked	inoculate	eligible	sphere	recommend

Exit

Corrected words:

1. _____   7. _____
2. _____   8. _____
3. _____   9. _____
4. _____   10. _____
5. _____   11. _____
6. _____   12. _____
                           13. _____

BONUS

What does the line suggest you might say when you reach the exit? Write it here:

_____

4–33 PRONUNCIATION

A number of words in our language are frequently misspelled because they are mispronounced. For example, if you pronounce the word *height* as *hīth* instead of *hīt,* you will probably spell it *heigth.* Fill in the missing letters in the words listed below and practice pronouncing them, paying particular attention to the sound of the letters you filled in. Then transfer the circled letters from the words into the spaces in the following sentence, which is an example of a $\overline{10}\ \overline{22}\ \overline{5}\ \overline{8}\ \overline{6}\ \overline{22}\ \overline{12}$:

$\underline{}\overset{q}{\underline{}}\ \underline{}\ \underline{}\ \underline{}$, $\underline{}\ \underline{}\overset{k}{\underline{}}\ \underline{}\ \underline{}\ \underline{}\overset{x}{\underline{}}\ \underline{}\ \underline{}\ \underline{}\overset{f}{\underline{}}\ \underline{}\ \underline{}\ \underline{}\overset{z}{\underline{}}\ \underline{}\overset{j}{\underline{}}\ \underline{}\ \underline{}$.

18 22 14 13 17   10 22 7   12 9   1 19   3 2 4 20   2 15 13   11 19   13 5   14 8 21

1. proba◯ly

2. pi◯_ture

3. san_◯ich

4. represen◯ative

5. gover◯ment

6. lib◯ary

7. Ar◯tic

8. reco◯nize

9. Feb_uar◯

10. su_◯rise

11. can◯idate

12. chi◯_ey

13. drown◯d

14. pron◯nciation

15. mischie◯___s

16. sherbe◯

17. ath◯etics

18. p_◯spiration

19. int_◯duce

20. lig◯t_ing

21. acros◯

22. burg_◯r

23. e◯cetera

BONUS

Write the word from the paragraph at the top that indicates what the sentence you filled in is. Then write a definition for this word. Look it up if necessary.

_____

_____

Here is another example of this: The quick brown fox jumps over the lazy dog. (This sentence is often used to test new typewriters to see whether all the keys work.)

4-34 SAME SPELLING BUT DIFFERENT PRONUNCIATION

Because some words have spellings that are basically the same, we would expect their pronunciations to be alike. For example, *beast* and *breast* both end with *east*, but one has the sound of long *e*, while the other has the sound of short *e*. Identify the two words for each sentence below that look as if they should be pronounced the same way.

1. Rex has never b_____ to Arizona nor s_____ the Grand Canyon, so I think he should go with us to see that region.

2. I really had a struggle trying to get this b_____ on my f_____.

3. You better not l_____ the prescription the doctor gave you because you need another d_____ of that medicine soon.

4. Though I can't s____ very well, I think I will try to mend a f____ of these garments.

5. This restaurant certainly serves g_____ f_____.

6. I don't know which is w_____ –trying to ride a h_____ that bucks a lot or one that just won't gallop at all.

7. I bought some stamps at the _____ office but _____ them on the way home.

8. Even though I was very ill, I n_____ had a f_____ over 100 degrees.

9. His _____ is 5'11″ and his _____ is 165 lb.

10. Don't be in such a r_____. We don't need to p_____ our way through this crowd.

11. I hope I can get this _____ before the _____ rings again.

12. The guard didn't say a _____ as he took the c_____ and wrapped it around the prisoner's hands.

BONUS

Imagine that you are a foreigner who has just arrived in the U.S., and you have learned a few English words. In the following sentence, for example, you know that the word *rough* is pronounced "ruff." If you saw this sentence written out, how would it sound when you read it aloud? (Use the logic a foreigner might use.)

Though I had a *rough* day and a bad *cough*, I was happy to get *through* early and head home, but on the way I was struck by the *bough* of a tree and ended up at the emergency room.

4–35 ACCENT SHIFT

Some of our two-syllable words can be changed from one part of speech to another by simply shifting the accent. The word *present,* for example, is a verb when accented on the second syllable (You may present' your speech now) and a noun or an adjective when accented on the first syllable (a Christmas pres'ent, at the pres'ent time). Identify the word that fits each pair of sentences below and indicate where the accent falls in each sentence. Then write the circled letters in the spaces at the left to form the answer to this question: Why did one bottle keep giving orders to the others?

Answer: Because it was a _____ _____.

_____ 1. A soldier in the Confederate Army was referred to as a __ __ (_) __ __ .

Will the members _____ if we enact this rule?

_____ 2. Joe won the __ (_) _____ easily.

Do you think the heirs will _____ the will?

_____ 3. In the last year there has been an ____ (_) _____ in the cost of living.

We must _____ our production.

_____ 4. For how many years did he __ (_) _____ the orchestra?

The teacher said my _____ could stand improvement.

_____ 5. Calling someone a "dork" is an _____ (_) _ .

Be careful not to say anything to _____ the boss.

_____ 6. I'm sure the jury will _____ (_) __ him.

After the _____ escaped from prison, he committed another crime.

_____ 7. _____ (_) me to escort you to the dining room.

You must get a building _____ to add a room to your house.

_____ 8. Please _____ (_) __ all these envelopes for me.

He didn't receive my letter because his _____ has been changed.

_____ 9. The (_) _____ is piling up because the garbage collectors are on strike.

How can I _____ your generous offer?

4–36 ENUNCIATION

Though you may pronounce words correctly, unless you also enunciate clearly, you still may not be understood. Each of the phrases at the left below can be mistaken for the words at the right if the enunciation is unclear. Practice saying the words in a manner that your classmates understand.

1. eye strain	iced rain, ice train
2. comic strip	comic's trip
3. helper	help her
4. summer school	summer's cool
5. insider	inside her, in cider
6. Caesar	seize her
7. some ice	some mice
8. Nick's car	Nick's scar
9. a narrow box	an arrow box
10. room 8	roommate
11. green isle	green Nile
12. icy	I see
13. ice cream	I scream
14. night rate	nitrate
15. an aim	a name
16. light housekeeper	lighthouse keeper
17. dresser	dress her
18. aspiring	a spy ring
19. makes two	make stew
20. Hispanic	his panic

BONUS

According to the *Guinness Book of World Records,* the following is the most difficult tongue twister: The sixth sick sheik's sixth sheep's sick.

Try writing a tongue twister of your own, using sounds that are particularly difficult to enunciate. Write it on the back of this sheet. Also print it on a larger sheet of paper so it can be displayed on the bulletin board. The class willl select the most difficult tongue twister as the winner.

5

NAMES OF PEOPLE, PLACES, AND THINGS

5-1 PLACES IN THE U.S. NAMED AFTER PEOPLE

Many places in the United States are named after famous persons. A few of these places are described below. The vertical column of letters, which spells out the words *United States,* gives you some clues. Fill in the missing letters.

1. The capital of Alaska, named after the man who discovered gold there
   _ U _ _ _ _

2. The capital of Nebraska, named after a president
   _ N _ _ _ _

3. The capital of Wisconsin, named after a president
   _ _ _ I _ _ _

4. A city and a state both named after the same president
   _ _ _ _ _ _ T _ _

5. A state named after the Quaker who established it
   _ E _ _ _ _ _ _ _ _ _ _

6. A river in New York and a bay, both named after an explorer
   _ _ _ D _ _

7. The capital of Ohio, named after an explorer
   _ _ _ _ _ _ _ _ S

8. A city in Texas named after a general who became the president of the Texas Republic
   _ _ _ _ T _ _

9. The capital of Mississippi, named after a president
   _ _ A _ _ _ _

10. The capital of Nevada, named after a frontiersman and scout
    _ _ _ _ _ _ _ _ T _ _

11. A peak in Colorado, named after an explorer
    _ _ _ E ' _ _ _ _ _

12. A state named after a French king
    _ _ _ _ S

BONUS

On the back of this sheet, list other places in the United States named after people. Try to find some named after women, such as *Virginia,* named after Queen Elizabeth I, the Virgin Queen.

Name _____ Date _____

5-2 PLACES IN THE WORLD NAMED AFTER PEOPLE

Many spots in the world are named after various famous people. A few of these are included in the exercise below. Identify the places described and place their names in the puzzle, where indicated, with items 1 and 2 placed horizontally and the others intersecting them vertically.

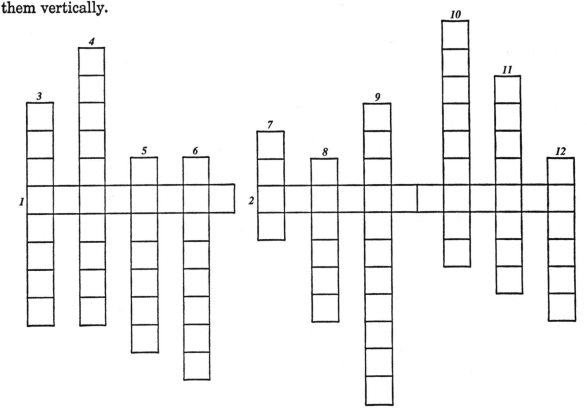

1. The capital of Liberia in Africa, named after the fifth president of the United States

2. A city in central Africa (later renamed Kisangani) named after the newspaper reporter who discovered Dr. Livingstone

3. An island state of Australia named after a Dutch explorer

4. A large city in Egypt named after the great conqueror from Macedonia

5. A South American country named after a famous liberator

6. The capital of British Columbia, named after an English queen

7. A sea and a large ice shelf in Antarctica named after an explorer

8. The capital of the Northern Territory of Australia, named after the scientist and explorer who wrote *The Origin of Species*

9. Asiatic islands formerly owned by the United States, named after a king of Spain

10. An island off the west coast of Canada named after an English explorer

11. A strait at the tip of South America named after a Portuguese explorer whose crew was first to circumnavigate the globe

12. A strait between Russia and Alaska named for a Danish explorer

Name _____ Date _____

5-3 MEANINGS OF PLACE NAMES

Many places in the world have names with interesting meanings. Some of these places are described below. Identify each place. In the marked vertical column, two other names will appear. These two place names are of Semitic origin. One of the names means "east" and one means "west." Which is which?

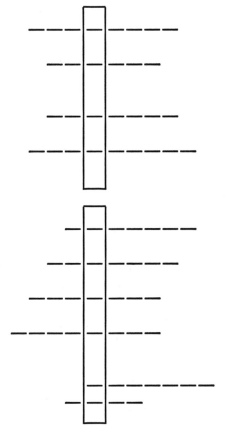

1. An island off the coast of California that used to have a large prison (Its name means "pelican.")
2. An island in the Pacific owned by Chile and named after the holiday on which it was discovered
3. The largest city in Illinois. (Its name means "wild onion place.")
4. A group of islands in the Pacific owned by Ecuador, inhabited by unusual animals, and with a name that means "tortoise"

5. A state with a French name that means "green mountain"
6. A country in South America given its name because it is on the 0° latitude line
7. A state with a name that comes from a Spanish word for "flowers"
8. A strait between European and Asiatic Turkey at the entrance to the Black Sea with a name that means "cow crossing"
9. A large ocean with a name that means "peaceful"
10. The capital of Switzerland, named after bears that inhabited the region

BONUS

On the back of this sheet, list several other places with interesting names and give the meanings of the names.

Name _____ Date _____

5–4 PLACES WITH COLORFUL NAMES

Fill the blanks below with the names of colors. (If there are two or more blanks in one sentence, all of the blanks will be filled with the same color.) Then take the circled letters and rearrange them to form a word that will fit into the blank in the last sentence.

Colors have supplied us with many names on the map. The Alps, for example, got their name from *albus,* the Latin word for __ _(_)__ , just as Lebanon's name came from a Semitic word for _____. Dublin, the capital of Ireland, comes from two Gaelic words that stand for (_)_____ pool, and in Germany we find the _____ Forest. Less frequent are names such as Kenya (in east Africa), which means __ _(_)_ (halfway between black and white).

The French words for "(_)___ stick" form the name Baton Rouge, the capital of Louisiana, and a Spanish word for _____ is also the name of Colorado. Amarillo in Texas comes from the Spanish for _____ _(_), and we have _____- stone Park in Wyoming, and the _____ Sea east of China.

The Spanish term *verde* refers to the color _____ _(_), as in Cape Verde and Mesa Verde, and a huge northern island is named _____land, even though it is a land of ice and snow. In Egypt we find the White Nile and the _____ Nile, and on the island of Capri, off the coast of Italy, is the _____ Grotto.

Both Florida and California have counties named (_)_____, which is quite appropriate. A number of places use _____ in their names, such as the former __ Coast of western Africa, which is now Ghana. A city at the southern tip of Texas is named _____sville. And in ancient times Phoenicia was given its name, which refers to the color _____, because the Phoenicians prepared a blue-violet dye from snails found in the area.

The world is so full of color and colorful names that we can say it resembles a

_____.

BONUS

On the back of this sheet, list several other colorful place names.

Name _____ Date _____

5–5 ITEMS NAMED AFTER PLACES

The following items were all named after certain places in the world. Match each one with its description by placing its letter in the space at the left of the item. Then shade in the letters you used in the diagram. The shaded area will form the answer to this question: What is the jolliest letter of the alphabet? _____ Can you think of a reason why?

A	D	G
L	F	N
C	M	I
J	H	K
E	O	B

A. Valencia   F. angora   K. dalmation

B. tuxedo   G. cologne   L. calico

C. currant   H. champagne   M. Edam

D. hamburger   I. Bible   N. tarantula

E. cantaloupe   J. Shetland   O. bayonet

_____ 1. A type of perfume named after a city in Germany

_____ 2. A type of large spider named after a city in Italy

_____ 3. A variety of small raisin from Corinth, Greece

_____ 4. A spotted dog originally from an area in Yugoslavia

_____ 5. An orange-colored melon from a city in Italy

_____ 6. A book of sacred writings named after a city in ancient Phoenicia

_____ 7. A daggerlike instrument attached to a gun and named after a city in France

_____ 8. A type of orange from a city in Spain

_____ 9. A type of small pony originally from islands near Scotland (also, a type of small dog)

_____ 10. A type of formal coat from the name of a park in New York

_____ 11. A type of cloth from a large city in India

BONUS

On the back of this sheet, list the items not shaded in the diagram. Look them up in the dictionary and find what part of the world each word comes from.

5-6 ORIGINS OF SURNAMES

Surnames come from a variety of sources, some of which are described in the paragraphs below. For each paragraph there is a set of words at the top. Select the correct set of words and rearrange their order to fit into the blanks. The first person to complete the exercise is the winner.

family	maiden	Italian	York
Iceland	members	colors	Hall
prefixes	hyphenate	Noble	towns
Irish	same	physical	river

Some English surnames come from the names of (1) _____, counties, or provinces in which people resided. Among such surnames are (2) _____, Kent, and London. Some surnames indicate locations in other ways, such as Banks (near a (3) _____), Hill, Atwell, and Underwood. Even buildings and other structures have supplied us with surnames—Church, (4) _____, Mill, Castle, and Gates.

Qualities of character form the basis for some surnames, such as (5) _____ and Meek. (6) _____ characteristics give us surnames such as Short, Long, and Young. Also used as surnames are various (7) _____, such as Black, White, Green, and Brown. In languages other than English these same methods are used. For example, Cortez means "polite" in Spanish, Gross means "big" in German, and Rossi means "red" in (8) _____.

Many surnames have (9) _____ or suffixes that mean "son of." Some examples are the *Mc* or *Mac* in McDonald (Scottish and Irish), the *O* in O'Brien (10 _____), *ivitch* in Ivanivitch (Russian), *sen* in Andersen (Danish), and *pulos* in Nicholopulos (Greek). In the country of (11) _____, the word *son* or *dottir* is added to the end of the father's name (Ragna Egvyndsdottir). As a result, the members of a (12) _____ have different last names.

In the United States, family (13) _____ ordinarily share the (14) _____ last name—that of the father. However, in recent years some women have chosen to retain their (15) _____ names, and in some instances their children combine the last names of both parents and (16) _____ them.

5-7 SURNAMES BASED ON OCCUPATIONS

Many English surnames came from occupations, such as *Chapman* (merchant) and *Cooper* (barrel maker). In Part 1, identify the surnames that refer to the occupations below by unscrambling the letters in the parentheses and placing them in the spaces at the right. The letters in the marked vertical column will form two more common occupational surnames. Some letters are provided to give you clues.

Part 1

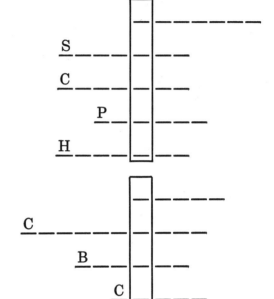

1. Manager of a household (RAWTEST)

2. One who shears sheep (NAMESHR)   S

3. Charcoal burner (RILELOC)   C

4. Bowl maker (TOPRET)   P

5. Chicken raiser (CHEATHR)   H

6. Bricklayer (SAMON)

7. Wagon maker (TRACTGHIRW)   C

8. One in charge of wines (LETRUB)   B

9. A record keeper, a scribe (RALCK)   C

10. One in charge of a forest (shortened from *Forrester*) (RFSTOE)

11. A lathe operator (RUNTRE)   T

Part 2

Write the two names that appear in the vertical column above and describe their occupations.

_____ : _____

_____ : _____

BONUS

On the back of this sheet, list examples of names from languages other than English that are based on occupations. (Maybe your own name or the names of your classmates will fit into this category.)

5–8 NAMES RELATED TO ANIMALS

Our given names are steeped in history, some going back to biblical times. *Mary,* for example, is a Hebrew name that means "distressed or tearful," and *David* means "beloved." *Christopher* is from Greek, and *Chester* is of Latin origin. Names come from many sources, and some of them have a connection with animals. Identify the animal source of each name below. The circled letters from the Boys' section below will spell another boy's name when rearranged, and the circled letters from the Girls' section will spell another girl's name.

Write them here: _____

ANIMAL

_ _ _Ⓞ

Ⓞ_ _ _

_ _Ⓞ_

_ _ _ _Ⓞ

_ _ _Ⓞ

Ⓞ_ _

_ _Ⓞ

_ _Ⓞ_ _ _

G_ _ _ _Ⓞ_

_ _Ⓞ_

BⓞO_ _ _ _ _

_ _Ⓞ_ _

BOYS' NAMES

1. Leonard and Leon (Latin), from the king of the jungle

2. Adolph (Teutonic), from a member of the canine family that is sometimes "in sheep's clothing"

3. Bernard (Teutonic), from a member of Smokey's family

4. Arnold (Teutonic), from the bird that is the symbol of the United States

5. Wilbur (Saxon), from an undomesticated relative of the pig

6. Alan (Gaelic), from man's best friend

GIRLS' NAMES

7. Deborah (Hebrew) and Melissa (Greek), from the name of a buzzing insect

8. Ophelia (Greek), from the reptile that deceived Eve

9. Dorcas (Greek) and Tabitha (Hebrew), from a member of the deer family in Africa

10. Jemima (Hebrew), from a bird that is a symbol of peace

11. Merle (Latin), from a bird of a very dark color

12. Rachel (Hebrew), from a woolly animal

BONUS

Look up your own first and middle names and discover their meanings and the language from which they come. Write the information on the back of this sheet.

5–9 NAMES OF WRITERS

Many of our well-known writers (poets, novelists, playwrights, etc.) have last names that represent common words, though in some cases the names are not spelled exactly the same as the word. Try to identify the writers whose names are defined below. Then write the circled letters in order in the following blanks to complete this statement by Richard Bach:

"A professional writer __ __   __ __   __ __ __ __ __ __ __ __   __ __ __ __   __ __ __ __ __ __ ,

q __ __ __ __ ."

1. Crafty, sly   Elinor _ _ _ _ _Ⓞ_

2. A layer of ice crystals on a cold surface   Robert _ _ _ _Ⓞ_

3. A swelling on the joint of the big toe   John _ _ _ _ _Ⓞ

4. A Christmas song   Lewis _Ⓞ_ _ _ _ _

5. Residences   Oliver Wendell _ _ _ _Ⓞ_ _

6. An organ of the body   Bret _Ⓞ_Ⓞ_

7. Sound made by a bull   Saul _Ⓞ_ _ _ _

8. Is in flames   Robert _Ⓞ_ _ _

9. A type of shrub   Nathaniel _ _Ⓞ_Ⓞ_ _ _

10. A type of head covering   Thomas _ _ _ _Ⓞ

11. Uncontrolled, not tame   Oscar_Ⓞ_Ⓞ_

12. Finished   John _ _Ⓞ_ _

13. One who makes bowls from clay   Beatrix _ _Ⓞ_ _ _

14. Sixteen ounces   Ezra _ _Ⓞ_ _

15. Fast   Jonathan _ _Ⓞ_Ⓞ

BONUS

On the back of this sheet, write definitions of last names of several other writers. Let your classmates guess them.

Name _____ Date _____

5–10 ITEMS NAMED AFTER PEOPLE

Some words we use, such as those described below, come from the names of people. Identify the words and transfer the circled letters to the corresponding spaces in the diagram to form a set of words in both directions.

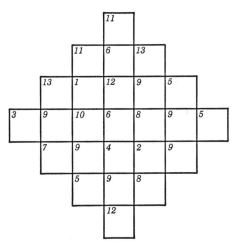

1. A candy bar (**named after President Coolidge's daughter**): B◯__ _____
2. A type of button-up sweater (**named after an English earl**): C____◯___
3. A tight-fitting garment with long sleeves and a high neck that is worn by dancers (**named after a French trapeze artist**): L_____◯
4. A Christmas flower (**named after a botanist**): P__◯_____
5. A type of engine (**named after its German inventor**): D__◯__
6. A method for sterilizing milk (**named after a French chemist**):
   P_____◯_
7. A beef dish containing sour cream (**named after a Russian count**):
   S__◯_____
8. A unit of electrical power (**named after a Scottish inventor**): W_◯_
9. A device found in amusement parks that consists of a huge wheel with seats on it (**named after an American engineer**): F◯_____
10. Denim trousers (**named after a German immigrant who participated in the California gold rush**): L_◯_'_
11. A hoisting device used on oil wells (**named after an English hangman**):
    D____◯_
12. A type of thin, crisp toast (**named after an Australian opera star**):
    M◯__
13. A kind of driver used on a four-slotted screw (**named after its inventor**):
    P_____◯_

BONUS

Look up *armalcolite* (the name of a mineral) and find out after whom it is named.

5–11 WORDS FROM MYTHOLOGY

Names of characters in mythology have provided us with a number of words. Identify the terms below. Then place the circled and boxed letters in the appropriate columns at the left. These letters will form the names of two characters in mythology. (One will have the letters in correct order, and the other will have them in reverse order.) Write the two names here, together with a brief statement about the context in which we use them today:

_____

_____

_____

☐ ◯

_____ _____ 1. A metallic element used in nuclear weapons (**named after a Greek god**): __ ◯ _____

_____ _____ 2. A day of the week (**named after the Norse god of the sky and thunder**): _____ ☐ _

_____ _____ 3. A process for curing rubber (**from the Roman god of fire**): ___ ◯ _____

_____ _____ 4. Pertaining to military matters (**from the Roman god of war**): __ ☐ ____

_____ _____ 5. An adjective that describes something of extraordinary difficulty (**from a Greek superhero who performed twelve impossible tasks**): ◯ _____

_____ _____ 6. An adjective meaning "huge" (**from the name of a group of giants in Greek mythology**): __ ◯ _____

_____ _____ 7. A strong, muscular woman (**from the name of a race of female warriors in Greek mythology**): _____ ☐ _

_____ _____ 8. A breakfast food (**from the Roman goddess of agriculture**): _____ ◯

_____ _____ 9. Any long journey (**from the name of a Greek king who had a long adventure at sea**): _ ☐ _____

_____ _____ 10. A very light, inert gas (**named after the Greek god of the sun**): __ ◯ ___

_____ _____ 11. A month (**named after the Roman two-faced god in charge of doors and beginnings and endings**): __ ☐ _____

_____ _____ 12. A planet (**named after the Roman goddess of love and beauty**): _ ◯ ___

_____ _____ 13. A book of maps (**from the name of a Greek giant who held the heavens on his shoulders**): ☐ _____

_____ _____ 14. A term psychologists use for a complex characterized by a child falling in love with the parent of the opposite sex (**named after a Greek youth who married his mother**): _____ ☐ ___

_____ _____ 15. A beautiful temptress (**from the name of some women who lured sailors to their death**): ◯ _____

5–12 ORIGINS OF BRAND NAMES

Many products we use every day have very interesting names. For example, the name *Kodak* was invented by George Eastman, the founder of the company. He wanted a forceful-sounding name, and he felt the letter *K* was forceful. Experimenting with different combinations of letters, he came up with *Kodak*. The name has no meaning whatsoever and is an entirely new word, not made from any preexisting elements. Such a word is a neologism. Identify the products described below and place the circled letters in the spaces at the left. These letters, in order, will form the name of a company that has produced many brand names.

Write the name here: _____

_____ 1. A soft drink named after a doctor who owned a drugstore: *Dr.* (_)_____

_____ 2. A candy bar with the name of a famous writer of short stories: __ ___(_)_

_____ 3. A soap whose name refers to the substance found in elephant tusks:
__ _(_)_ _

_____ 4. A cleanser whose name refers to a celestial body with a nucleus and a long tail:
(_)_____

_____ 5. A bath soap that has a name meaning "seashore": _____(_)

_____ 6. A cigarette with the name of a humped animal: ____(_)_

_____ 7. A dry copying process with a name that comes from a Greek word for "dry":
__(_)_ _

_____ 8. A line of cosmetics named after a river in England along which Shakespeare's home was located: (_)____

_____ 9. A decaffeinated coffee with a name derived from two French words meaning "without caffeine": __(_)__

_____ 10. A paper cup with a name that is slang for the "Old South": (_)_____

_____ 11. A bus line named after a fast dog: (_)_____

_____ 12. A milk product (both canned and powdered) with a flower name:
_(_)_____

_____ 13. A baking soda named after a part of the body and a carpenter's tool:
__(_) ____ _____

_____ 14. A line of frozen products named after its founder, whose name refers to part of a bird's anatomy: (_)_____

_____ 15. A zipper named for a bird's claw: ___(_)__

_____ 16. A laundry detergent with a name that refers to the rising and falling of the ocean surface: ____(_)

BONUS

On the back of this sheet, write a definition for another product and let your classmates guess it.

5-13 NAMES OF CARS

Over the years cars have been given fascinating names. Identify the car names described below, placing each in the puzzle where indicated. (The manufacturer of each car is listed to assist you.)

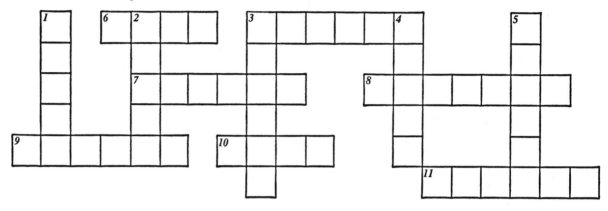

DOWN

1. Juliet's beau (**Alfa**)
2. A constellation of a hunter with a belt and sword (**Ford**)
3. A bird of prey (**Ford**)
4. The constellation between Pisces and Taurus that is pictured as a ram (**Dodge**)
5. An optical illusion (**Mitsubishi**)

ACROSS

3. Spanish term for a party or celebration (**Ford**)
6. A game played on horseback with mallets and balls (**Volkswagen**)
7. An African antelope (**Chevrolet**)
8. A resort area on the southern coast of France (**Buick**)
9. A rectangular game piece with two equal parts, each of which has from one to six dots on it (**Daihatsu**)
10. A young horse (**Plymouth, Dodge**)
11. A small piece of matter in the solar system that makes a streak of light when it enters the atmosphere (**FORD**)

BONUS

In the space below, write the definitions for several other interesting car names. Let your classmates guess the names.

_____

_____

_____

_____

_____

Name _____ Date _____

5-14 NAMES OF BIRDS

Many birds have names that also have other meanings. Try to identify the birds whose names have the meanings listed below. The letters in the marked vertical column will form the first four words of a common rhyming expression. Write them here and complete the expression:

_____

_____

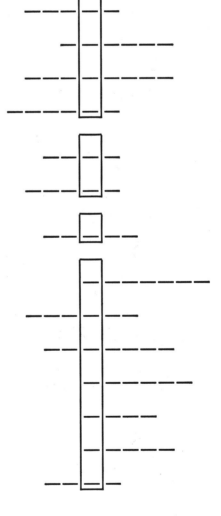

1. Tapping a baseball lightly without swinging

2. To lose courage

3. A baseball player from Baltimore

4. A high official of the Catholic Church

5. To complain or grumble

6. To boast or brag

7. Fast

8. A machine for hoisting objects

9. To burn with an unsteady flame

10. A person who is easily deceived

11. To eat; to accept without question

12. Three strikes in a row in bowling

13. To sell on the street by calling out to passersby

14. Two below par on a hole in golf

15. A frolic

BONUS

On the back of this sheet, write the definitions of several other birds' names. Let your classmates guess the names.

5–15 NAMES OF FLOWERS

Using a little imagination, you should be able to identify the flowers described below. Example: If the definition is "a joyful metal," an appropriate answer would be *marigold* (merry gold). After identifying the names, transfer the circled letters to these spaces to form the names of three flowers that also are the names of colors:

$$\overline{1}\ \overline{2}\ \overline{9}\ \overline{10}\ \overline{11}\ \overline{14}\ \overline{4}\ \overline{13} \qquad \overline{5}\ \overline{16}\ \overline{6}\ \overline{12} \qquad \overline{9}\ \overline{8}\ \overline{7}\ \overline{15}\ \overline{3}\ \overline{17}$$

1. A closing device on the garment of an unmarried man:

   _ _ _ _ _Ⓞ_ _ ' _   _ _ _ _ _ _ _

2. A country that has many automobiles: _Ⓞ_ _ _ _ _ _ _ _ _

3. The air that escapes from the mouth of an infant: _ _ _ _ _ ' _   _ _Ⓞ_ _ _ _

4. A British slang term for one's mother: _ _ _ _ (short for

   _ _ _ _ _ _ _ _ _ _Ⓞ_ _ _)

5. A possible nickname for father: _ _Ⓞ_ _

6. Don't put me out of your mind: _ _ _ _ _ _ _ _-_ _ _-Ⓞ_ _

7. Groups of sheep: _ _ _Ⓞ_

8. The colored part of the eye: _ _Ⓞ_

9. What a certain four-legged, wild animal might wear on its paw: _ _ _ _ _ _ _Ⓞ_

10. A small, flavorful green vegetable: _ _Ⓞ_ _   _ _ _ _

11. A shiny metallic bar: _ _ _ _ _Ⓞ_ _ _

12. A stiff spine on the leg of a certain songbird: _ _ _ _Ⓞ_ _ _ _ _

13. Got up: Ⓞ_ _ _ _

14. A command to someone to take a picture of a fire-breathing monster:

   _ _ _ _Ⓞ_ _ _ _

15. An unhappy ringing device: _ _ _ _ _ _ _ _Ⓞ

16. A vital organ that has been wounded: _ _ _ _ _Ⓞ_ _   _ _ _ _ _ _

17. A container for holding a dairy product: _ _Ⓞ_ _ _ _ _ _

BONUS

On the back of this sheet, list several other flowers with interesting names.

Name _____ Date _____

5–16 OCCUPATIONAL NAMES

At a business luncheon, a group of men and women discussed the names of their children, and it became apparent that all of them had given their children names related to their occupations. For example, the boxer had named his son *Knox,* and the ornithologist had named her two daughters *Phoebe* and *Robin.* Find the names of the sons and daughters of the following persons by unscrambling the letters. The names in each set will be in alphabetical order.

BOYS

1. Dentist   NEKIA   _____
2. Calendar manufacturer   TUSGUA   _____
3. Telephone company executive   TOOBH   _____
4. Coffee pot manufacturer   TRESWEBR   _____
5. Artist   WERD   _____
6. Barber   YAHRR   _____
7. Credit manager   ENOW   _____
8. Handbag manufacturer   CERYP   _____
9. Fisherman   DRO   _____

GIRLS

10. Gambler   TEBYT   _____
11. Construction engineer   DIGTREB   _____
12. Songwriter   LARCO   _____
13. Restaurant manager   HANDI   _____
14. Weather forecaster   ALGI   _____
15. Liquor salesman   NINYG   _____
16. Flour mill operator   LIMYL   _____
17. Deep-sea diver   LERAP   _____
18. Florist   TELIVO   _____

BONUS

The florist's other daughters are Pansy, Fern, Flora, Iris, and Ivy. Try to think of names for other sons and daughters for the persons listed above.

5–17 NAMES OF IMAGINARY PEOPLE

Occasionally you encounter people whose names in some way suit their professions. For example, there actually is a dentist named Peter Hertz, and there is a James Bugg who is an exterminator. A search through a phone book will yield many more such names. The people below, however, are strictly imaginary. You are to pretend that these people are all authors. The titles of their books are given, along with their first names. Think of appropriate last names. Examples: A book entitled *Car Repair* might be authored by *Otto Mobile,* and a book with the title *Writing Editorials* might be written by *Ed Itor.* (There may be more than one appropriate last name for some of the authors below.)

BOOK TITLES	AUTHORS
1. *Successful Gambling*	Jack _____
2. *Bacteria*	Mike _____
3. *Synthetic Fabrics*	Polly _____
4. *Treating Arthritis*	Ben _____
5. *Aging*	Jerry _____
6. *Coastal Areas*	Sandy _____
7. *The Dangers of Tobacco*	Nick _____
8. *The Lumbering Industry*	Tim _____
9. *Garden Salads*	Tom _____
10. *Autumn Flowers*	Chris _____
11. *Maintaining Public Buildings*	Jan _____
12. *Mounting Photographs*	Al _____
13. *Vocal Music*	Sarah _____
14. *Common Birds*	Bob _____
15. *Roadside Signs*	Bill _____
16. *Building Canoes*	Doug _____
17. *Minnesota Cities*	Minny _____
18. *Thorny Problems*	Rose _____
19. *Cops and Robbers*	Dee _____
20. *Recipes for Cool Drinks*	Ginger _____
21. *Musical Instruments*	Clara _____
22. *Optimism*	Rosie _____
23. *Cuts of Beef*	Chuck _____
24. *Outdoor Cooking*	Barbie _____
25. *The Story of the Pilgrims*	May _____

6

LANGUAGE
AS AN ART FORM

A BLOSSOM IS A WONDROUS THING WHEN IT BURSTS FORTH IN EARLY SPRING ENTICING INSECTS ON THE WING DELIGHTING RAMBLER JUST AS KING WITH JOYFUL HUES THAT MAKE US SING

6–1 TECHNIQUES IN PROSE WRITING

A girl was being courted by two young men. One was an aspiring poet, and the other was a dairy farmer. She couldn't ———————— whether to ———————— for ———————— or ————————. To find the missing words, first fill the blanks in the statements below that deal with the ways writers employ language. Select from the list of words at the top. The four words remaining will fit into the blanks above.

verse	roundabout	unsaid	verbs	caricature
lightning	stereotype	visualize	vivid	butter
assume	marry	dialogue	active	decide

To help readers (1) ———————— situations, writers use (2) ———————— descriptions of sights, sounds, and smells to suggest images. But writers often also leave some things (3) ————————. For example, if the writer mentions the fact that there is a saucer of milk on the floor, the reader can (4) ———————— a cat lives in the house without being told.

A writer can develop characters through (5) ———————— and through the interaction of the characters. The characters may be presented in a variety of ways. A (6) ———————— is a character that fits a preconceived notion, such as a "typical politician" or a "typical yuppie." A (7) ———————— is a character with one aspect of its personality extremely exaggerated. In serious writing, authors try to develop complex, dynamic characters that are changed by the events of the story.

Good prose writers use vivid (8) ———————— and nouns rather than an excess of adverbs and adjectives. (Example: The eagle soared and circled overhead. *Not*: The eagle flew up and then slowly swung around and around in circles above us.) (9) ———————— verbs are preferable to those in the passive voice, since such constructions are generally weak. Avoid all (10) ———————— forms of expression. (Example: Bad weather caused his absence. *Not*: The reason he was absent was that the weather was bad.)

With the right choice of words a writer can create a work of art. Mark Twain once said that the difference between the right word and one that is almost right is like the difference between (11) ———————— and a (12) ———————— bug. (**same word in both**)

Name _____ Date _____

6-2 TERMS USED BY WRITERS

The definitions below refer to terms used by novelists, playwrights, poets, journalists, and other writers. Identify them. The letters in the marked vertical column will complete this quotation from W. H. Auden: "A real book is not one that's read but

____ _____ _____ __."

1. An essay in a newspaper on a subject of interest to the public
2. Verse with no end rhyme but with meter

3. A speech at the end of a play

4. A serious drama with a disastrous conclusion
5. An interruption in the action by interjection of events that occurred earlier
6. The use of humor and wit to ridicule human nature or human institutions
7. A novel characterized by mysterious settings and an atmosphere of unknown terror

8. Poetry relying on melody and emotion rather than story content
9. A long narrative poem about the adventures of a hero
10. A written work, such as a parable or fable, that describes one set of concrete items that have another abstract significance
11. A type of exaggerated drama in which the characters (either very good or very bad) get what they deserve

12. A division of an act of a play

13. A speech in a play delivered by a character who is alone on the stage
14. One section of a longer poem, consisting of a certain grouping of lines

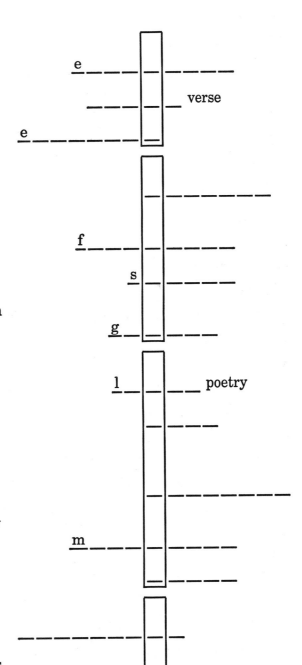

6-3 FIGURES OF SPEECH

Figures of speech are methods writers use to produce interesting images and twists of thought. Select a set of letters from each of the three columns below to form the name of a figure of speech and write the name next to its definition. (To simplify the process, cross out letters as you use them.)

EU	THE	ICATION
META	RON	PHE
APOS	PHEM	SIS
SIM	NY	BOLE
I	ONIF	OR
METO	I	MY
PERS	TRO	ISM
ANTI	PER	Y
HY	PH	LE

_____ 1. Giving lifelike qualities to inanimate objects: **The sun smiled and the wind caressed my cheek.**

_____ 2. Stating something in such a way that the exact opposite is implied: **Robin Hood calling the biggest member of his band "Little John"**

_____ 3. Extreme exaggeration to create an effect: **mile-high ice cream cones**

_____ 4. Speaking directly to an absent person or a lifeless object as if it could reply: **Oh, death, where is thy sting?**

_____ 5. Understatement by substituting a softer or more pleasant term for a shocking or unpleasant one: **saying "passed away" instead of "died"**

_____ 6. A comparison using *like* or *as*: **Her eyes were as blue as tropical lagoons.**

_____ 7. A direct comparison without the use of *like* or *as*: **The ship plowed the sea.**

_____ 8. Substituting a term associated with another for the original term: **He took up the cross. (The cross represents Christianity.)**

_____ 9. Using contrasting expressions balanced against each other: **Thought without action is futile; action without thought is fatal.**

BONUS

In your literature book, find an example of one or more of the above items. Write them on the back of this sheet, and let the class identify the figure of speech involved.

6-4 SIMILES AND METAPHORS

A simile is a comparison of two unlike items by using *like, as,* or similar terms, such as *resembles.* Like items that are compared do not constitute a simile. The following sentence, for example, is not a simile: His tie is exactly like mine. Many of our old sayings are similes, such as those below. Fill in the missing words and transfer the circled letters to this statement:

The doctor's diagnosis showed the writer was suffering from

$$\overline{}\ \overline{}\ \overline{}\ \overline{}\ \overline{}\ \overline{} - \overline{}\ \overline{}\ \overline{}\ \overline{}.$$
8 1 3 6 10 4   2 5 7 9

1. as poor as a __ __ (__) __ __ __   __ __ __ __ __ __

2. as __ __ (__) __ __ as a bat

3. as warm as __ __ __ __ __ (__)

4. as __ (__) __ __ __ __ __ as a picture

5. as __ __ __ __ __ (__) as rain

6. a memory like an __ __ __ __ __ (__) __ __ __

7. as quick as a __ (__) __ __

8. as slow as __ __ __ __ (__) __ __ __ __ __ in January

9. as __ __ (__) __ as taking candy from a baby

10. as __ (__) __ __ as a cucumber

Bonus 1

Try writing a simile of your own—something really striking, not trite like the clichés above. (Example: In that crowd I felt as conspicuous as a single radish in a green salad.) Write your best simile here:

_____

_____

_____

Bonus 2

A metaphor resembles a simile in that it also is a comparison, but it does not use *like* or *as.* For example, in the following description, the fresh snow is compared to ermine, ribbons, and lace: **When I awoke I was greeted by a lacy fence, white ribbons strung from pole to pole, and ermine-clad trees.** Write a metaphor of your own in the space below. Try to make it as interesting as possible. The winner is the one the class selects.

_____

_____

6–5 EUPHEMISMS

Euphemisms are understatements. Many in common use are expressions tactfully designed to soften the blow that blunt terms would inflict. For example, we might say that someone's statement is "inexact," when we really mean that it is a lie. Some euphemisms are designed to be humorous, such as "trachea tweaker" (hangman). Others imply status, such as the term "domestic engineer" used in place of *housewife*. And some serve the purpose of deliberate deception. One example is the use of the term "revenue enhancement" by some politicians to obscure the fact that they are actually talking about tax increases. Match each harsh term at the left with its euphemism by placing the circled letter from the term in the space at the left. Then transfer the letters to this quotation from the Bible about euphemisms:

$\overline{15}$ $\overline{5}$ $\overline{3}$ $\overline{2}$ $\overline{6}$ $\overline{13}$ $\overline{11}$ $\overline{5}$ $\overline{12}$ $\overline{9}$ $\overline{10}$ $\overline{6}$ $\overline{8}$ $\overline{10}$ $\overline{11}$ $\overline{9}$ $\overline{1}$ $\overline{4}$ $\overline{15}$ $\overline{12}$ $\overline{13}$ $\overline{7}$ $\overline{12}$ $\overline{10}$ $\overline{13}$ $\overline{1}$ $\overline{14}$.

Letter

_____ 1. kickback

_____ 2. repossessing a car

_____ 3. illegal alien

_____ 4. loneliness

_____ 5. ghetto

_____ 6. poor

_____ 7. accidental shelling of your own troops

_____ 8. blind

_____ 9. recession

_____ 10. slavery

_____ 11. retreat

_____ 12. strike

_____ 13. gases that don't kill but impair

_____ 14. crippled

_____ 15. garbage

1 • strategic (w)ithdrawal of services

2 • economically disadvan(t)aged

3 • stimulus impoveri(s)hment

4 • n(e)gative growth

5 • accommoda(t)ion payment

6 • friendl(y) fire

7 • vis(u)ally impaired

8 • p(h)ysically challenged

9 • involuntary trans(f)er of a mobile proprietary asset

10 • retrograde ma(n)euver

11 • und(o)cumented transborder migrant

12 • involuntary ser(v)itude

13 • solid w(a)ste

14 • life(s)tyle enclave

15 • benevolent inc(a)pacitators

BONUS

Take one of the following words and write as many euphemisms for it as you can: tyrant, loud-mouthed, stupid, cowardly, skinny. Use the back of this sheet for your answers.

6-6 ANTITHESIS

An antithesis is a contrasting statement, such as the one John Kennedy used when he said, "Ask not what your country can do for you; ask what you can do for your country." By filling the two blanks in each sentence below with the same word, you can form an antithesis. (Some clue letters are given to help you figure out the word to use.) Whenever the author is known, this is indicated. Then write the circled letters in order in the spaces in this story:

Two men played five games of checkers, and each one won three games. How is this

possible? Answer: Each one played _____ _____ _____.

1. "The secret of happiness is not in doing ()___t you like but in liking _____t you do." *James Barrie*

2. New York is a perfect model of a large c()___, but not a model for a perfect large

   c____.

3. Those who are ()__l k_____ don't know what's going on, and those who know

   aren't ___l k_____.

4. Peace on _____() or the _____ in pieces.

5. Wise men talk because they have something to ()___, but fools talk because they

   have to ____ something.

6. When the occasion a__()___, he a_____ to the occasion.

7. There's no ()__n__y in poetry and no poetry in ____n__y.

8. An optimist __()___ an opportunity in every calamity; a pessimist _____ a

   calamity in every opportunity.

9. A man who trusts no ()___ is the kind of man no _____ trusts.

10. He didn't p___() to fail; he just failed to p_____.

11. "Defeat the f()___ of death and welcome the death of f_____." *G. Gordon Liddy*

12. It's better to d__b___() a question without settling it than to settle it without

    d__b____.

13. It's easier to ()__v__ it up than to ____v__ it down.

14. Better than counting your y____() is to make your y_____ count.

15. Tradition doesn't mean that the living are __()___ but that the _____ are

    living.

6–7 BIBLICAL ALLUSIONS

Writers frequently paint pictures in our minds by using allusions (references to characters or situations in history or in literature with which the readers are familiar). For example, if a writer describes someone as a "Romeo" or a "Don Juan," we have an immediate impression of the man. Characters in the Bible are often used in allusions. If you were writing about persons of the type described below, what biblical character might you compare each to? Unscramble the names of the persons described to find out. (The names will be in alphabetical order.) Write the names in the spaces at the left.

_____ 1. A man who, out of jealousy, murdered his own brother (**INAC**)

_____ 2. A small person with great courage who went up against a giant and won (**VIDDA**)

_____ 3. An evil woman who died a violent death (**ZEELBEJ**)

_____ 4. A man who suffered a great deal but did not lose faith (**OJB**)

_____ 5. A man whose dreams foretold his future success (**SOPHJE**)

_____ 6. A great military hero (at the Battle of Jericho) (**SOJAHU**)

_____ 7. A man who betrayed his master for thirty pieces of silver (**SUDAJ**)

_____ 8. A man who was revived after being dead (**AZRSAUL**)

_____ 9. A man who lived an extremely long time (**SUTHEMHALE**)

_____ 10. A great leader who led his people into a new land (**SEMSO**)

_____ 11. A survivor of a flood (**HANO**)

_____ 12. A beautiful woman who performed sensual dances (**MELOSA**)

_____ 13. A strong man defeated by a deceitful woman (**MANOSS**)

_____ 14. A very wise ruler and judge (**MOOSNOL**)

_____ 15. A man who doubted things unless he could see for himself (**STOHMA**)

Name _____ Date _____

6–8 ALLUSIONS TO FABLES, MYTHS, AND LITERATURE

Often writers refer to people, places, and things in famous novels, poems, myths, and fables in order to make a point and to create an image in the mind of the reader. From the list at the bottom, select the phrase that indicates what is meant by each underlined allusion at the top. Place its circled letter at the left. The letters will form the name of another person to whom allusions are often made.

Letter

_____ 1. He grasshoppered his life away. (**Aesop fable**)

_____ 2. He cried wolf once too often. (**Aesop fable**)

_____ 3. Saying she was glad that her fiancée broke the engagement was really **a case of** sour grapes. (**Aesop fable**)

_____ 4. He may be a tortoise, but I'm betting on him. (**Aesop fable**)

_____ 5. His obsession with gambling is his Achilles' heel. (**mythology**)

_____ 6. She has been struck by Cupid's arrow. (**mythology**)

_____ 7. She's no Helen of Troy! (**mythology**)

_____ 8. Like a phoenix he recovered after his bankruptcy and is again the **head of a big** corporation. (**mythology**)

_____ 9. He isn't going to get me to whitewash his fence. (**literature**)

_____ 10. I'm through fighting windmills. (**literature**)

_____ 11. It's like a Montague-Capulet feud. (**literature**)

_____ 12. The Kennedys appeared to be living in Camelot. (**literature**)

1 • trick me into completing his job for him
2 • mythical bird that arose from its own ashes
3 • slow but steady, yet likely to beat a sprinter
4 • a place of perfection and great happiness
5 • had a good time instead of working
6 • taking on things against which one can't cope
7 • weakness and possible ultimate downfall
8 • a great beauty over whom a war was fought
9 • lied frequently and now cannot be believed even when telling the truth
10 • fallen in love
11 • a struggle between the two feuding families of *Romeo and Juliet*
12 • pretending not to want something that one really does want

Name _____ Date _____

6–9 SYMBOLISM

A symbol is something that represents something else. Writers use symbols to paint pictures with deeper meanings. In the poem "Sea Fever" by John Masefield, the sea voyage can be interpreted as representing life and the "quiet sleep" death. Many of our proverbs contain symbolism. From the list in the box, select the words that represent the deeper meaning symbolized by the underlined words. Write your answers in the blanks in the sentences following the symbolic expressions. Then, in the box, connect the dots of the words you used in items 1 to 6 with a single line and those in items 7 to 9 with another line. These lines will form two numbers that are a clue to another proverb that contains them.

Write it here: _____

_____

goal •	• opportunity	wealth •	• child
venture •	• sadness	decision •	• truth
grievances •	• possessions	people •	• trouble

1. Hitch your wagon to a <u>star</u>. (Always keep a _____ before you.)

2. Make hay while the <u>sun</u> shines. (Act when the _____ exists.)

3. Into each life some <u>rain</u> must fall. (Everyone must experience some _____ along with the joy.)

4. Don't put all your eggs in one <u>basket</u>. (Don't risk everything on one _____.)

5. Let sleeping <u>dogs</u> lie. (Don't stir up old _____.)

6. Half a <u>loaf</u> is better than none. (Be thankful for whatever _____ you have, even though they may not be great.)

7. As the <u>twig</u> is bent, so grows the tree. (As a _____ is trained, so it develops into an adult.)

8. Where there's smoke, there's <u>fire</u>. (Behind the rumors there is probably some

_____.)

9. A stitch in time saves <u>nine</u>. (Taking care of a problem when it first arises will save lots

of _____ later on.)

BONUS

On the back of this sheet, write another proverb and explain its symbolism.

6-10 PARALLEL PROVERBS

Proverbs are found in most languages dating back to ancient times. They might be described as pithy generalizations of human experience. Since human experiences vary little from region to region, the proverbs relating to them are very similar. Match each American proverb at the top with its counterpart at the bottom by placing the circled letter from the matching item in the space at the left. These letters will form the name of the theory that all languages came from a single source.

Write it here: _____

Letter

_____ 1. One man's meat is another man's poison.

_____ 2. Too many cooks spoil the broth.

_____ 3. Don't bite off more than you can chew.

_____ 4. Actions speak louder than words.

_____ 5. Speech is silver; silence is golden.

_____ 6. Spare the rod and spoil the child.

_____ 7. A word to the wise is sufficient.

_____ 8. Call a spade a spade.

_____ 9. Great oaks from little acorns grow.

_____ 10. Slow and steady wins the race.

_____ 11. The truth will out.

1 • **(France)** Drop by drop fills the tub.

2 • **(Denmark)** Give to a pig when it grunts and to a child when it cries, and you will have a fine pig and a bad child.

3 • **(Romania)** Don't stretch yourself till you're longer than the blanket.

4 • **(Spain)** Call bread bread and wine wine.

5 • **(Tanzania)** The heap in the barn consists of single grains.

6 • **(Italy)** With too many roosters crowing the sun never comes up.

7 • **(Czechoslovakia)** To a wise man just whisper; to a fool you must spell out everything.

8 • **(Finland)** Fire cannot destroy truth.

9 • **(Russia)** What is healthy to a Russian is death to a German.

10 • **(China)** Talk cooks no rice.

11 • **(East Africa)** To speak is good; not to speak is better.

6-11 MALAPROPISMS

In a play by Richard Sheridan, a character named Mrs. Malaprop constantly misused words. The words she used sounded similar to the ones she intended to use, but they conveyed an entirely different meaning. Usually such malapropisms are unintentional, but writers and speakers sometimes use them to create humorous effects. Each sentence below contains a term used inappropriately. Underline the incorrect word or words and write the correct, similar-sounding term in the puzzle where indicated.

ACROSS

1. She suffers from very close veins in her legs.
2. Some people consider capital punishment a good detergent for crime.
3. The escaping prisoner clamored up the wall.
4. When the man was choking, the waiter used the Heimlich remover on him.
5. When the votes were counted, it was found that the decision was anonymous.

DOWN

2. The difference between ten cents and ten dollars is the dismal point.
6. Don't worry about him. He's just going through a phrase.
7. This lemonade will really clench your thirst.
8. Did you mail the package by partial post?
9. When Moses came down from the mountain, he brought the ten amendments.
10. Thomas Gray wrote an allergy in a country churchyard near London.
11. He doesn't have a large vocabulary. Mostly he speaks in words of one cylinder.

Name _____ Date _____

6-12 OXYMORONS

A man visits a friend on the seventeenth floor. He leaves, walks to the elevator, and goes down several floors when the elevator suddenly stops. Ten minutes later the power is restored and, as the elevator goes down, the man cries because he knows his friend has died. How does he know? To find out, select a word from the right column below to place with a word at the left in order to form an oxymoron (an expression apparently contradictory in meaning yet readily understood, such as "awfully good" or "important trivia"). Place the word you selected in the blank and place its circled letter in the space at the left. These letters will form the answer to the question above. Write the answer here:

_____

____	1. light _____	new(s)
____	2. vague _____	m(i)sunderstood
____	3. bitter _____	leth(a)l
____	4. strangely _____	(a)wful
____	5. oddly _____	gr(i)ef
____	6. clearly _____	froze(n)
____	7. plastic _____	unfinishe(d)
____	8. freezer _____	chocola(t)e
____	9. completely _____	(O)pinion
____	10. civil _____	ic(e)
____	11. somewhat _____	app(r)opriate
____	12. guest _____	defi(n)ition
____	13. even _____	(w)ar
____	14. fresh _____	bur(n)
____	15. perfectly _____	(s)weet
____	16. barely _____	glasse(s)
____	17. dry _____	d(r)essed
____	18. old _____	(p)hony
____	19. real _____	sh(r)imp
____	20. good _____	ho(s)t
____	21. jumbo _____	(f)amiliar
____	22. definite _____	so(r)row
____	23. white _____	(h)eavyweight
____	24. unbiased _____	(o)dds
____	25. sweet _____	m(a)ybe

Name _____ Date _____

6–13 CONNOTATION

Writers and speakers can change the tone of a situation through their choice of words. Two sets of words that have approximately the same definitions may have entirely different connotations. The pairs of items below illustrate a complimentary and an uncomplimentary way of saying the same thing. In the space under the examples (or on another sheet of paper), write two paragraphs that describe an imaginary person, phrasing one in a critical way and the other in a complimentary way. The class will select the winning pair of paragraphs.

Complimentary	Uncomplimentary
1. She's a vision.	She's a sight.
2. She's a kitten.	She's a cat.
3. He is a born leader.	He is power hungry.
4. He pays close attention to detail.	He's a fussbudget.
5. She's petite and delicate.	She's weak and helpless.
6. She's in the prime of life.	She's no spring chicken.
7. He's a well-rounded person with many interests.	He's a jack-of-all-trades and a master of none.
8. He's a good listener.	He's uncommunicative.
9. He dresses casually.	He's a sloppy dresser.
10. She certainly has perseverance.	She doesn't know when to quit.

_____

_____

_____

_____

_____

_____

_____

_____

_____

6-14 SOUND EFFECTS

By using various devices, writers can create interesting musical sound effects. Four such techniques are described below. Unscramble the name of each and write it in the space provided. The circled letters, in order, will form the initials and last name of a poet who frequently employed such sound effects. Write his name here: _____

TILTALRANEIO

1. _ _ _ _ _ ◯ _ _ _ _ _ is the repetition of the same consonant sound at the beginning of several words or accented syllables.

   Examples: "The *fair* breeze blew, the white *foam flew,*
   The *furrow followed free.*"–*Samuel Taylor Coleridge*

   "*H*ome is the sailor, *h*ome from the sea,
   And the *h*unter *h*ome from the *h*ills."–*Robert Louis Stevenson*

NOSACANSE

2. _ _ _ _ _ ◯ _ _ _ is the repetition of the same vowel sound in a series of syllables.

   Examples: "Break, break, break
   On thy c*o*ld gray st*o*nes, *O* sea."–*Alfred Lord Tennyson*

   "...birds and a wh*i*te l*i*ght
   In the back of m*y* m*i*nd to gu*i*de me."–*Louis MacNeice*

ATEAMOONPOIO

3. _ _ _ _ _ _ ◯ _ _ _ _ is the use of words whose sound suggests the meaning. The association may be direct as in the case of *dingdong, hiss,* and *swish,* or it may be merely suggestive. For example, the word *mournful* has a mournful sound.

   Examples: "But when the loud *surges lash* the sounding shore,
   The hoarse, rough word should like the torrent *roar.*"–*Alexander Pope*

   "The sea was *moaning* and *sighing* and saying, *"Hush!"*–*John Masefield*

SOONCANECN

4. ◯ _ _ _ _ _ _ ◯ is the repetition of consonant sounds at the ends of words although the vowels preceding them differ. For example, *stroke* and *luck* may be used at the end of two lines of poetry, repeating the *k* sound. Similarly, the words *begun* and *afternoon* repeat the consonant *n,* and *all* and *kill* repeat *l.*

6–15 TAUTONYMIC EXPRESSIONS

Some words contain their own sound effects, since they repeat the same syllable, such as the term *baa baa*, which represents the sound made by a sheep. Some names are also tautonymic, such as *Lulu, Mimi,* and *ZsaZsa.* Identify the expressions defined below. Then, in the diagram connect the circled letters in order. This line will form another expression of the same type. (You may have to go through some letters in getting from one to another.)

```
 F  R  L  U  H  C
 J  K  E  T  S  P
 N  D  A  O  Q  G
 B  M  Y  W  V  X
```

1. A foolish mistake or blunder
2. A type of candy
3. An Indian drum
4. An extinct bird
5. A laugh
6. The sound made by a train
7. Perfect vision
8. A toy on a string
9. An African fly that transmits diseases
10. A Hawaiian dance
11. A short skirt worn by a ballerina
12. A type of bullet (also slang for a stupid person)
13. A French dance involving high kicks
14. The capital of American Samoa
15. Neither very good nor very bad
16. To express contempt for

BONUS

Another term of this type is *atlatl.* Look up this word and write its meaning below.

Name _____ Date _____

6-16 INNER RHYME

Some English words may be thought of as small poems within themselves, since they have inner rhyme. Two examples are *kudu* (a type of African antelope) and *solo*. Identify the terms below. The letters in the vertical column spell the words *inner rhyme*, as shown.

1. A New Zealand bird   _ I _ _

2. A stupid person   N _ _ _ _ _

3. To associate closely   _ _ _ N _ _

4. Outstanding, exceptional   _ _ _ E _ - _ _ _ _ _

5. An organ grinder's instrument   _ _ R _ _ - _ _ _ _

6. Intricate maneuvers to confuse an opponent   R _ _ _ _ _ - _ _ _ _ _

7. Equipment for reproducing a full range of clear musical notes   H _ - _ _

8. Trickery, mischief   _ _ _ _ Y - _ _ _ _

9. Dull, boring   _ _ M _ _ _

10. An Indian tent   _ E _ _ _

BONUS

For some unknown reason, there are more words with inner rhyme that start with the letter *h* than any other letter. (Five of them are in the exercise above.) Look through your dictionary under the letter *h* and find at least ten others. List them below.

_____

_____

_____

_____

_____

_____

_____

_____

_____

6-17 VOWEL CHANGE

Part 1

Interesting sound effects are produced by words in which the second half of the compound is exactly like the first except for the vowel. One example is Ping-Pong. Identify the words below that fit this pattern. The letters spelling *vowel change* in the vertical column will give you clues to the words.

1. Having a monotonous tone or rhythm   _ _ _ _ **V** _ _
2. To send signals with flags by using a code   _ _ _ **O** _ _
   _ _ _ **W** _ _
3. The sound of rain on a roof   _ _ _ _ **E** _ - _ _ _ _ _
4. To trick or deceive   _ _ _ _ **L** _ _

5. Idle conversation, small talk   _ _ _ _ **C** _ _ _
6. Inconsistent, undependable   _ _ _ _ **H** _ - _ _ _ _
7. A mixture, a jumble   _ _ _ _ **A** _ _
8. A small ornamental article   _ _ _ _ _ _ **N** _ _
9. To make short, sharp turns from side to side   _ _ **G** _ _
10. Nonsense   _ _ _ _ **E** - _ _ _ _ _

Part 2

In some short, one-syllable words we can switch the vowels and produce new words with all of the vowels substituted in turn. For example, we can take the word *mass* and replace the *a* with *e, i, o,* and *u* and produce new words (*mess, miss, moss,* and *muss*). Identify the words defined below, all of which contain an *a.* Then substitute the other vowels to obtain four other words, as was done with *mass* in the example.

1. To stow; to bundle up: _ _ **a** _ _, _____, _____,
   _____, _____

2. Final: _ **a** _ _, _____, _____, _____,
   _____

3. An object that is used in sports: _ _ **a** _ _, _____, _____,
   _____, _____

4. A group of musicians: _ _ **a** _ _, _____, _____,
   _____, _____

5. A small, flat piece of butter: _ _ **a** _, _____, _____,
   _____, _____

6 A cloth or paper container: _ _ **a** _, _____, _____,
   _____, _____

© 1992 by The Center for Applied Research in Education

Name _____ Date _____

6-18 ECHOIC WORDS (ONOMATOPOEIA)

Among the first words created by humans probably were words that imitated natural sounds around them. The word *boom*, for example, may have originated when someone imitated the sound of thunder. Other words, rather than being direct imitations, have sounds that merely suggest their meanings, such as the word *slimy*. The words defined below are of the first type. Try to identify them and then transfer the circled letters to the spaces at the top to form three additional words of this type.

‾1‾ ‾17‾ ‾10‾ ‾8‾ ‾3‾ ‾16‾   ‾15‾ ‾6‾ ‾9‾ ‾15‾ ‾2‾ ‾12‾ ‾14‾   ‾7‾ ‾11‾ ‾5‾ ‾4‾ ‾13‾

1. Sound made by a rock falling into water   s _ _ _ _ Ⓞ

2. Sound made by a tiny bell   Ⓞ _ _ _ _ _

3. Sound made by a bee or a saw   _ Ⓞ _ _

4. Sound made by a snap of a whip   Ⓞ _ _ _ _

5. Sound made by a snake   _ Ⓞ _ _

6. Sound made by a barking dog   _ _ _ _ _ Ⓞ

7. Sound made by a dove   Ⓞ _ _

8. A bird named after a sound it makes
   (Its name is a slang term for "crazy.")   Ⓞ _ _ _ _ _

9. Sound made by frying bacon   s Ⓞ _ _ _ _

10. Sound made by a breaking dish when it falls   Ⓞ _ _ _ _

11. Sound made by a large bell   c Ⓞ _ _ _

12. Sound made by someone having difficulty in breathing   w _ _ Ⓞ _ _

13. Sound made by a rusty door or a mouse   _ _ _ _ _ Ⓞ

14. Sound made by words spoken very softly   _ _ _ _ _ _ Ⓞ

15. Sound made by dry leaves when you walk through them   r _ _ Ⓞ _ _

16. Sound made by a rubber band when you pull it and then let it go   _ _ _ Ⓞ

17. Sound made when you walk in mud   s _ _ Ⓞ _ _

BONUS

Find a copy of Robert Southey's poem "The Cataract of Lodore." It is full of interesting sound effects. Read it aloud to get the full effect.

Name _____ Date _____

6–19 RHYME

Writers use various types of rhyme to produce interesting and artistic effects. Several types of rhyme are described below. Study the examples at the bottom and place the number of the example next to its description. Then transfer the numbers to the diagram, where the total will be equal in all directions. **Note:** There is one extra example that is not considered to be a rhyme. Which one is it?

Write its number here: _____

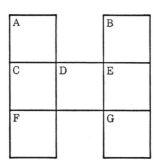

_____ A. Masculine rhyme involves one rhyming accented syllable. A forceful rhyme with a single punch, it is used in serious works.

_____ B. Feminine rhyme, or double rhyme, involves two consecutive rhyming syllables, one accented and one unaccented.

_____ C. Triple rhyme involves three consecutive rhyming syllables. It is used mainly in humorous, light verse.

_____ D. Internal rhyme, or leonine rhyme, employs rhymes within the lines as well as at the ends.

_____ E. Slant rhyme can involve words with corresponding vowel sounds (assonance) or words with corresponding end consonant sounds (consonance) but no true rhyme.

_____ F. Rhyming locutions are sayings or common expressions that involve rhyme, thus making them easy to remember.

_____ G. Refractory rhymes are those that are forced, either by changing the spelling of one word to match another, by dropping or adding a syllable, or by placing just part of the word at the end of a line and the rest on the next line.

1. She was radiant and glamorous;
   He was helpless and amorous.
2. "I sing of brooks, of blossoms, birds, and bowers,
   Of April, May, of June and July flowers." *Robert Herrick*
3. "What they often cure the sick wid
   Is either pills or liquid."—*author unknown*
4. "Ah, distinctly I remember, it was in the bleak December
   And each separate dying ember wrought its ghost upon the floor."—*Edgar Allan Poe*
5. "Where the bee sucks, there suck I
   In a cowslip's bell I lie."—*William Shakespeare*
6. Snug as a bug in a rug.
7. "I married her for love
   As my fancy did me move."—*Izaak Walton*
8. Into the gloomy night
   Rode the gallant knight.

Name _____ Date _____

6-20 RHYME SCHEMES AND STANZAS

To plot the rhyme scheme of a poem, the first line is labeled line *A,* and whatever lines in the stanza rhyme with it are also designated with an *A.* The next line is *B,* and so on through the alphabet. Identify the stanzas described below by placing the number of each next to its description. Then place these numbers in the diagram. Items A, G, and D will have the same total as items B, G, and E and items F, G, and C.

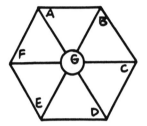

1. acrostic
2. ode
3. couplet
4. haiku
5. tercet

6. sonnet
7. quatrain
8. limerick
9. clerihew

_____ A. This stanza consists of two rhyming lines expressing a complete thought.

_____ B. This stanza consists of four lines that may rhyme in different ways–ABCB (ballad stanza), ABAB (heroic stanza), ABBA, AABB, or even AAAA.

_____ C. This type of stanza consists of three lines with a rhyme scheme of ABA or AAA.

_____ D. This type of humorous poem has five lines with the rhyme scheme of AABBA. Lines 1, 2, and 5 have three accented syllables, while lines 3 and 4 have just two.

_____ E. This type of short poem consists of three lines in which lines 1 and 3 contain five syllables, and line 2 contains seven (a total of seventeen syllables altogether). Usually the rhyme scheme is ABC.

_____ F. This type of poem contains fourteen lines and may have various rhyme schemes. One popular form that Shakespeare used had this rhyme scheme: ABAB CDCD EFEF GG

_____ G. This poem is named after the man who devised it. The first line is always the name of a person who is being ridiculed in the poem. The rhyme scheme is AABB.

Two items are left in the list of nine at the top. Which of them fit these descriptions?

_____ H. A poem in which the first letters of the lines spell out words or names vertically. (It may be of any length and may rhyme in any manner.)

_____ I. A poem of praise that does not follow any particular meter or rhyme

BONUS

Select one of the types of stanzas or poems and write one of your own by following the pattern described.

6-21 RHYTHM

Through the use of accented and unaccented syllables, writers create rhythms. In prose the rhythm is haphazard, but in poetry it is more well-defined, thus producing a pattern. The basic metric unit is known as a *foot.* Five types of metric feet are illustrated below by the names of girls. Identify each by unscrambling the letters. Also identify the various line lengths described. Then transfer the circled letters to this quotation for John Ciardi:

"___ ___ ___ ___ _y_   ___ ___ ___ ___   ___ ___ ___   _w_ _y_   ___ ___   ___ ___ ___   ___ ___ _u_ ___ ___."
10 6 12 13 9   4 5 11 3   7 8 3   1   13 6   8 2 11   13 9   8 2

TYPES OF FEET

1. Adelle   _Ⓞ_____ (BACIMI)

2. Hazel   _____Ⓞ____ (CHAIRCOT)

3. Antoinette   _____Ⓞ___ (CPINASEAT)

4. Gloria   _____Ⓞ__ (CATDILCY)

5. Mimi   _____Ⓞ_ (DOPSANCI)

LENGTH OF LINE

6. One foot   _Ⓞ___ meter

7. Two feet   _Ⓞmeter

8. Three feet   Ⓞ__ meter

9. Four feet   ____Ⓞ_ meter

10. Five feet   Ⓞ_____ meter

11. Six feet   _Ⓞ__ meter

12. Seven feet   _Ⓞ___ meter

13. Eight feet   __Ⓞ_ meter

BONUS

What type of meter did Shakespeare use in many of his writings? Study the lines below and mark the accented and unaccented syllables. Determine the type of foot involved and the length of the lines.

Write the two words here: _____

"That time of year thou mayst in me behold
When yellow leaves or none or few do hang
Upon those boughs which shake against the cold,
Bare ruined choirs, where late the sweet birds sang."

Name _____ Date _____

6-22 CONCRETE POEMS (CALLIGRAMS)

Poets sometimes arrange their words in a shape that is related to the subject of the poem, as in the illustration of the lamp below. In the space at the bottom of this page, try to compose a short concrete poem of your own on any subject. Then redraw it on another sheet of paper. Display all the calligrams on the bulletin board. The class will select a winner.

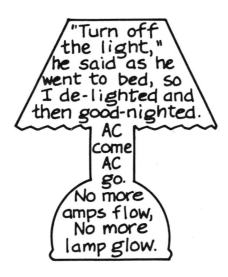

7

MISCELLANEOUS WORD GAMES

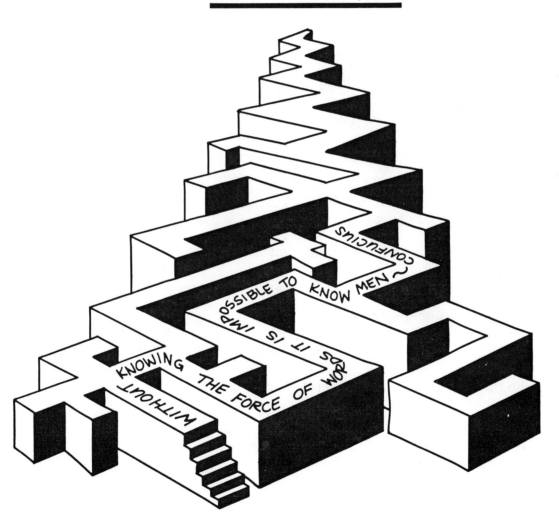

KNOWING THE FORCE OF WORDS IT IS IMPOSSIBLE TO KNOW MEN ~CONFUCIUS WITHOUT

7–1 OCTOBER QUIZ

The prefix *octo-* refers to the number eight. Originally October was the eighth month on the calendar. All of the words below have a connection with the number eight. Match each word with its definition by placing the letter of the word in the space at the left of the definition. Then, in the diagram, connect all the letters in the order in which you listed them, connecting the last letter on your list to the first. This connecting line will form a shape related to this quiz.

OCTODONT Ⓐ   Ⓑ OCTAGON
OCTAMETER Ⓒ   Ⓓ OCTAHEDRON
OCTANE Ⓔ   Ⓕ OCTAVE
OCTARCHY Ⓖ   Ⓗ OCTET
OCTOGENARIAN Ⓘ   Ⓙ OCTOPOD

_____ 1. A chemical in petroleum containing eight carbon atoms

_____ 2. Government consisting of eight rulers

_____ 3. A person between the ages of eighty and ninety

_____ 4. A mollusk with eight arms, such as an octopus

_____ 5. A group of eight singers

_____ 6. A series of eight notes

_____ 7. A line of poetry with eight metrical feet

_____ 8. Having eight teeth

_____ 9. A plane figure with eight sides

_____ 10. A solid figure with eight sides

Thought question: How many zeros must be placed after the number 1 in order to form the number octillion? _____

BONUS

October is the month of ghosts and goblins. Can you figure out these "crossing" jokes below?

1. What do you get when you cross a witch and a kettle?

2. What do you get when you cross ghosts and a meeting?

3. What do you get when you cross a washing machine and a wild animal?

4. What do you get when you cross a vampire with the edge of a river?

5. What do you get when you cross a ghost and a small chicken?

7-2 THANKSGIVING

How would you like to eat the items listed below? They don't sound very appetizing, but each one represents a food. Some of the items are slang terms. Identify each one, and you will have a fabulous menu for Thanksgiving dinner.

1. A province in France   _____

2. Thick fog   _____

3. A short person and a rooster's appendage   _____

4. Military campaign ribbons placed on money   _____

5. Pretty girls   _____

6. Difficult situations, dilemmas   _____

7. Low-grade humor   _____

8. Something embarrassing or troublesome that one doesn't want to touch   _____

9. An ocarina (a musical instrument)   _____

10. A country in the Middle East with a bandage   _____

11. An actor who overacts   _____

12. Lists of names   _____

13. An island in Indonesia   _____

14. Young Girl Scouts   _____

15. A state prepared in the oven   _____

16. Totally organized and in order   _____

17. Small metal blocks that hold bolts in place   _____

18. Places where coins are made   _____

Name _____ Date _____

7–3 YULETIDE

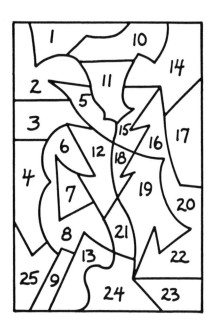

On a separate sheet of paper, number from 1 to 25. Then look at the underlined words below and decide which ones are spelled correctly. Rewrite the incorrect ones and leave the others blank.

Then, in the diagram, shade in the spaces of the words you believe to be correct. Turn the diagram upside down to reveal a shape related to Christmas. If you don't see a recognizable shape, go back and find what you did wrong. Use a dictionary if necessary.

It was Christmas Eve. The church was decorated with (1) holy and (2) wreathes made from (3) bows of (4) ceder. Red velvet bows hung on all the doors. First, the (5) choir sang some (6) hyms. Then the (7) preist spoke from the (8) alter. Next, the children came down the (9) isle and presented a (10) pagent. Some were dressed like shepherds, while others were (11) seraphim and (12) Magi bringing gold, frankincense, and (13) myrr. The (14) pues of the church were filled with happy people thinking about Christmas and (15) Epiphany (the day the Wise Men arrived at the (16) manager).

When Jeremy returned to his home and opened the door, he saw the table set with a (17) sumptious feast and a (18) poinsettia centerpiece. The tree was decorated with (19) tinsle, festooned with strings of lights, and covered with shiny (20) bobbles. Above the door was a sprig of (21) mistletoe, and on the (22) harth was a (23) creshe. Jeremy was so happy that he started to sing a (24) caroll as he lit the candles in the (25) candleabra.

Name _____ Date _____

7–4 JANUARY GAME

January is a good time to look ahead at the next year. You can do just that with the words below, each of which starts with the first three letters of the name of a month. Then, in each set of four sentences, connect the circled letters in order. (Notice that some words contain more than one circled letter.) The three lines formed by connecting the letters will form shapes that have a significance in terms of the calendar.

• •
T R   1. Caretaker of a building: _ _ _ _ _○_○

• •   2. Feverish: _ _ _ _ _ _○_
S L

       3. Any animal that carries its young in a pouch:
• •
C P   _ _ _ _○_○_ _ _

       4. A small, orange-colored fruit: _ _ _ _ _○_ _
_____
• •   5. A dressing made of eggs, oil, and vinegar: _ _ _ _ _ _○_ _ _ _○
N K

• •   6. A type of evergreen shrub or tree: _ _ _ _ _ _ _ _○
E P

• •   7. An alcoholic drink garnished with mint that is popular in the South:
R L
       _ _○_○
_____
       8. A tool for boring holes: _ _ _ _○_

• •   9. A tomb: _ _ _ _ _○_ _ _ _○
R L
• •   10. A group of eight vocalists or instrumentalists: _ _ _ _ _○
T C
• •   11. A beginner: _ _ _ _ _○_
E P   12. To cut the head off: _ _ _ _ _○_ _ _ _○

"Swift calendar, thy pages fall

To doom our dreams and mock us all."–*Author unknown*

7–5 BE MY VALENTINE

February is the month for valentines, hearts, and flowers. We have many expressions involving the word *heart.* For example, when we speak of our innermost feelings, we might refer to the "heart of hearts," and when we speak of the central part of a country, we refer to it as the "heartland." Identify the expressions defined below. Then transfer the circled letters to the spaces in this story: A certain young man could not decide whether to continue his education or get married and find a job. He decided to get married, thus putting

‾‾ ‾‾ ‾‾   ‾‾ ‾ ‾ ‾ ‾‾   ‾ ‾‾ ‾ ‾‾ ‾ ‾‾   ‾‾ ‾‾ ‾   ‾‾ ‾ ‾‾ ‾ ‾ ‾‾ .
18 14 6   18 9 1 3 13   7 15 5 17 2 10   13 16 8   11 4 12 3 6 10

1. Be kind: H◯___ _♡

2. I promise: C◯____ my ♡

3. Made me sad: B◯____ my ♡

4. Made me happy: D___ my ♡ _◯__

5. With total sincerity: ◯____ ____ _____ of my ♡

6. Unalterably opposed: H_____ my ♡◯__ _____ __

7. From memory: ◯_♡

8. In line with my own tastes: A___◯_ my own ♡

9. Reversed a decision: ____ _ C_____◯ ___♡

10. Consider seriously: T__◯ __♡

11. As much as I want to: T__ my ♡'s ◯_____

12. Noticeably in love with someone: W_____ your ♡ on __◯_

   _____

13. Speaking frankly to someone: H_____ a ♡ -to- ♡ ◯____

14. To desire something intensely: ____ your ♡ ___ ◯_

15. To listen to; to encourage: G___◯♡ to

16. Cruel: ◯____ ♡ed

17. Depressed: _◯__ ♡ed

18. A love interest: ♡T◯____

Name _____ Date _____

7-6 PRESIDENTS' DAY

Part 1

Listed below are definitions of the last names of some of our presidents. Identify them by using a little imagination. (The names of some of the presidents may not be spelled the same as the words being defined.) The vertical line indicated will form the names of two additional presidents who had something in common. Can you figure out what it is?

Write it here: _____

_____

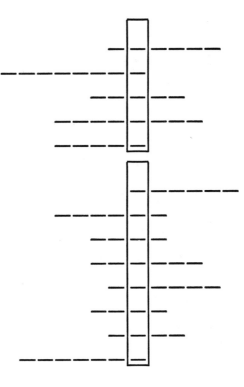

1. One who makes or alters clothing

2. A popular cartoon cat

3. To bestow; to give

4. To supply an additional amount

5. Grasses used as cattle feed

6. A brand of vacuum cleaner

7. An honest, loyal male

8. A brand of car

9. One who transports things in a light vehicle

10. To penetrate; to perforate

11. A shrub

12. To punch; to jab; to prod

13. An angry male offspring

Part 2

Take the circled letters from the names of the presidents listed below and rearrange them to form a Roman numeral that has a great significance in our history. Write the Roman numeral in the spaces indicated and state its significance.

Roman numeral: _ _ _ _ _ _ _

Significance: _____

Calvin Coolidge   Grover Cleveland
Martin Van Buren   Theodore Roosevelt
James Knox Polk   Warren Harding
Richard Nixon   James Buchanan
Abraham Lincoln

Name _____ Date _____

7-7 MARCH GAME

Part 1

March is a month of melting ice and snow. Figure out the words defined below, all of which end with *ice*. Just as the words decrease in size, so the ice and snow gradually disappear during March.

1. A failure by a professional, such as a doctor, to perform services in a proper manner
2. One involved in a crime but who does not actually commit the crime
3. To suffer a loss for what one believes in
4. A black candy flavored with an extract from a certain plant root
5. Fairness and impartiality, according to the law
6. A recommendation or suggestion on a decision or course of action
7. A seasoning for food, such as nutmeg, ginger, pepper, etc.
8. A grain that is a principal food in much of the world

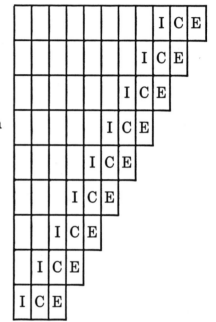

Part 2

March comes in like a lion and goes out like a lamb, according to an old saying. Change the word *lion* to *lamb* by replacing one letter at a time in each item below.

1. A boy's name

2. Thin, lanky

3. Money lent

4. The cut of meat between the hip and ribs

5. Past participle of *lie*

6. Past tense of *lay*

7. The part of the earth's surface that is not water

8. A narrow passageway or route

9. Crippled

Name _____   Date _____

7–8 EASTER EGGS

Part 1

Test your "eggspertise" by thinking of words that start with the sound of "eggs" (*ex*) that fit the definitions below. The letters in the marked vertical column will form a two-word Easter-like term to describe nurses. Write it in this sentence:

Nurses are _____

1. Costly
2. To live
3. Tired, worn out
4. Of high quality
5. Outside

6. Excessive, extreme
7. To carry out; to kill
8. To inspect carefully
9. No longer in existence
10. To state emphatically
11. An illustration
12. A departure

Part 2

For each of the following persons, think of an egg dish that would be appropriate. For example, a person who has been pampered might like a coddled egg.

1. Taxidermist: _____
2. Warlock or witch: _____
3. Optimist: _____
4. A cruel person: _____
5. An illegal hunter: _____
6. A traitor: _____
7. A sunburned person: _____
8. A jogger: _____
9. A person in a hurry: _____
10. An acrobat: _____

Name _____ Date _____

7–9 ARBOR DAY

Arbor Day is a day dedicated to the planting of trees. The date on which it is celebrated varies from state to state, but it is usually in April. Pretend that you are at the top of a tree and the only way you can get down is to use the rope shown below, which connects the letters that are the same in the answers. The definitions give clues to the various names of common trees. **Hint:** The names of some of the trees may not be spelled the same as the words being defined.

1. What's left after wood is burned

2. A kind of flavoring or syrup

3. To suffer from longing or desire

4. To make oneself neat and trim

5. A sandy stretch of coast

6. An odd game played to break a tie

7. To measure the depth by using a lead weight attached to a line

8. An insect in the grasshopper family

9. A bottle stopper

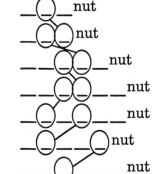

You thought you were all the way down, didn't you? Not quite. In order to reach the ground, you must identify the following nuts, all of which grow on trees, except one. **Another Hint:** Once again, spellings may differ from those of the words being defined.

10. A side of a room

11. A small vegetable

12. A girl's name

13. A South American country

14. A sneeze

15. Container for pirate treasure

16. A golden spread made from milk

BONUS

Which of the nuts above does not grow on a tree? _____

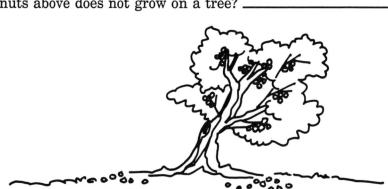

Name _____ Date _____

7-10 MOTHER'S DAY AND FATHER'S DAY

Mother's Day (in May) and Father's Day (in June) are occasions for thinking about all that our parents have done for us. All of the words below contain *ma, pa, mom, pop, mum,* or *dad,* as indicated. Fill in the missing letters.

1. An instant   mom _ _ _ _

2. To damage, make worse   _ _ pa _ _ _

3. A flower   _ _ _ _ _ _ _ _ _ _ _ _ mum

4. A type of tree   pop _ _ _ _

5. A type of spider   dad _ _ _ _ _ _ _ _ _ _

6. Result, consequences   _ _ _ _ _ _ ma _ _

7. A device for determining directions   _ _ _ _ pa _ _ _

8. The number of inhabitants in a region   pop _ _ _ _ _ _ _ _

9. A vegetable   _ _ pa _ _ _ _ _

10. To speak indistinctly   mum _ _ _ _

11. A play   _ _ _ _ ma

12. An unbound booklet   pa _ _ _ _ _ _ _

13. A beginner   _ ma _ _ _ _ _

14. Nonsense   pop _ _ _ _ _ _ _

15. Important, of great consequence   mom _ _ _ _ _ _ _

16. To go   _ _ _ pa _ _ _

17. One skilled in international relations   _ _ _ _ _ _ ma _

18. The smallest allowable amount   _ _ _ _ _ mum

19. A scolding   _ _ _ _ _ _ ma _ _

20. Restless   _ _ pa _ _ _ _ _

21. Another name for a crayfish   _ _ _ _ _ dad

22. More than half   ma _ _ _ _ _ _

23. A plant from which the Egyptians made paper   pa _ _ _ _ _ _

Name _____ Date _____

7-11 SHOPPING FOR RHYMES

Pretend you are shopping for the items described below. To obtain the item, all you need to do is to identify each item by a pair of rhyming words. For example, if you are shopping for a home for a pet rodent, you must ask the clerk for a *mouse house*. A one-syllable rhyming pair of words is a hink pink. If each word has two syllables, it is a hinky pinky, and a pair of three-syllable words is a hinkety pinkety. (If you get all the answers right, you can label yourself as a *proper shopper*.)

HINK PINKS

1. A rabbit trap   _____ _____
2. A burglar alarm   _____ _____
3. An imitation reptile   _____ _____
4. A place for holding reading matter   _____ _____
5. A stable for a giraffe   _____ _____
6. A container for a banner   _____ _____
7. A garbage can   _____ _____
8. A scarecrow   _____ _____
9. A wig   _____ _____

HINKY PINKIES

10. A musical instrument from an island near Florida   _____ _____
11. A mystery novel about a murder   _____ _____
12. A coffeemaker   _____ _____
13. A bird feeder   _____ _____

HINKETY PINKETIES

14. An almanac   _____ _____
15. Peanut butter (or margarine, jelly, etc.)   _____ _____
16. A yellow fruit from the capital of Cuba   _____ _____

BONUS

Think of one example of your own in each of the categories above and write definitions for them on the back of this sheet. Let your classmates guess them. (You may also be able to think of some four-syllable rhymes, such as *uranium geranium*.)

Name _____ Date _____

7–12 HINK PINK PEOPLE

All the types of individuals described below can be identified by two-word rhyming expressions. For example, an angry father is a *mad dad*. This is a hink pink, since each word has a single syllable. A hinky pinky involves two-syllable words. (Example: A nicer-looking horn player is a *cuter tooter*.) When the rhyming pair consists of words with three or more syllables, it is a hinkety pinkety. If you can identify all the people described below, you can label yourself as a *quiz whiz*.

HINK PINKS

1. A deceased Communist   _____ ____

2. Chief of police   ____ ____

3. Leader of a gang of robbers   _____ _____

4. A female from Paris   _____ _____

5. A tardy husband or wife   _____ _____

6. A well-groomed man from Athens   _____ _____

7. A Scandinavian who has been killed   _____ _____

8. A man from a certain city in Belgium   _____ _____

HINKY PINKIES

9. A cowardly man   _____ _____

10. A librarian   _____ _____

11. A part-time law enforcement officer   _____ _____

12. A car salesman   _____ _____

13. A doctor who specializes in stomach ailments   _____ _____

14. A snake charmer   _____ _____

15. An eye doctor   _____ _____

16. A false friend   _____ _____

HINKETY PINKETIES

17. A nonmilitary person from Rio de Janeiro: _____

_____

18. An underground dweller in Pittsburgh or Philadelphia:

_____ _____

19. A moody person from China or Japan: _____

_____

20. An evil clergyman: _____ _____

7-13 TOM TWISTIES

At one time Tom Swifties were a craze. They are expressions using descriptive adverbs with a relationship to what Tom said. (Examples: "Where are my crutches?" Tom asked lamely. "I don't like Sinatra," Tom stated frankly.) The items below represent a twist, since you are asked to supply a descriptive verb rather than an adverb. (Examples: "I have been to Hawaii but not to Alaska," Tom stated. "I'm under a lot of pressure," Tom stressed.) Using a bit of imagination, try to supply verbs that would be descriptive of what Tom said in each sentence below. (There may be more than one suitable answer.)

1. "Isn't that baby bird cute!" Tom _____.

2. "The tip of this arrow is defective," Tom _____ out.

3. "But I wanted a purebred dog," Tom _____.

4. "Get all those men out of here," Tom _____.

5. "Cuts of meat have funny names," Tom _____.

6. "She really *is* my sister," Tom _____.

7. "I wanted Burgundy, not Chablis," Tom _____.

8. "Moby Dick bit off my leg," Tom _____.

9. "Your Honor, I'm not guilty," Tom _____.

10. "I wish I were back in the forest," Tom _____.

11. "My raven is the winner," Tom _____.

12. "She sang off-key," Tom _____.

13. "The faucet's broken," Tom _____.

14. "Give me that rubber band," Tom _____.

15. "That's the worst train I've ever ridden," Tom _____.

16. "You must have left the gas turned on," Tom _____.

17. "I may need new glasses," Tom _____.

18. "Don't worry. I'll fix your shoe," Tom _____.

19. "I'll help out at the Red Cross," Tom _____.

20. "*Hound* is not the subject of the sentence," Tom _____.

Note: The term *Tom Swifty* came from a character named Tom Swift in books written by Victor Appleton, who used many descriptive adverbs.

7-14 ANIMALS IN SAYINGS

Animals play a significant role in our lives, as shown by the sayings below, which represent only a small portion of those in our language. On the line at the left, write the word that belongs in the blank. All these animal names will be in alphabetical order. The first person to complete the list is the winner.

_____ 1. To go _____ over something (**to be very enthusiastic**)

_____ 2. An eager _____

_____ 3. To take the _____ by the horns

_____ 4. To sing like a _____

_____ 5. To bell the _____

_____ 6. To _____ out (**to give up, to quit**)

_____ 7. To be in the _____ house (**out of favor**)

_____ 8. A memory like an _____

_____ 9. Like a _____ out of water

_____ 10. Sly as a _____

_____ 11. A big _____ in a little pond

_____ 12. The _____ that laid the golden egg

_____ 13. A road _____ (**a driver who is discourteous**)

_____ 14. _____-hearted (brave)

_____ 15. Crazy as a _____

_____ 16. Stubborn as a _____

_____ 17. Wise as an _____

_____ 18. To buy a _____ in a poke

_____ 19. To play _____ (**to pretend to be dead or asleep**)

_____ 20. To _____ on someone (**to betray a person**)

_____ 21. Slow as a _____

_____ 22. To _____ away your money (**save your money and hide it**)

_____ 23. To take a _____ by the tail (**to tackle a difficult problem**)

_____ 24. To talk _____ (**to get down to the facts**)

_____ 25. A _____ in sheep's clothing

BONUS

Try to write a statement of comparison similar to those above—but one you originate yourself. (Example: Her thinking was like a zebra—only black and white, with no gray areas.) Write your statement on the back of this sheet.

7–15 TERMS RELATED TO ANIMALS

Part 1

What did the firefighters name their two dalmatian dogs? To find out, match each baby animal below with the name of its parent by placing the letter of its parent in the space at the left. Notice that there are two items with the letter *T*, so they are identified as *T (1)* and *T (2)*. The letters will form the names of the dogs.

Write them here: _____ _____

_____ 1. cut	D.	goose
_____ 2. calf	I.	sheep
_____ 3. fawn	O.	horse
_____ 4. lamb	Q.	whale
_____ 5. cygnet	R.	swan
_____ 6. kid	S.	lion
_____ 7. gosling	T.	(1) kangaroo
_____ 8. colt	T.	(2) goat
_____ 9. joey	U.	deer
_____ 10. spat	Z.	oyster

Part 2

What did the seamstress name her two cats? To find out, match each animal below with its proper collective noun by placing the letter of the collective noun in the space at the left. Notice that there are two items with the letter *E,* so be sure to identify each by its number as shown below. The letters will form the names of the two cats.

Write them here: _____ _____

_____ 1. ants	A.	brood
_____ 2. chicks	C.	flock
_____ 3. kangaroos	D.	covey (or bevy)
_____ 4. sheep	E.	(1) pod
_____ 5. bees	E.	(2) gaggle
_____ 6. geese	H.	swarm
_____ 7. elephants	M.	pack
_____ 8. wolves	N.	pride
_____ 9. whales	P.	army
_____ 10. lions	S.	herd
_____ 11. quail	T.	mob
_____ 12. fish	Y.	school

7-16 MORE ANIMAL TERMS

Part 1

Identify the female or male in each pair of animals below and transfer the circled letters to the spaces in the diagram in order to form a square with words in both vertical and horizontal positions. The first word in the square will name something that animals have.

6	7	1	4	
				T
7	8	2	7	4
1	2	1	3	7
4	7	3	5	9
	4	7	9	10
T				

MALE

1. __◯____
2. ◯___
3. lion
4. ◯__
5. fox
6. cock
7. ____◯
8. horse
9. __◯___
10. stag

FEMALE

goose

cow

_____◯_

ewe

_◯____

◯__

duck

◯___

jenny

◯__

Part 2

Match each adjective below with the animal to which it refers by placing the letter of the corresponding animal at the left. These letters will form another animal adjective.

Write it here and tell what animal it refers to: _____ _____

_____ 1. canine		E. pig
_____ 2. equine		I. cow
_____ 3. feline		L. dog
_____ 4. bovine		N. bear
_____ 5. ursine		P. cat
_____ 6. porcine		U. horse

7-17 SOUNDS ANIMALS MAKE

Part 1

What did the florist name his dog? To find out, match each animal below with the sound it makes by placing the letter of the matching sound at the left. Notice that there are two items labeled *A,* and they are further identified by the numbers beside them.

Write the name of the florist's dog here: _____

_____ 1. frog   A. (1) roar

_____ 2. lion   A. (2) bray

_____ 3. hyena   G. laugh

_____ 4. pig   I. gibber

_____ 5. sheep   L. neigh, whinny

_____ 6. horse   N. squeal, grunt

_____ 7. ape   O. bleat

_____ 8. donkey   W. croak

Part 2

What two-word name did the minister give his horse? To find out, match each bird below with the sound it makes. When you use either of the two items labeled *A,* be sure to identify each by its number, as shown.

Write the name of the horse here: _____

_____ 1. dove   A. (1) hiss

_____ 2. crow   A. (2) crow

_____ 3. cock   E. caw

_____ 4. duck   G. chirp

_____ 5. eagle   I. cluck

_____ 6. owl   L. scream

_____ 7. sparrow   P. coo

_____ 8. goose   R. quack

_____ 9. hen   T. chatter

_____ 10. magpie   Y. hoot

BONUS

Crickets chirp and beetles drone. List a couple of other insects on the back of this sheet and name the sound they make.

Name _____ Date _____

7-18 DOGS

Dogs play an important role in our lives, as indicated by the numerous expressions we have in reference to them. Identify the "doggy" expressions below. The circled letters, in order, will fit into this story:

A man went to a psychiatrist and said, "I need help. I keep thinking I'm a dog."

"Well," said the psychiatrist, "lie down on my couch and we'll discuss this."

"I can't," said the man.

"I'm _____ allowed _____!"

1. An exclamation: dog___◯_

2. Highest official: _◯_ dog

3. A metal disk for military identification: dog◯___

4. A type of shrub or tree: dog__◯___

5. Destruction, ruination: ____◯_ ___ ____ dogs

6. Extremely weary: dog◯_____

7. Aerial warfare between two fighter planes: dog____◯_

8. A simple swimming stroke: dog _____◯

9. A soldier, an infantryman: dog◯_____

10. Someone not favored in the odds: ◯_____dog

11. A snug-fitting necklace: dog _____◯

12. Heavy downpour: ____◯____ _____ ____ dogs

13. A miserable existence: a dog's _◯___

14. A type of hard cracker: dog _____◯

15. Out of favor: ___ ____ dog__◯___

16. Sirius: the dog ____◯

17. An inferior type of humorous verse: dog__◯____

BONUS

On the back of this sheet, write a couple of additional expressions involving dogs.

7–19 COLORFUL EXPRESSIONS

A certain young man always described his girlfriend as "_ _ _ _ in

_____."

To find the answer, first fill the blanks in the phrases below with the names of colors. Then, in the string of letters preceding each set of phrases, cross out the first letters of the colors you used. The remaining letters, when rearranged, will form a word, and the two words formed will provide the answer. Then try to guess why he might refer to his girl this way.

Write your guess here: _____

_____

B B B E G N O O P P R Y

1. _____ alert: an emergency state of readiness

2. to _____-bag: to take your lunch to work

3. a _____ movie: pornographic film

4. in the _____: in good health

5. born to the _____: royal, imperial

6. Agent _____: a chemical used in the Vietnam war to defoliate trees

7. _____ journalism: printing sensational material

8. _____ Panthers: an organization of senior citizens

9. _____ hole: a point in space

E G G I I L L M N O R S V W

10. _____ flight: movement of middle-class whites from the centers of cities to the suburbs

11. _____ revolution: the use of high-yield grains to increase farm production and feed the hungry peoples of the world

12. _____ lining: the bright side of a bad situation

13. good as _____: of high value

BONUS

Can you think of the name of a color to put in the following blank to create a phrase that sounds like the name of one of Shakespeare's plays?

"_____ Like It"

Name _____ Date _____

7–20 EXPRESSIONS USING *UP*

Up is a very short word but a very useful one. We have a number of words that contain *up*, such as *upstart.* We also have numerous phrases using *up,* such as "not up to snuff." Identify the words and phrases below. Then connect the circled letters in order in the diagram to form a shape that has a connection with this game. (Not all the expressions contain circled letters.)

```
B   E   A   F   H
J   T       C   L
S   R       U   O
M   P       K   Q
W   D       V   Y
X   G   Z   N   I
```

WORDS

1. One's early training   up _ _ _ _ ◯ _ _ _
2. Upward movement of air   up ◯ _ _ _ _ _
3. Maintenance   up _ _ _ _ _
4. Snobbish, arrogant   up ◯ _ _ _ _
5. Extreme disorder   up _ _ _ _ _ _ _
6. To improve to a higher rating   up _ _ _ _ _ _
7. Erect   up ◯ _ _ _ _ _
8. To pull out or displace   up _ _ _ _ _
9. To turn over; to cause disorder   up ◯ _ _
10. Tense, nervous   up _ _ _ _ ◯

PHRASES

11. Current, modern   up–_ _ _ –_ ◯ _ _
12. To confront a problem   _ _ ◯ _ up _ _ _ _ _
13. To hide   _ ◯ _ _ up
14. To rob   _ _ _ _ _ up (or stick up)
15. To go faster   _ ◯ _ _ _ up (or speed up)
16. Confused   _ _ _ _ _ _ up
17. Cosmetics   _ _ ◯ _ up
18. To withstand something   _ _ _ _ up _ _ _ _ _ _ _ _
19. To have unrestrained fun _ _ ◯ _ _ _ _ up
20. To end something   _ _ _ _ _ _ _ up
21. To raise the stakes   up _ _ _ _ _ ◯ _ _
22. Alert and likely to succeed up–_ _ _ _ –_ _ _ _ _ _

Name _____ Date _____

7-21 EXPRESSIONS INVOLVING A SERIES

A number of expressions we use in everyday speech contain a series of three items. For example, we refer to the flag as "the red, white, and blue." In such expressions the words are always spoken in the same order. You would not be likely to hear the flag spoken of as "the white, blue, and red." In each expression below, one of the three terms is missing. Fill in the missing item. The circled letters will then spell three words that also form an expression of this type. Write them here and tell what they refer to:

_____, _____, and _____.

_____

1. Beg, ◯_____, or steal

2. I ____◯, I saw, I conquered

3. Lock, stock, and _____◯

4. First, last, and __◯_____

5. Of the people, ◯__ the people, and for the people

6. Food, __◯_____, and shelter

7. __◯__, Dick, and Harry

8. Stop, ____◯, and listen

9. Reading, writing, and _____◯

10. ◯_____, vegetable, and mineral

11. ___◯, place, or show

12. Eat, ◯_____, and be merry

13. Ready, __◯_____, and able

14. Wine, ____◯__, and song

BONUS

Can you complete this four-item expression Winston Churchill spoke as prime minister on May 13, 1940?

"I have nothing to offer but _____, _____, _____, and _____."

Think of at least one other common expression involving a series and write it on the back of this sheet.

Name _____ Date _____

7–22 EXPRESSIONS INVOLVING FOOD

Food is something we think about several times a day and also something that crops up in our speech in regard to items not related to food. Fill the blanks in the story below with the names of foods. The first person to complete the exercise is the winner. (In several of the blanks more than one correct answer is possible.)

John Foster was in a bad humor. When he started his new job, he thought life would be a bowl of (1) _____, but his boss turned out to be a real (2) _____ (**grouch**), and there seemed to be no way to (3) _____ him up. John still owed a lot of money on his new car, which had turned out to be a real (4) _____. And his daughter, who was the (5) _____ of his eye, was ill. He was really in a (6) _____ (**dilemma**). Should he sell the car to pay for the hospital bills, or should he ask his boss for a raise? He thought he'd go (7) _____ worrying about it.

To relax, he picked up his guitar and went to his friend's house for a (8) _____ session. His friend told John to go to the boss and ask for a promotion to supervisor, but John didn't think he could cut the (9) _____ as a supervisor. His friend said, "If you just stay cool as a (10) _____ when you go in to talk to the boss, it will be a piece of (11) _____ to get the job. And you know you can handle the job as well as anyone." But John feared the idea was just (12) _____ in the sky.

Deciding to go for it, John said, "I'm a pretty smart (13) _____. If I use my (14) _____ (**head**), maybe I can handle it." He psyched himself up until he felt full of (15) _____ (**pep**).

The next morning he walked into the boss's office and chewed the (16) _____ for a few minutes before making his move. Much to John's amazement, the boss agreed to let John try the position of supervisor. John was pleased as (17) _____. The boss was a good (18) _____ after all!

John wanted to keep the promotion a surprise, but he spilled the (19) _____ at dinner. His wife, Priscilla, also had a surprise–the doctor had reported that their daughter did not need surgery after all. John and Priscilla drank a (20) _____ to their good luck. They were as happy as (21) _____ in a cloudburst, for now they would have enough (22) _____ (**money**) to take care of all their needs.

7–23 MISLEADING EXPRESSIONS

Suppose someone asked you, "Did you ever see a nuthatch?" Would you picture a bird, or would you imagine a nut hatching by coming out of its shell? A number of compound words or two-word terms can be misinterpreted in this manner. Such terms are usually intended to be nouns, but the second half of the term can be thought of as a verb as well. Supply the second half of each term below. The intended meaning is given. After completing the exercise, select one of the items (or another similar item of your own choosing) and make a drawing illustrating the misinterpreted version of the words. Place these drawings on the bulletin board and select a winner.

DID YOU EVER SEE...

1. a fish_____?   a glass container for goldfish

2. a beauty _____?   a place where hairdressing and manicures are done

3. a cow_____?   leather made from a cow

4. a home_____?   the final part of a race

5. a dragon_____?   an insect

6. a banana _____?   a dessert

7. a man_____?   an order from an authority

8. a salad _____?   a seasoned sauce

9. a cat_____?   a mint-like herb

10. an ear_____?   an ornament for the ear

11 a fox-_____?   a type of dance

12. a house_____?   housekeeping

13. a kid_____?   an abduction of a person

14 a sun_____?   a time-keeping device

15. a tool_____?   a place for storing tools

16. a jelly _____?   a sheet of sponge cake spread with jelly, rolled up, and sliced

17. an apple _____?   a pastry made by folding the crust over the filling

18. coffee _____?   a rest period for consuming refreshments

19. a cake_____?   a competition with a cake as a prize

7-24 TERMS CONTAINING BODY PARTS

Fill the blanks in the story below with names of parts of the human body.

Amanda, wearing a sweater made of (1) mo_____, a gold (2) _____lace, and a bracelet with several (3) ch_____s dangling from it, waited for her boyfriend, Arnold, a (4) ro_____ fellow who had been a (5) _____ball player. He always had a (6) s____shod appearance. Although he was the (7) ri_____ man in town, he was also a real (8) _____flint who hated to spend money. Generosity was not one of his (9) att_____utes. And that is why Amanda was so surprised when he arrived (10) b_____ing a large package.

"I'm early because I got a (11) _____ start," Arnold said as he (12) _____ed her the package. Inside was a (13) _____chilla coat. How delighted Amanda was! She put it on and stepped into the Porsche that Arnold always kept (14) s_____shape. It was (15) _____ing because it had just been waxed. Even the chrome on the (16) w_____s sparkled.

They rode off. Arnold, not paying attention, made an (17) il_____al turn and was suddenly (18) _____d by a policeman, who (19) _____d him suspiciously. "Aren't you the same fellow who (20) de_____d the monument downtown with graffiti?" Arnold wanted to talk (21) _____, but he knew that if he became (22) in_____nt, he would be in trouble, having been involved in the prank. "You better (23) _____ the mark from now on," said the policeman.

(24) Down_____ed, Arnold took Amanda home. The whole affair really (25) r_____d him, but he decided to put it behind him and be more careful next time, since he didn't want another (26) _____-lashing from a policeman—or from his mother. In fact, he even went (27) _____ to the monument and removed the graffiti, since he wanted Amanda to be proud of him. He (28) _____d down to business and made a huge fortune. When he and Amanda were married, everyone in town attended the wedding, and they all agreed that they were the (29) _____somest couple anyone had ever seen.

7–25 EXPRESSIONS INVOLVING BODY PARTS

Many expressions we use contain names of parts of the body. For example, we speak of a "private eye," "the long arm of the law," etc. Fill in the body part in each phrase below. Then, on another sheet of paper, draw a human figure, using just the parts mentioned in this exercise. The person with the funniest drawing is the winner.

1. Deceitful, not trustworthy   two-_ _ _ _ d

2. Jealous   green-_ _ _ d

3. Working hard   keeping your _ _ _ _ _ to the grindstone

4. A marine   leather_ _ _ _ _

5. Going through the mind without making an impression   in one _ _ _ _ and out the other

6. A scolding   _ _ _ _ _ _ _ _-lashing

7. Being casual and unrestrained   letting your _ _ _ _ _ _ down

8. To use force   to strong-_ _ _ _

9. Near death   on your last _ _ _ _ _

10. Cruel   hard-_ _ _ _ _ _ _ed

11. Cowardly   lily-_ _ _ _ _ _ _ed

12. To pay the expenses   _ _ _ _ _ _ the bills

13. Shallow, superficial   _ _ _ _ _ _-deep

14. Used, recycled   second_ _ _ _ _ _

15. To follow rules precisely   _ _ _ _ the line

16. To accuse someone   To _ _ _ _ _ _ _ _ _ a suspect

17. All out, in a fierce manner   _ _ _ _ _ _ _ and nail

18. To accept the burden   _ _ _ _ _ _ _ _ _ _ _ the responsibility

19. To poke fun at someone   to _ _ _ _ _ someone

20. To get relief by telling something to someone   to get it off your _ _ _ _ _ _

21. An instant response without careful consideration   a _ _ _ _ _ _-jerk response

Name _____ Date _____

7-26 DOUBLE MEANINGS

Test your sense of humor by thinking of double meanings for each of the statements below and then coming up with a silly remark to make in response. Example: Two men were on a golf course, and one said, "Harry just shot a birdie." The other one might say, "I hope it wasn't a robin."

1. A student said to the art teacher, "Please teach me to draw." The teacher replied, "_____

_____"

2. A man who was obviously ill said to another, "Call me a doctor." The other man said, "_____

_____"

3. It was Sally's turn to cook, and she asked, "Where is the pot?" Jane replied, "_____

_____"

4. One boy tells another that he asked a certain girl to a party before his friend asked her. He says, "I sure beat Jack to the punch." The second boy says, "_____

_____"

5. One nurse explained to a new employee, "Dr. Jackson is the head doctor in this hospital." The new nurse said, "_____

_____"

6. The English teacher, pleased with one of her students, said, "He has a great thirst for the classics." Another teacher then remarked, "_____

_____"

7. "I think I'll vote for him. He's a promising politician," said Barbara. Her friend replied, "_____

_____"

8. One man said to another, "Tonight my wife will be entertaining." The other man said, "_____

_____"

9. One girl said to another, "For my birthday Jim gave me a compact in a pink box with a rose on top." The other girls said, "_____

_____"

10. One man, speaking of the latest in men's fashions, said, "Men's ties are narrower this year, pant legs are wider, but there is little change in men's pockets." A listener remarked, "_____

_____"

Name _____ Date _____

7-27 MISINTERPRETATIONS

A man speaking to a friend said, "I keep seeing spots before my eyes." When the friend asked, "Have you seen a doctor?" the man replied, "No, just spots." This story illustrates how words can be interpreted in two different ways. Read the pairs of sentences below and, in the space under each pair, write the words that might have been spoken and interpreted in both of those ways. For example, here are two interpretations: **He often goes on safaris and kills large animals. He is a gambler looking for action with high stakes.** What words could be interpreted in both of these ways? Answer: He is a big game hunter.

INTENDED MEANING	**MISINTERPRETATION**
1. He is nervous.	He has been hanged.
2. The prisoner has escaped.	The prisoner has developed a rash.
3. Grandma doesn't use any devices to aid her vision.	Grandma drinks out of the bottle.
4. Get out of here.	Stir it up vigorously.
5. I have a better apartment now.	I am using better coins now.
6. I purchased a car for my wife.	I traded my wife for a car.
7. He attracts women.	He makes portraits of women.
8. The door was slightly open.	The door was damaged.
9. I'll call you.	I'll give you a piece of jewelry.
10. She was detained.	She was mugged.
11. Stop.	Clip it out with scissors.
12. They are filming the sample episode of a TV show.	They are firing a gun at the man flying the plane.
13. He hits his wife.	He gets up earlier than his wife.
14. I have serious problems.	I have problems with wrinkles in my clothes.

Name _____ Date _____

7–28 MONEY TERMS

We may never feel that we have enough money, but we surely have plenty of slang terms for it. Money in general is referred to as *bread, do-re-me* (or *dough*), *moolah,* etc. Terms for paper money include *alfalfa, toad hides, lettuce, cabbage,* and *long green,* while coins have terms of reference such as *clinkers* and *shekels.*

Three boys each had the amounts shown below, and they wanted to combine their money for an investment. List the amounts represented by each slang term, total the amount for each boy, and then get the grand total. For their investment the boys need $1,300. Would they have enough with the amounts shown below?

Write your answer here: _____

1. **Les**   C-note   = _____
              sawbuck   = _____
              fin   = _____
              two bits   = _____
                              TOTAL [____]

2. **Bruce**   grand   = _____
              skin   = _____
              four bits   = _____
              a copper   = _____
                              TOTAL [____]

3. **Ken**   double sawbuck = _____
              thin one   = _____
              blip   = _____
              Brown Abe   = _____
                              TOTAL [____]
                      GRAND TOTAL [____]

Interesting facts about money: The words *money* and *mint* come from *Moneta,* an alternate name for the Roman goddess Juno. At her temple in Rome, some of the first money was minted. The word *dollar* comes from the German word *thal,* meaning valley, because the first such coins were minted at St. Joachimsthal. The *picayune* (a half dime) was the smallest coin every minted in the U.S. The two-dollar bill is considered unlucky by some, who clip off one corner to ward off bad luck. But most people consider it twice as lucky to have a two-dollar bill as a one-dollar bill.

7-29 POSTAL ABBREVIATIONS

By combining the United States postal abbreviations for the states listed below, you can form the four-letter words needed in the puzzle.

ACROSS

1. Rhode Island and Mississippi
2. Colorado and Alabama
3. Hawaii and Delaware
4. Michigan and Nebraska
5. South Carolina and Arizona
6. Massachusetts and Idaho

DOWN

4. Missouri and Oregon
7. Maine and North Dakota
8. Pennsylvania and Connecticut
9. Virginia and Indiana
10. Washington and Illinois

BONUS #1

Which three state abbreviations might a boy use if he is startled by his father approaching unexpectedly? Write them here.

_____

BONUS #2

Can you combine any other state abbreviations to make something interesting? If so, write your idea on the back of this sheet.

Name _____ Date _____

7-30 GOBBLEDYGOOK

Gobbledygook is highfalutin speech designed either to impress or to baffle listeners. Government bulletins often use such language. Good speakers and writers avoid the overuse of long words. Some examples of gobbledygook are given below. Match each with its meaning by placing the corresponding letter at the left. These letters, when transferred to the spaces in the following sentence, will form a quotation from Winston Churchill:

"$\overline{12}\,\overline{5}\,\overline{13}$ $\overline{10}\,\overline{5}\,\overline{8}\,\overline{9}\,\overline{12}$ $\overline{6}\,\overline{8}\,\overline{9}\,\overline{11}\,\overline{10}$ $\overline{7}\,\overline{9}\,\overline{13}$ $\overline{4}\,\overline{13}\,\overline{10}\,\overline{12}$' $\overline{7}\,\overline{2}\,\overline{11}$ $\overline{12}\,\overline{5}\,\overline{13}$ $\overline{8}\,\overline{3}\,\overline{11}$

$\overline{6}\,\overline{8}\,\overline{9}\,\overline{11}\,\overline{10}$ $\overline{7}\,\overline{9}\,\overline{13}$ $\overline{4}\,\overline{13}\,\overline{10}\,\overline{12}$ $\overline{8}\,\overline{1}$ $\overline{7}\,\overline{3}\,\overline{3}$."

_____ 1. Feathered bipeds

_____ 2. Aerodynamic personnel decelerator

_____ 3. People expressways

_____ 4. Educational edifices

_____ 5. Cubic random number generators

_____ 6. Wooden interdental stimulator

_____ 7. Interlocking slide fastener

_____ 8. Orthopedic immobilization appliance

_____ 9. Theological place of eternal bliss

_____ 10. Expansible amorphous absorption module

_____ 11. Audiovisual electronic troubleshooter

_____ 12. Circumorbital hematoma

_____ 13. Celestial incandescent mass

A. zipper

B. school buildings

D. TV repairman

E. star

F. birds

H. dice

L. sidewalks

N. parachute

O. cast (for a broken leg or arm)

R. heaven

S. sponge

T. black eye

W. toothpick

BONUS

An example of bureaucratic gobbledygook is this title of a former HUD study on bicycle safety: "Evaluation and Parameterization of Stability and Safety Performance Characteristics of Two-and Three-Wheeled Vehicular Toys for Children." Find other examples of this type of speech and write them on the back of this sheet.

7–31 LETTERSPEAK

These letters represent an entire sentence: **L-N N K-T R QTT.** (Ellen and Katie are cuties.) Thinking along the same lines, supply the letter combinations that produce words with the meanings given below. Write the letters and also write the word the letters represent. Then take the circled letters and rearrange them to form a sentence you might use in reply to an alien from outer space when he asks, "Who are you?" Write your answer here:

_____

COMBINATIONS OF TWO DIFFERENT LETTERS   LETTERS   WORD

1. Christmas
2. Jealousy
3. Frosty
4. Containing nothing
5. To add or attach something
6. An award for excellence on TV
7. A Native American's home
8. An English composition
9. An alcoholic beverage
10. A type of vine

PAIRS OF THE SAME LETTER

11. To bother or harass
12. Is in debt to
13. Has good judgment
14. Hints
15. Freedom from discomfort
16. Put into service, employ

THREE-LETTER COMBINATIONS

17. A Native American
18. A dog, a cat, or a cow, etc.
19. Loveliness
20. A foe, an opponent
21. A type of flower
22. Strength, pep
23. Great joy
24. To look at carefully

FOUR-LETTER COMBINATION

25. Title for a high official

Name _____ Date _____

7-32 DAFFY DEFINITIONS

Sometimes when we encounter new words, we can analyze them and determine their meanings. Many times, however, we can be wrong. For example, if you heard the word *cartoon* for the first time, you might think it refers to a song on a car radio. In the same way, you might conclude that *childhood* refers to something a child wears on its head. Look at the definitions below and match each one with a word from the list at the top to which it could logically apply. Then transfer the letters to the following spaces, which will form a sentence giving you some interesting information about teachers:

‾‾ ‾‾ ‾‾ ‾‾ ‾‾ ‾‾ ‾‾ ‾‾ ‾‾ ‾‾ teachers ‾‾ ‾‾ ‾‾ ‾‾ ‾‾ ‾‾ ‾‾ ‾‾ ‾‾ ‾‾ ‾‾ .
6 11 13 4 5 10 12 7 13 1   3 8 9 13 11 12 2 10 8 14 14

A. kindred   H. protein   P. lagoon
B. scintillate L. doleful   S. acquire
C. curate   M. dismembered   U. pasteurize
D. stardust   N. contents   V. crestfallen
E. catalyst   O. popcorn   Y. Chinese checker

_____ 1. What's left of a famous movie actor after cremation

_____ 2. The speed with which a doctor gets you over your disease

_____ 3. In favor of teenagers

_____ 4. Kicked out of the club

_____ 5. A French hoodlum

_____ 6. Beyond your field of vision

_____ 7. An oriental grocery clerk

_____ 8. Fear of relatives

_____ 9. Dropped your toothpaste

_____ 10. Filled with pineapple

_____ 11. A place where criminals spend the night

_____ 12. Dad's silly jokes

_____ 13. A roster of cow's names

_____ 14. Singers in church

_____ 15. To drink and gamble until the wee hours

BONUS

Think of other words that could be misinterpreted. Write daffy definitions for them and let your classmates guess the words.

7-33 BASEBALL AND FOOTBALL TERMS

Many baseball and football terms have applications to things outside of sports. For example, the terms *plate* and *pitcher,* used in baseball, are used in the kitchen to refer to quite different objects. Identify the terms defined below. Then, in the diagram, shade in the first letters of all the words you used. The unshaded portion will form the shape of something related to this exercise. (Several words may start with the same letter. Fill one space in the diagram for each such word.)

BASEBALL

1. A foundation, a support   _____

2. A Greek poet   _____

3. A locked chest for storing valuables   _____

4. A lawn-mower attachment for holding clippings   _____

5. An insect   _____

6. A ship belonging to a steamship company   _____

7. A semiliquid mixture of flour and milk   _____

8. A work stoppage   _____

FOOTBALL

9. Soft, fluffy feathers   _____

10. Two bits   _____

11. Fishing gear   _____

12. In a city, a rectangular space surrounded by streets   _____

13. Static on a radio   _____

14. A free ticket   _____

15. An electrical device that captures electrical signals
    and converts them to sound   _____

7–34 WORDS CONTAINING ROMAN NUMERALS

When certain words are printed in capital letters, they may appear to contain Roman numerals, since certain letter combinations form those numerals. Given below are definitions of such words. The circled portions of the words contain the numerical value indicated. How quickly can you identify these words?

1. To come to one's destination	— — — ⊂◯⊃ — —	**4**
2. To quiver or shake	⊂◯⊃ — — — — —	**6**
3. A group of letters added to the front of a word	— — — — ⊂◯⊃	**9**
4. To live; to be	— ⊂◯⊃ — —	**11**
5. The shaft on which a wheel turns	— ⊂◯⊃ — —	**40**
6. The largest organ of the body	⊂◯⊃ — — —	**54**
7. More than enough	— ⊂◯⊃ — —	**90**
8. To repeat from memory	— — ⊂◯⊃ — —	**101**
9. An African member of the cat family	⊂◯⊃ — — — —	**104**
10. Faraway	⊂◯⊃ — — — —	**501**
11. Permanent legal separation from one's spouse	⊂◯⊃ — — — —	**504**
12. The Deep South	⊂◯⊃ — — —	**509**
13. To allow	— — — ⊂◯⊃ —	**1001**
14. A blend, a combination	⊂◯⊃ — — — —	**1009**
15. A warm season	— ⊂◯⊃ — —	**2000**

BONUS

Can you think of any word with a higher value in Roman numerals than the last item above?

If so, write it here: _____

What is the value of your entire name in Roman numerals? For example, a name such as *Lionel* can be considered to have the value of 101, since it contains *LI* and another *L* (51 plus 50). Print your name on the back of this sheet, circle the Roman numerals, and total them.

Name _____ Date _____

7–35 NUMERICAL PREFIXES

Look at the prefixes contained in the words below and determine the number represented by each. Write the numbers in the spaces. Then follow the mathematical procedure indicated here:

$$A + B + C \div D + E - F - G \times H \div I - J - K + L + M \div N - O - P = \underline{\ ?\ }$$

Your answer should be a nice round number. Write it here: _____

A. Quatrain: a stanza with _____ lines

B. Sextant: one-_____th of a circle

C. Octopod: a mollusk with _____ arms

D. Bilingual: able to speak _____ languages

E. Heptarchy: rule by _____ people

F. Triplex: a building with _____ apartments

G. Unicellular: having _____ cell

H. Decathlon: an athletic contest consisting of _____ events

I. Quintuplets: _____ babies born at the same time

J. Monochromatic: having _____ color

K. Dioxide: containing _____ atoms of oxygen

L. Hexagram: a star with _____ points

M. Nonagon: a figure with _____ sides

N. Trefoil: a plant with _____-fold leaves

O. Pentameter: poetry with _____ beats per line

P. Septennial: occurring every _____ years

BONUS

Using your dictionary, look up several other words with numerical prefixes. Write definitions for them on the back of this sheet and let the other members of the class guess them.

7–36 THE WICKED WITCH

A certain wicked witch turned a bunch of boys and girls into various objects. You can reverse the spell by taking the names of the objects listed below, adding one letter to them, and rearranging the letters to form the names of the boys and girls. For example, if the word is *cider,* you add a *C* and rearrange the letters to form *Cedric*. The letter that you must add is indicated. Ignore the circled letters until you get to the bottom of the page.

BOYS

1. cars   **O**   _ (_) _ _ _

2. kite   **H**   _ _ _ _ (_)

3. wine   **D**   _ _ _ _ _

4. mules   **A**   _ _ _ (_) _ _

5. file   **X**   _ _ _ _ _

6. bear   **N**   _ _ _ _ (_)

7. trees   **L**   _ _ _ (_) _ _

8. barn   **I**   _ _ _ _ (_)

GIRLS

1. land   **I**   _ _ _ _ _

2. coal   **R**   (_) _ _ _ _

3. mail   **W**   _ _ _ (_) _

4. cream   **N**   _ (_) _ _ _ _

5. lime   **Y**   _ _ _ _ (_)

6. ram   **Y**   (_) _ _ _

7. metal   **H**   _ (_) _ _ _ _

8. veil   **O**   _ _ _ _ (_)

BONUS

Shakespeare said, "A rose by any other name would smell as sweet." Take the circled letters from the names above and rearrange them to form the name of a flower that will fit into this parody of Shakespeare's line: "A _____ by any other name would be easier to spell."

7-37 BREAK-APARTS

The English language contains many compound words, such as *headache*, that can be broken into two separate words from which the compound was originally formed. Certain other words can also be broken apart to form separate words, though they are not compounds. For example, the word *hatred* can be separated into *hat* and *red*—words that have no connection with the original word. From the second column below, select words to add to the words in the first column in order to form new words with the definitions indicated. Also place the circled letter from your choice in the space at the left. These letters will form the answer to this question: What happened to the silkworms in the race?

Answer:

_____

____	1. pan_____	lad(y)	A storage place for food items
____	2. asp_____	i(n)ning	A substance for paving roads
____	3. sea_____	(n)est	Closed tightly
____	4. ma_____	(t)ry	A disease or disorder of the body
____	5. bud_____	acr(e)	A spending plan
____	6. ear_____	(u)s	Sincere
____	7. leg_____	(i)ce	A story handed down from the past
____	8. mass_____	ge(t)	Wanton murder
____	9. imp_____	rid(t)	Expressed indirectly
____	10. sin_____	(h)alt	A cavity in the skull
____	11. pa_____	(a)le	Pertaining to the Pope
____	12. not_____	ev(i)l	An announcement
____	13. beg_____	or(e)	A start
____	14. fin_____	lie(d)	An ending
____	15. pat_____	l(e)d	One who loves his country
____	16. we_____	en(d)	An insect
____	17. rest_____	(p)al	To renew; to bring back to its original state

BONUS

Find one other word that is not a compound but that can be broken apart. Write its definition on the back of this sheet. Let your classmates guess it.

7-38 PHOBIAS

Everyone experiences fear, even newborn infants, who, for example, have an instinctive fear of falling. Most of the time our fears are "normal" and temporary. If they get out of control and become chronic, they may be considered to be phobias. There are literally hundreds of phobias, including some very unusual ones, such as *cheimaphobia* (fear of cold), *pogonophobia* (fear of beards), and *homichlophobia* (fear of fog). Some of the more common phobias are listed below. Match each one with the "fearful" item it is associated with. Use a dictionary for this exercise if you need to. Then connect the letters in the diagram in the order in which you used them, making a separate line for items 1 to 5 and another for items 6 to 16. These lines will reveal something else that some people fear.

```
F   C   J   N

L   D   S   Q

P   B   O   E

A   M   R   T

H   G   K   I
```

_____ 1. claustrophobia
_____ 2. agoraphobia
_____ 3. acrophobia
_____ 4. pyrophobia
_____ 5. zenophobia
_____ 6. autophobia
_____ 7. gynephobia
_____ 8. algophobia
_____ 9. hemophobia
_____ 10. toxicophobia
_____ 11. aviophobia
_____ 12. ailurophobia
_____ 13. mysophobia
_____ 14. ergasiophobia
_____ 15. zoophobia
_____ 16. thanatophobia

A. fire
B. poison
C. being alone
D. snakes
E. cats
F. closed spaces
G. death
H. strangers
I. work
J. women
K. animals
L. wide open spaces
M. thunder
N. pain
O. flying
P. heights
Q. men
R. fur
S. blood
T. germs and dirt

What phobia involves fear of everything? **Answer: panphobia**

7-39 REPEATED WORDS

Seldom do we use the same word two times in succession in a sentence, but in some instances this is correct. *Example:* If I *had had* my hay fever medicine with me, my eyes would not be so swollen now. From the list of words at the top, select those that can be repeated in each sentence and make sense. Write the word twice in the sentence and write its letter in the space at the left. These letters will form the two words to complete this statement:

The English language is _____ _____.

A. no	L. sing	R. whether
C. to	M. on	S. so
E. stayed	O. is	T. arrived
I. did	P. sin	U. all

_____ 1. The principal is not aware of what goes _____ _____ the playground.

_____ 2. What this _____ _____ no laughing matter.

_____ 3. I failed to do _____, _____ I have no excuse.

_____ 4. I didn't think anyone was coming because all those who _____ _____ late.

_____ 5. Don't mince words. Call _____ _____.

_____ 6. Those who _____ _____ because they wanted to meet Congressman Stenner, whose plane was late.

_____ 7. He does not do a bit more than he has _____ _____ meet the minimum requirements.

_____ 8. Despite our harrowing experience we are _____ _____ right.

_____ 9. If you must _____, _____ on key.

_____ 10. What you _____ _____ not meet with the approval of the boss.

_____ 11. He definitely means _____, _____ doubt about that.

_____ 12. I don't know _____ _____ is a conjunction or a preposition.

BONUS

Try to think of a sentence of your own in which it is appropriate to use the same word twice. Write it on the back of this sheet.

7-40 MOST BEAUTIFUL WORDS

Wilfred Funk, the dictionary publisher, once selected the ten words of the English language that he considered the most beautiful—beautiful both in sound and in meaning. These ten are defined below. Identify them, and you will see that they are all in alphabetical order. Then take the circled letters and rearrange them so they will fit into the first word below. The boxed letters, when rearranged, will form the second word. These two words, according to Dorothy Parker, are the two most beautiful words in English.

C _ _ _ K _ _ _ _ _ _ _ _

1. A set of musical bells

2. Daybreak

3. Having the color of a precious metal

4. Stillness, silence

5. A song for putting babies to sleep

6. Shining, glowing brightly

7. Haze, moisture in the air that blurs vision

8. A tune, a song

9. Speaking in a soft, low voice

10. Calm, peaceful

BONUS

Other beautiful words that have been suggested are *sea sands* (suggested by Edwin Markham) and *oriole* and *translucent* (mentioned by Rupert Hughes). When the words *cellar door* were suggested, one mother promptly named her new baby daughter *Cellador.* In the space below, list several words that you consider beautiful, not only in sound but also in meaning.

_____

_____

_____

_____

Note: Hawaiian words all have soft, fluid sounds produced by the consonants H, K, L, M, N, and P, along with the vowels. *Examples: Aloha* (hello or good-bye), *malihini* (stranger), *mahalo nui* (many thanks), *lei* (wreath), and *huapala* (sweetheart).

7–41 THE END

Identify the words defined below, all of which end with *end*. Place the circled letters from the words in the spaces at the left. These letters will form a three-word Latin expression that means "The end crowns the work." Write it here:

_____

_____ 1. To insult; to cause hurt feelings   _ (_) _ e n d

_____ 2. A share of profits distributed to stockholders   _ (_) _ _ _ e n d

_____ 3. To rise above or go beyond   _ _ _ _ (_) _ _ e n d

_____ 4. A buddy, a pal   _ _ (_) e n d

_____ 5. To pay out; to use up   (_) _ _ e n d

♦ ♦ ♦ ♦

_____ 6. To go up   _ _ (_) e n d

_____ 7. To endorse as being worthy   _ _ _ _ (_) _ _ e n d

_____ 8. To act out; to make believe   _ (_) _ e n d

_____ 9. To give a sign of the future   _ (_) _ _ e n d

_____ 10. The number from which the subtrahend is subtracted   _ _ (_) _ e n d

_____ 11. To change or modify   (_) _ e n d

_____ 12. To lengthen   _ _ (_) e n d

♦ ♦ ♦ ♦

_____ 13. To understand   _ (_) _ _ _ _ _ e n d

_____ 14. To arrest   _ (_) _ _ _ e n d

_____ 15. To hang up; to set aside temporarily   _ (_) _ _ e n d

_____ 16. Money paid for services performed   (_) _ _ _ e n d

ANSWER KEYS

Section 1 DEVELOPMENT OF THE ENGLISH LANGUAGE

1–1 Stages of Development

1. Y	5. R	9. I
2. H	6. G	10. X
3. P	7. O	11. E
4. A	8. C	12. L

The letters in reverse spell LEXICOGRAPHY, the art of dictionary making.

1–2 Synonyms from Anglo-Saxon and Latin

1. fragile
2. diminutive
3. consternation
4. audacious
5. interrogate
6. people
7. commence
8. profound
9. solitary
10. story
11. abandon
12. juvenile
13. domicile

The circled letters are: I M N A T P N P T S N J L ("I am in a tepee and Petey is in jail.")

1–3 Latin and Greek Synonyms

1. perimeter
2. sorcery
3. criticize
4. migratory
5. melancholy
6. dilemma
7. worship
8. ecstasy
9. lunatic
10. yardstick
11. childlike
12. dynamic
13. dictionary
14. enigma
15. smother
16. tantalize
17. humorous

The circled letters complete this sentence: "Because he only *preyed* on *weak knights*." This answer is unusual because it is a triple pun.

1–4 Latin Phrases

Part 1
1. In the year of our Lord
2. Peace be with you
3. The voice of the people is the voice of God
4. Let the buyer beware
5. Before the war
6. For the good of the public
7. Always faithful
8. Time flies
9. One from many

The circled letters spell NEOLOGISM, a term which refers to a new word—one made from entirely new elements that did not exist before.

Part 2

Annuit coeptis: He has smiled on our undertakings.
Sic semper tyrannus: Thus always to tyrants
Nil sine numine: Nothing without providence
Semper paratus: Always prepared

1–5 Words from European Countries

1. Czech	8. Irish
2. Dutch	9. Italian
3. French	10. Portuguese
4. German	11. Romanian
5. Greek	12. Russian
6. Hungarian	13. Scottish
7. Icelandic	14. Swedish

1–6 Words from the Romance Languages

1. garage	11. casino
2. fiancée	12. cigar
3. brunette	13. adobe
4. rendezvous	14. mosquito
5. restaurant	15. canyon
6. antiques	16. mesa
7. soprano	17. tapioca
8. violin	18. molasses
9. studio	19. cashew
10. macaroni	20. palaver

1–7 Words from Asia, the Middle East, and the Pacific Islands

1. G	7. A
2. C	8. R
3. N	9. L
4. D	10. E
5. I	11. P
6. M	

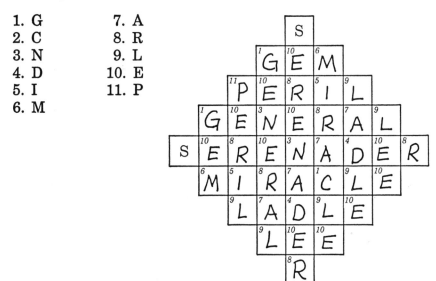

1–8 Words from Native American Languages

1. woodchuck	5. moccasin
2. hickory	6. pecan
3. succotash	7. wigwam
4. moose	8. skunk

9. wampum   12. mackinaw
10. hominy   13. sequoia
11. squash

The letters in the column spell WYOMING and KANSAS.

Bonus
Wyoming means "large prairie place" and Kansas means "south wind people."

1–9 Words from William Shakespeare

1. green-eyed
2. obscene
3. assassination
4. hint
5. gloomy
6. frugal
7. leapfrog
8. dwindle
9. laughable
10. hurry
11. courtship
12. excellent
13. lonely
14. rely
15. premeditated

The completed statement is as follows: "Macbeth doth murder sleep."

1–10 Phrases from William Shakespeare

1. wit
2. end
3. self
4. beat
5. world
6. idiot
7. Greek
8. blind
9. elbow
10. hot
11. bag
12. there
13. fall
14. cold

1–11 Phrases from Miguel de Cervantes

1. kettle
2. word
3. leaf
4. limit
5. pie
6. yet
7. pudding
8. fair
9. born
10. eggs
11. throw
12. haves
13. bond
14. wise
15. forgive

The remaining words form this sentence: "Give the devil his due."

1–12 Proverbs from John Heywood

1. waste
2. leap
3. heads
4. pitchers
5. gift
6. Paul
7. broom
8. hay
9. turn
10. nail
11. hands
12. hot

The remaining letters in the puzzle form the
following proverb: "A penny for your thoughts."

1-13 Doublets

1. cap
2. prune
3. vow
4. parson
5. hospital
6. ration
7. chapel
8. employ
9. fragile
10. cancer
11. channel
12. jettison
13. guard
14. tweed

1-14 Prefixes

1. trans
2. circum
3. pre
4. inter
5. avi
6. omni
7. sub
8. super
9. pseudo
10. pan
11. bio
12. micro
13. semi
14. ex
15. neo
16. photo
17. auto
18. biblio

The circled letters spell FACETIOUS and UNORIENTAL. Both words contain all the vowels. "Facetious" has them in alphabetical order; "unoriental" has them in reverse order.

1-15 Suffixes

1. amusement
2. childhood
3. darkness
4. agreeable
5. different
6. breakage
7. phraseology
8. comical
9. elementary
10. homeward
11. authenticate
12. dangerous
13. friendship
14. hopeless
15. secondary
16. poisonous
17. collection
18. foolish
19. absorbent
20. clockwise
21. sailor

The circled letters spell the following words: "The beggar was her sister."

1-16 Roots

A. 16
B. 2
C. 3
D. 13
E. 5
F. 11
G. 10
H. 8
I. 9
J. 7
K. 6
L. 12
M. 4
N. 14
O. 15
P. 1

A 16	B 2	C 3	D 13
E 5	F 11	G 10	H 8
I 9	J 7	K 6	L 12
M 4	N 14	O 15	P 1

The numbers in all
directions total 34.

1–17 Origins of Words

1. escape
2. nucleus
3. dandelion
4. onion
5. hogwash
6. dessert
7. ukulele
8. curfew
9. fiasco
10. nifty

The words in the diagram appear in the following order: curfew, dandelion, dessert, fiasco, onion, nifty, ukulele, nucleus, escape, hogwash.

1–18 More Word Origins

1. ladybug
2. petticoat
3. polecat
4. ramshackle
5. aftermath
6. surly
7. crowbar
8. butterscotch
9. sophomore
10. assassin
11. daily

```
L  B (R  A  M  S  H  A  C  K  L  E)
A  E (P) T (P) W  E  ■  E  N  T  ■
D  H (E)(S)(O) P  H  O  M  O  R  E)
Y (S) T  E  L  D  E  ■  V  I  ■  L
(B)(U) T  T  E  R  S  C  O  T  C  H)
U  R  I  A (C  R  O  W  B  A  R) N
(G) L  C  D (A  S  S  A  S  S  I  N)
T (Y) O  H (T) E  D  ■  E  E  P  ■
B  ■ (A  F  T  E  R  M  A  T  H) L
■  U (T) E  S (D  A  I  S  Y) E  A
```

The remaining letters spell the following words: "between the devil and the deep blue sea." (A devil was a seam near the edge of the deck that a sailor sometimes had to caulk. This was a dangerous job.)

1–19 Compounds

Answers will vary.

1–20 Clipped Words

1. gasoline
2. properties
3. facsimile
4. convict
5. corduroy
6. raccoon
7. influenza
8. sea lion
9. mathematics
10. permanent
11. politician
12. perquisite
13. magazines
14. hoodlum

The shaded letters form the shape of the letter "I," which when inserted six times with the given letters spells INDIVISIBILITY.

1–21 Blends

1. confound
2. lunch
3. broadcast
4. communication
5. spiced
6. inflation
7. digit
8. hazardous
9. channel
10. pedal
11. oxygen
12. tangerine
13. cremation

```
A   B   C   D
E   F   G   H
I   J   K   L
M   N   O   P
```

The circled letters form the shape of "S" in the diagram. Inserted properly among the letters "AIN," these letters form the word ASSASSIN.

1–22 Acronyms

1. Without
2. Petroleum
3. Scholastic
4. Space
5. Drunk
6. Committee
7. Women
8. People
9. Safety
10. Society
11. American
12. Immune
13. White
14. Force
15. Surgical
16. Radio
17. Missing
18. Living
19. Number
20. Trade
21. Weapons

The circled letters spell these words: HE HAD ONLY ONE HOUR SLEEP.

1–23 Eponyms

Part 1

A. 7   F. 3
B. 0   G. 6
C. 2   H. 9
D. 4   I. 1
E. 5   J. 8

Part 2
Answers will vary.

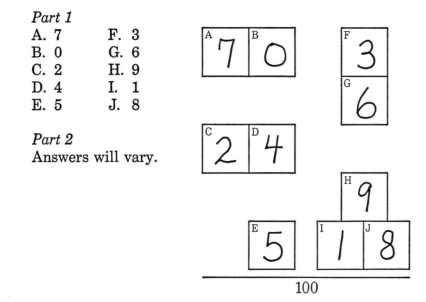

100

1–24 Words from Brand Names

1. escalator
2. Sanforized
3. thermos
4. Formica
5. Teflon
6. Realtor

7. aspirin
8. Vaseline
9. Ping-Pong
10. Dacron
11. Technicolor
12. Band-Aid

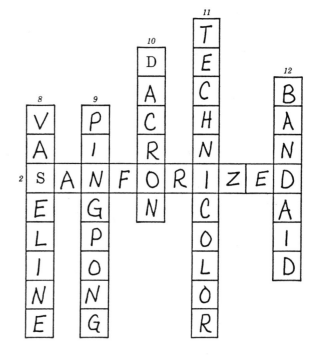

1–25 Generalization and Specialization

Part 1
1. A pink who is in the pink
2. A greenhorn on the green
3. A blue blue blood
4. A yellow fellow involved in yellow journalism
5. A white buying a white elephant
6. Blackballed by those in the black arts
7. A brownshirt browning meat
8. A gray day for the Gray
9. A goldbricking gold digger
10. A silver-tongued man with a pocketful of silver

Part 2
1. starve
2. meat
3. deer

4. corn
5. liquor

1–26 A Mysterious Example of Generalization

The mystery word is RUN, which has more than 100 definitions in an unabridged dictionary.

1-27 Elevation and Degeneration

1. minister
2. lady
3. chivalry
4. knight
5. steward
6. fond
7. knave
8. disease
9. vile
10. wiseacre
11. cretin
12. silly
13. villain

1-28 Functional Shift

1. sardine
2. crazy
3. leaflet
4. rethink
5. tube
6. junk
7. gift
8. den
9. fries
10. prowl
11. basics
12. umbrella

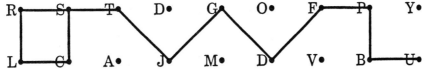

1-29 Back Formation and Fold Etymology

1. pea
2. stave
3. cherry
4. statistic
5. beg
6. burgle
7. an apron
8. a nickname
9. pea jacket
10. woodchuck
11. Pig

1-30 Slang

1. shock
2. jargon
3. color
4. poetry
5. convenient
6. fleeting
7. permanent
8. habitual
9. standard
10. appropriate

The circled letters spell TOMATO and DOLL.

1-31 Obsolescent and Obsolete Words

1. *bangled:* frittered, wasted
   jollification: fun, partying
2. *dabbly:* rainy
   sposhy: muddy, soggy
3. *yaffle:* woodpecker
   janglesome: nerve-wracking
4. *peruke:* wig
   carked: worried

5. *soodled:* strolled, wandered
   pillygrubs: hairy worms
6. *fell:* elevated field, moor
   glints: fragments of rainbow
7. *gormless:* stupid
   fibster: liar
8. *ordinary:* tavern
   settle: storage place under a bench or chair

1–32 Neologisms and Nonce Words

1. quiz
2. Kodak
3. googol
4. skedaddle
5. gobbledygook

1–33 New Words in Politics and Government

1. Miranda
2. disinformation
3. quota
4. gag
5. third
6. fairness
7. floater
8. shuttle
9. linkage
10. polemologist
11. humint
12. hegemony

Stevenson's statement: "Politics is perhaps the only profession for which no preparation is thought necessary."

1–34 New Words in Business and Industry

1. deskilling
2. wasteplex
3. turnaround time
4. middle manager
5. product liability
6. flextime
7. kilobyte
8. deman
9. gentrification
10. give-back
11. garbology
12. bankable

The circled letters spell SLUMPFLATION, a term referring to a decline in business as prices rise and unemployment increases.

1–35 New Terms in Science and Medicine

1. biomaterial
2. autotransfusion
3. cryopreservation
4. ecodoom
5. zootoxins
6. seed bank
7. exobiology
8. ozone shield
9. astration

^{2}H	^{9}E	^{4}A	^{8}R	^{3}T
^{9}E	^{9}E	^{8}R	^{5}I	^{9}E
^{4}A	^{8}R	^{1}O	^{7}S	^{9}E
^{8}R	^{5}I	^{7}S	^{9}E	^{6}N
^{3}T	^{9}E	^{9}E	^{6}N	^{7}S

Bonus

The three extra words are as follows:

echocardiogram—a visual record of the heart made by using sound waves
controlled substance—any drug regulated by law
infrasonics—sound waves of a frequency below that audible to humans

1–36 New Terms in Art and Music

1. T	5. L	9. O
2. H	6. I	10. E
3. N	7. C	11. G
4. A	8. M	12. W

The title of the picture is THE WELCOME WAGGIN'.

Bonus

The two extra words are:

sound sculpture–a structure consisting of materials that produce sound, such as metal rods

rocker–either a rock musician or a rock fan

1–37 New Terms in Sports

A. 11	I. 15
B. 17	J. 16
C. 9	K. 14
D. 12	L. 10
E. 2	M. 5
F. 18	N. 13
G. 7	O. 4
H. 1	

Bonus

The three extra terms are as follows:

superfecta–the first four horses to finish in a race in the exact order in which they place

crackback–a block at knee level in football

Fosbury flop–a type of high jump in which the jumper goes over the bar back first

1–38 New Terms for Types of People

A. 2	G. 1
B. 9	H. 7
C. 15	I. 12
D. 3	J. 4
E. 10	K. 13
F. 14	L. 6

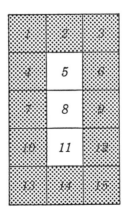

The shaded blocks form the letter O, which is the oldest letter of the alphabet.

Bonus

aerophobe–a person who fears flying

right-to-lifer–a person opposed to abortion

TMer–a person who practices transcendental meditation

1–39 New Words for Foods and Fashions

1. chili dog
2. granola bar
3. junk food
4. Reuben sandwich
5. liquid protein
6. piña colada
7. body shirt
8. bolo tie
9. leg warmers
10. tube socks
11. layered look
12. safari hat
13. leisure suit

The circled letters spell SARA LEE and the boxed letters spell ADIDAS.

1–40 New Names for New Products

An *optacon* is an electronic machine used by the blind that converts printed letters into shapes that can be felt.
Gasohol is a blend of gasoline and grain alcohol.

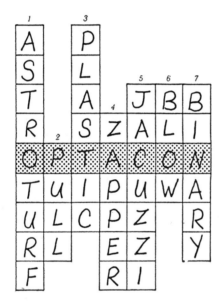
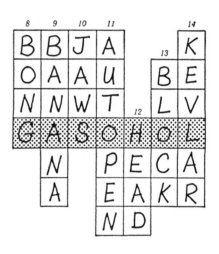

1–41 British English

1. muffler
2. dessert
3. link sausage
4. biscuit
5. fruit pie
6. fender
7. cracker
8. gasoline
9. traffic circle
10. potato chip
11. peanut
12. truck
13. horn
14. oatmeal
15. hamburger
16. molasses
17. hood
18. windshield
19. overpass
20. trunk

The circled letters spell these words: "Give me a tinkle on the blower." The American translation is "Give me a call on the phone."

1–42 Australian English

1. O
2. H
3. A
4. B
5. I
6. C
7. D.
8. K.
9. R
10. Q
11. S
12. L
13. E
14. T
15. G
16. N
17. U

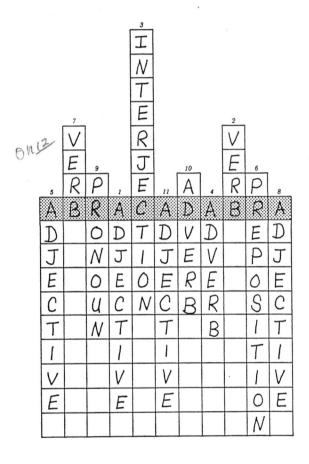

When the letters are connected, they spell POM, the Australian term for an English-man and an acronym for "Prisoner of Her Majesty."

Section 2 GRAMMAR AND USAGE

2–1 Parts of Speech

The word ABRACADABRA is unusual because it starts and ends with the same four letters.

Bonus

In the two extra sentences, *but* is used as a noun and a conjunction.

2–2 Types of Nouns

1. singular
2. plural
3. verbal
4. masculine
5. feminine
6. neuter
7. possessive
8. common
9. proper
10. compound
11. phrasal
12. collective
13. concrete
14. abstract

When transferred, the circled letters form this statement: "God, to me it seems, is a verb, not a noun, proper or improper."

2–3 Types of Objects

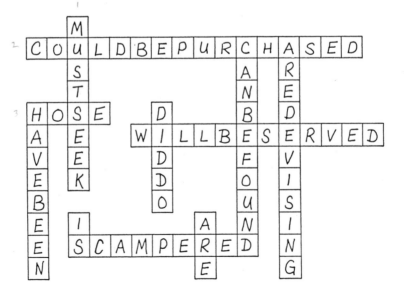

1. zebra, apple, bag
2. Yolanda, book, Houdini
3. Theresa, bowl, fruit
4. son, house, Florida
5. me, kit, tools
6. her, rules, tennis
7. Debbie, trick, school
8. Carrie, variety, stories
9. Bob, volleyball, tournament
10. apples, zest, juice

The words in the first column are in reverse alphabetical order, while those in the second column are in alphabetical order. (The A to Z groupings for the first and last items should give students a clue.)

2–4 Direct Objects

1. pebble
2. radio
3. ocean
4. silverware
5. eagle
6. pears
7. organ
8. eggs
9. truthfulness
10. ranch
11. yards
12. berries
13. edition
14. samples
15. title

The three words that fill the blanks are PROSE, POETRY, and BEST.

2–5 Recognizing Verbs

1. can be found
2. are
3. do want
4. scampered
5. are devising
6. could be purchased
7. will be served
8. must seek
9. did do
10. have been
11. is
12. hose

2–6 Principal Parts of Verbs

1. gave
2. eaten
3. went
4. borne, born
5. lose
6. fought
7. skiing
8. burst
9. frozen
10. lie
11. catching
12. hopped
13. sped
14. seeing
15. fallen
16. risen
17. hope

The transferred letters spell PRESENT PARTICIPLE.

2–7 Transitive, Intransitive, Active, and Passive Verbs

1. sang
2. will be launched
3. seems
4. am
5. are swimming
6. soared
7. came
8. have
9. were planted
10. are hung
11. contain
12. smells
13. was written
14. should obey
15. has been
16. look

Transitive active verbs: 1, 8, 11, 14 = 34
Transitive passive verbs: 2, 9, 10, 13 = 34
Intransitive complete verbs: 5, 6, 7, 16 = 34
Intransitive linking verbs: 3, 4, 12, 15 = 34

2–8 Lie *and* lay

1. lies
2. lie
3. laid
4. lay
5. lying
6. lain
7. lain
8. lying
9. lay
10. laid
11. lie
12. lies

The remaining letters spell the names WILL and SHALL.

Bonus

Mary named her twin kittens Shall and Will because she couldn't tell the difference.

2-9 Verb Tense

1. bought
2. does
3. have forgotten
4. will see
5. go
6. has written
7. lay
8. had known
9. swung
10. has spoken
11. had executed
12. will confront

on 24

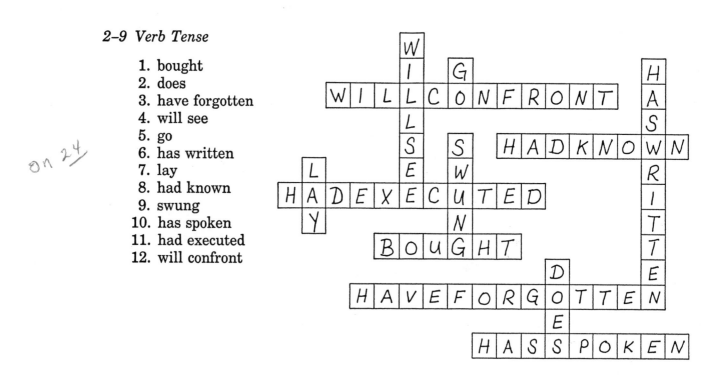

2-10 Subjunctives

R 1. were
C 2. had come
E 3. were
+ 4. expected
A 5. waited
m 6. had made
O 7. told
w 8. were
B 9. had been

G 10. had gone
N 11. had given
H 12. had known
D 13. had met
k 14. knew
L 15. landed
S 16. was
i 17. had studied
F 18. had found

On 36

All the verbs are subjunctive except 4, 7, 14, and 16. The title of the picture is A CROW IN THE BLACK FOREST AT MIDNIGHT.

2-11 Nouns or Verbs?

1. noun
2. verb
3. noun
4. verb
5. verb
6. verb
7. noun
8. noun
9. verb
10. noun
11. verb
12. noun

on 14

The letters in the two columns spell PENCIL and HAMMER.

2-12 Agreement of Subjects and Verbs

1. singular (refers to *nobody*)
2. plural (refers to *apples*)
3. singular (refers to *problem*)
4. plural (because *assistants* is closer to the verb than *Sheldon*)
5. singular (because just one of the two will be driving)
6. singular (because *sister* is closer to the verb than *Johnsons*)

On 30

7. plural (refers to *parts*)
8. plural (because *sisters* is closer to the verb than *Betty*)
9. plural (refers to *cats*)
10. plural (both paper and pencils)

The completed poem is: Squirrels in the Urals
Have singular problems
Dealing with plurals.

2-13 Pronouns

Part 1
1. whole (who)
2. whimper (him)
3. sour (our)
4. theme (he, them, me)
5. thatched (that, he)
6. dishes (I, she, he)
7. heart (he)
8. weapon (we)
9. customer (us, me)
10. thistle (this, his)
11. bayou (you)
12. ermine (mine)
13. chisel (his)
14. appendectomy (my)
15. cherub (her)

Part 2
1. self
2. selves
3. ever

2-14 Types of Pronouns

1. I
2. F
3. A
4. D
5. L
6. N
7. C
8. K
9. G
10. E
11. J
12. M
13. B

F H D K N M B
I A L G C J E

2-15 Recognizing Adjectives

1. E (exciting)
2. O (outstanding)
3. O (older)
4. E (exact)
5. A (ancient)
6. I (instantaneous)
7. N (nervous)
8. S (sensible)
9. L (latest)
10. V (vigorous)
11. C (crucial)
12. N (neglected)
13. X (xeric)

The transferred letters spell SAXON VIOLENCE.

Bonus
Some common adjective suffixes are *-ous, -able, -ic, -ful, -ing, -ant,* etc.

2-16 Recognizing Adverbs

1. T (there)
2. Y (yesterday)
3. A (about)
4. T (tactfully)

5. H (harder)
6. R (really)
7. O (often
8. T (too)
9. O (on)
10. H (here)
11. U (ultimately)
12. T (tragically)

The transferred letters spell AT TOOTH HURTY.

Bonus
Adverbs describe verbs, adjectives, and other adverbs.

on 14

2-17 Adjectives or Adverbs?

W 1. adjective
N 2. adverb
O 3. adverb
E 4. adjective
S 5. adverb
R 6. adjective
K 7. adverb
D 8. adjective
C 9. adverb
N 10. adjective
A 11. adverb
A 12. adjective
J 13. adverb

When read from the bottom up the letters in the two columns spell the **name of** ANDREW JACKSON.

2-18 Recognizing Prepositions

on 12

S	I	N	C	E		A	R	O	U	N	D		A	B	O	A	R	D				
	N			X		C				E				E		F					O	
	S			C		R				X				H		T	H	R	O	U	G	H
	I		B	E	Y	O	N	D		T				I		E				T		
	D			P		S				T			N		R		A	L	O	N	G	
	E			T		S		T	O	W	A	R	D						F			

2-19 Conjunctions

1. and
2. consequently
3. either, or
4. unless
5. but
6. not only, but also
7. either, or
8. and
9. what
10. neither, nor
11. and
12. when
13. which
14. both, and
15. or

on 30

Coordinate conjunctions: 1, 5, 8, 11, 15 = 40
Subordinate conjunctions: 2, 4, 9, 12, 13 = 40
Correlative conjunctions: 3, 6, 7, 10, 14 = 40

2-20 Prefixes and Suffixes

1. laughable
2. away
3. defiant
4. decoration

on 22

5. movement
6. endurance
7. European
8. sunless
9. memorize
10. swiftly
11. peaceful
12. backward
13. review
14. typist
15. Catholicism
16. glorious
17. friendship
18. befriend
19. describe
20. co-exist
21. childish

The letters spell BANANA, PEEL, PARTS, and SPEECH, which fit into Clifton Fadiman's statement.

2-21 Dependent Clauses

1. When <u>Annie</u> did not turn in her report
on 2l 2. Because <u>Betsy</u> left the gate open
3. <u>that</u> are <u>high</u> in protein
4. <u>we</u> played tennis with at camp
5. What <u>Joe</u> said
6. <u>whoever</u> attends
7. <u>which</u> has sixteen miles of corridors
8. where <u>we</u> are now standing
9. When <u>they</u> are lost
10. <u>who</u> represents our company in the Southwest

The letters remaining in the two sets spell SUCH FUNGIS.

Bonus

Noun clauses: 5, 6
Adjective clauses: 3, 4, 7, 10
Adverb clauses: 1, 2, 8, 9

2-22 Subordinate Clauses

1. I like (adjective)
2. what he eats (noun)
3. that I didn't apologize (noun)
4. because it was frightened by the big dog (adverb)
5. Whenever I visit my grandparents (adverb)
6. with which he was killed (adjective)
7. what she told me (noun)
8. that is worth more than a hundred dollars (adjective)
9. who thoroughly enjoys reading (adjective)
10. that he almost collapsed (adverb)
11. Whatever is worth doing (noun)
12. Since snakes can't hear airborne sounds (adverb)
13. that moves (adjective)

The circled letters spell MR. AND MRS. SANTA.

2-23 Simple, Compound, and Complex Sentences

Simple sentences: 2, 4, 9, 12, 13 = 40
Compound sentences: 1, 5, 8, 11, 15 = 40
Complex sentences: 3, 6, 7, 10, 14 = 40

on 15

2-24 Sentence Fragments

Fragments: 2, 6, 7, 8, 10, 13, 14 = 60
Complete sentences: 1, 3, 4, 5, 9, 11, 12, 15 = 60

on 15

Note: Point out to students that imperative sentences, such as items 3 and 9, have understood subjects but are still complete sentences even though the subject does not appear in the sentence.

2-25 Misplaced Modifiers

The words that the phrases should modify are as follows:

1. dog
2. Hilda
3. drawing
4. babies
5. tourist
6. Deborah
7. calculator
8. body
9. boys
10. bat

on 30

					T		C					
		D	E	B	O	R	A	H				
					U		L					
	D	█	█	█	R		C					
	R				I		U					
B	A	B	I	E	S		L					
	W				T		A		B	A	T	
H	I	L	D	A			T		O			
	N		o			B	O	D	Y			
	G		G				R		S			

2-26 The Importance of Capital Letters

1. china
2. bronco
3. polish
4. mercury
5. davenport
6. rolls
7. afghan
8. coke
9. welsh
10. march
11. homer
12. pan
13. visa

on 14

The circled letters spell RARE STAMPS ON THE ENVELOPES.

2-27 Capitalization

The letters that need to be changed in each sentence are as follows:

on 33

1. n, o, f
2. r, o, s, t
3. f, o, r, m
4. s, o, n
5. t, h, e, o
6. t, s, i
7. d, e
8. o, f, w
9. i, n
10. d, o, w, s

The solution formed by the letters: NO FROST FORMS ON THE OUTSIDE OF WINDOWS.

2-28 Parallel Construction

A. 12   F. 7
B. 6   G. 5
C. 4   H. 10
D. 14   I. 13
E. 8   J. 9

The total is 88. This is the number of constellations and also the number of keys on a piano. (Sentence B refers to constellations, and sentence D refers to pianos.)

SUGGESTED ACTIVITY: Have the students identify the items in each parallel construction—adjectives, verbs, etc.

2-29 Unnecessary Words

A. between them (2)   H. together (1)
B. past (1)   I. on (1)
C. penniless (1)   J. lady (1)
D. free (1)   K. all alone (2)
E. three (1)   L. very (1)
F. of flowers (2)   M. brilliant (1)
G. from abroad (2)   N. with his hands (3)

The total of the crossed out words is 20. This multiplied by 5 equals 100, the total number of squares and rectangles in the diagram.

2-30 Usage

A. any   I. bad
B. finds   J. into
C. number   K. among
D. have   L. persuade
E. that   M from
F. as   N. well
G. fewer   O. those
H. stole   P. let

The four numbers remaining form the date 1828.

2-31 Preferred Usage

1. X   8. R
2. A   9. I
3. N   10. C
4. T   11. H
5. H   12. O
6. O   13. U
7. T   14. S

These letters spell XANTHOTRICHOUS.

The facts can be put together in a variety of ways, but each paragraph should deal with a particular set of facts. In the following sample composition, the first paragraph deals with Mark Twain's early life, the second with his later life and writings, and the third with his death.

Samuel Langhorne Clemens, born in 1835, spent his boyhood in Hannibal, Missouri, on the Mississippi River. Incidents from his childhood provided him with material for his books *Tom Sawyer* and *Huckleberry Finn*, and his experience as a pilot on a Mississippi steamboat provided him with his pen name, Mark Twain, which came from a call used by pilots to mark the depth of the water.

As a newspaperman and later as a lecturer, Twain traveled widely. His book *Roughing It* is based on his trip to a Nevada silver mine, and *Innocents Abroad* was inspired by his travels in Europe. Among his other works are *A Connecticut Yankee in King Arthur's Court* and *The Prince and the Pauper*. Many of his writings are still popular today, and he is often quoted.

Though this famous humorist was born in the heart of America, he made his permanent home in the East, where he died in 1910 on the day Halley's comet reappeared, just as it had appeared on the day of his birth.

Section 3 PUNCTUATION

3–1 The Importance of Punctuation

1. Don't do anything, stupid.
2. The committee consists of Mary, Jane, Sue, Ann, and Louise.
3. "The team," said the coach, "is great."
4. Let's talk, turkey.
5. We'll leave it alone.
6. The ladies have cast-off clothing at the garage sale.
7. Bring four-gallon jugs.
8. Go fetch, Fido.
9. Listen to me. That doesn't make sense.
10. Don't eat. Fast.

3–2 Types of Punctuation Marks

A. 8 (period after *Mr.*)
B. 11 (comma after *burglarized*)
C. 13 (apostrophe in *I'm*)
D. 1 (semicolon after *illegal*)
E. 10 (colon after *ingredients*)
F. 9 (ellipsis after *but*)
G. 6 (exclamation point after *moonlight*)
H. 14 (parentheses around *Food and Drug Administration*)
I. 7 (hyphen in *two-thirds*)
J. 4 (dash after *profit*)

The connecting line forms the shape of a question mark.
Explanation of additional marks:
Single quotation marks are used for quotations within quotations. Brackets are used to enclose side remarks within parentheses. A virgule or slash is used to show alternatives (he/she).

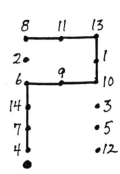

3-3 Punctuation Rules

1. T	6. X
2. I	7. T
3. M	8. E
4. D	9. R
5. E	

Tim (Timothy) Dexter was the author of the book without any punctuation marks.

3-4 Which Punctuation Mark?

1. comma	7. apostrophe
2. period	8. comma
3. colon	9. colon
4. apostrophe	10. quotation marks
5. period	11. comma
6. semicolon	

The connecting line forms several triangles.

3-5 End Punctuation

1. imperative	7. imperative
2. declarative	8. declarative
3. interrogative	9. interrogative
4. imperative	10. exclamatory
5. exclamatory	11. interrogative
6. declarative	

The letters in the vertical column spell PERIOD PIECE, the title of the picture.

3-6 Punctuating a Series

1. piano, sings (2)	6. lawn, hedge (2)
2. uneducated (1)	7. club, choir (2)
3. smallpox, bubonic plague (2)	8. exciting (1)
4. hulking (1)	9. beaches, mountains (2)
5. hand-painted (1)	10. excellent (1)

When sentences 2, 4, 5, 8, and 10 are connected, they form a pentagon. Numbers 1, 3, 6, 7, and 9 form a star inside the pentagon.

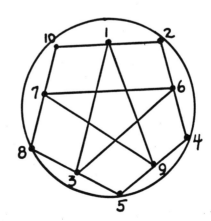

3–7 Punctuating Appositives and Adjective Clauses

A. Burton, class, Burton (3)
B. (0)
C. calcium (1)
D. garage, team (2)
E. (0)
F. Buttons, cat (2)
G. Carrington (1)
H. Carroll, *Wonderland* (2)
I. Squeezer, constrictor, Tusk, elephant (4)
J. (0)
K. Eileen, friend, Matt (3)
L. Wilburn, Corporation (2)

The three totals (6, 5, and 9) indicate the escape is on June 5 at 9:00.

3–8 Punctuating Interrupters

1. *c*ontrary
2. *a*ccording
3. *T*om
4. *c*overing
5. *h*as
6. *e*xpects
7. *R*achel
8. *in*
9. *n*evertheless
10. *t*he
11. *H*annah
12. *E*velyn
13. *R*osemary
14. *y*esterday
15. *e*very

The letters spell the book title *CATCHER IN THE RYE.*

3–9 Punctuating Quotations

1. I
2. N
3. G
4. R
5. S
6. E
7. V
8. E
9. R
10. P

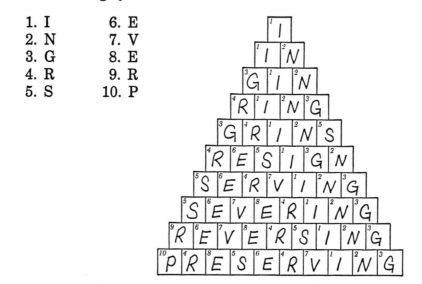

3–10 Apostrophes in Possessive Nouns

The correct items are B, O, B, D, I, C, K, H, I, C, K, O, and X, which spell BOB and DICK HICKOX. These names, when written in capital letters and then turned over and upside down, still spell the same thing when viewed through the other side of the paper.

The corrected items are as follows:

A. Ben's	J. Wayne's
C. bullet's	O. city's
E. teachers'	N. men's
R. world's	E. ladies'
O. Florida's	G. thieves'
Y. students'	S. books'

3–11 Apostrophes in Contractions

Part 1	Part 2
1. It's	10. can't
2. Whose	11. He'd
3. you're	12. Let's
4. Their	13. You'll
5. There's	14. We've
6. Who's	15. he'll
7. your	16. wasn't
8. its	17. mustn't
9. They're	

Items 1, 3, 5, 6, 9, 12, 16, and 17 have one letter missing.
Items 10, 13, 14, and 15 have two letters missing.
Item 11 has four letters missing.

Bonus

In *ma'am*, a *d* is missing. In *o'clock*, the missing letters are *of the*.

3–12 The Importance of Periods and Apostrophes

Part 1	Part 2
1. gal	11. wed (we'd)
2. Phil	12. hell (he'll)
3. Jan	13. well (we'll)
4. pop	14. shell (she'll)
5. ant·	15. shed (she'd)
6. long	
7. cent	
8. bus	
9. sing	
10. chap	

The circled letters, when rearranged, spell SLEEPLESSNESS.

3–13 Common Abbreviations

1. Attorney	8. Company
2. Bachelor	9. glutamate
3. Boulevard	10. latitude
4. postscript	11. hour
5. rest	12. ounce
6. revolutions	13. bushel
7. cubic	

Section 4 SPELLING AND PRONUNCIATION

4–1 Rules for Spelling Plurals

1. singular
2. es
3. consonant
4. vowel
5. men
6. both
7. f
8. plurals
9. compound
10. same
11. irregular
12. dictionary

The transferred letters spell: NO, I AM A FRAYED KNOT.

4–2 Irregular Plurals

1. beau
2. hypotheses
3. strata
4. alumni
5. cherub
6. phenomenon
7. wolf
8. datum
9. crises
10. criterion
11. species
12. sheep
13. insignia
14. salmon
15. bacterium
16. sons-in-law

The transferred letters spell A PAIR OF MEN'S PANTS.

4–3 Silent Letters

Horizontal words: league, caught, psalm, plumber, wrestle, knife, ghastly, tight, tongue

Vertical words: wreath, crumb, height, listen, rhyme, knead, gnarled

The remaining letters form these words: A MOUTHWASH FOR MIDGETS.

4–4 I Before E

The correctly spelled words are numbers 2, 3, 5, 8, 9, 12, 14, 15, 17, 20, 21, 24, 26, and 27. When these words' numbers are shaded in on the diagram, they form the shape of the number 8. The word *eight* contains *ei* and follows the old rule, since it has the sound of long *a*.

1	2	3	4
5	6	7	8
9	10	11	12
13	14	15	16
17	18	19	20
21	22	23	24
25	26	27	28

4–5 The Schwa

1. a	6. e	11. i	16. e
2. e	7. a	12. e	17. o
3. i	8. e	13. o	18. e
4. o	9. a	14. a	19. o
5. i	10. e	15. i	20. e

When the letters are transferred, the message reads: DOC, NOTE I DISSENT. A FAST NEVER PREVENTS A FATNESS. I DIET ON COD. This set of words is a palindrome. When all the letters are reversed, they spell exactly the same message!

4–6 Words with Repeated Letters

1. aardvark	11. orthodontist
2. hubbub	12. peppery
3. distended	13. rearrange
4. gentlemen	14. success
5. giggle	15. untruthful
6. highlight	16. sullenness
7. whirligig	17. committee
8. lullaby	18. commonness
9. mammoth	19. bookkeeper
10. nomination	20. aggressiveness

The circled letters spell HITCH PITCH.

4–7 The "Eyes" Words

Part 1
1. polarize
2. pluralize
3. glamorize, dramatize
4. harmonize
5. exercise
6. advise, legalize
7. devise
8. supervise

Part 2
9. serialize, fictionalize
10. baptize, evangelize, sermonize
11. sterilize, hospitalize
12. penalize
13. militarize, generalize
14. energize
15. analyze
16. paralyze

Note: Accept any other words that suit the situation and end with the "eyes" sound.

4–8 The "Seed" Words

1. proceed	7. exceed
2. concede	8. recede
3. intercede	9. supersede
4. precede	10. accede
5. secede	11. antecedent
6. succeed	

The transferred letters form this sentence: He had three college degrees but did not let his education go to his head.

Bonus

Other suffixes that can be used are *-ion, -ure, -or, -ent, -ive, -ing,* etc.

4-9 Words Containing E's

Part 1
1. eke
2. ease
3. eagle
4. empire
5. eclipse
6. eligible
7. elaborate
8. emancipate
9. enfranchise
10. exsanguinate

Part 2
11. esteem
12. beetle
13. determine
14. enumerate
15. sequence
16. electrocute
17. emerge
18. keepsake
19. precede
20. depreciate

Bonus

The word for a horsewoman is EQUESTRIENNE.

4-10 Words Containing the Sound of O̅O̅

1. doer
2. duplicate
3. soup
4. two
5. rheumatism
6. canoe
7. pursue
8. withdrew
9. bamboo
10. nuisance
11. rendezvous
12. ragout
13. through
14. Sioux

Bonus

Answers will vary.

4-11 Words Containing the Sounds of A̅ and ÂR

1. age
2. stray
3. trait
4. steak
5. gauge
6. vein
7. sleigh
8. they
9. puree
10. gourmet
11. souffle
12. gaol
13. croquet
14. despair
15. compare
16. bear
17. elsewhere
18. solitaire
19. ne'er
20. prayer
21. their
22. Pierre
23. Croix de Guerre

The circled letters, when rearranged, form the word DECOMPOSING.

4-12 Words Containing the Sounds of E̅ and I̅

1. absentee
2. plead
3. stampede
4. seize
5. shriek
6. tambourine
7. monkey
8. botany
9. rye
10. Thailand
11. ally
12. thigh

13. edelweiss
14. aye
15. alkali

16. height
17. untie

The circled letters, when transferred, spell PERMANENT PRESS.

4–13 Words Containing the Sound of SH

1. shrink
2. migration
3. ocean
4. sure
5. pension
6. missionary
7. chaps
8. schnauzer
9. suspicion
10. conscious
11. fuchsia
12. pshaw

The circled letters spell HEROINE.

Bonus
HEROINE contains HE, HER, and HERO.

4–14 Unusual Vowel Combinations

1. squeeze
2. silhouette
3. plateau
4. virtuous
5. courageous
6. fleeing
7. quaint
8. squeak, squeal
9. vicious
10. canoeing
11. Hawaiian
12. onomatopoeia
13. sequoia
14. queueing
15. strength
16. splotch
17. rhythm
18. myrrh
19. crypt
20. nymph

The circled letters spell LATCHSTRING, which has six consecutive consonants.

4–15 Words with -able *and* -ible

1. a
2. a
3. i
4. i
5. a
6. a
7. ea
8. a
9. i
10. a
11. a
12. i
13. a
14. e

The completed sentence is as follows: A basin is a place where Australians wash their face.

4–16 Doubling Letters Before Suffixes

1. admitted
2. barred
3. mannish
4. profitable
5. opening
6. drummer
7. controlled
8. occurrence

9. marvelous	13. labeled
10. revved	14. beginning
11. riddance	15. shining
12. riding	16. traveler

The transferred letters form this sentence: When a health food salesman comes to your door, go ahead and vitamin.

4–17 Adding Prefixes

A. 2 B. 1 C. 2 D. 2 E. 1 (total = 8)
F. 2 G. 2 H. 1 I. 2 (total = 7)
J. 2 K. 1 L. 2 M. 1 (total = 6)
N. 1 O. 2 P. 1 (total = 4)
Q. 1 R. 1 S. 1 (total = 3)
T. 2 (total = 2)

876 reversed and subtracted yields 198, as does 432 when reversed and subtracted.

4–18 Similar Words Often Confused

A. 4   F. 2
B. 9   G. 1
C. 3   H. 7
D. 5   I. 1
E. 8   J. 6

The number 12345679 × 18 = 222222222.

4–19 Synonyms

1. absurd
2. audacious
3. apprehend
4. alliance
5. apparel
6. authentic
7. attractive
8. adversary
9. apparent
10. assistant
11. alleviate

4-20 Synonyms Inside Words

Part 1	Part 2
1. equal	11. gigantic
2. dead	12. exists
3. last	13. struggle
4. slid	14. fragile
5. bloom	15. curtail
6. idle	16. observe
7. urge	17. masculine
8. joy	18. hatred
9. lies	19. cavern
10. apt	20. separate

4-21 Oodles of Synonyms

Part 1
Answers may vary from the following examples:

1. *green*—emerald, chartreuse, peridot, grass, jade, kelly, lime, mint, moss, olive, pine, teal, etc.
2. *happy*—cheerful, joyful, delighted, glad, pleased, elated, joyous, gleeful, etc.
3. *crazy*—nutty, screwy, cracked, kooky, flaky, balmy, bats, cuckoo, looney, wacky, bonkers, etc.

Part 2
4. wind
5. bravery
6. walked
7. mixture

4-22 Antonyms

1. primitive
2. peculiar
3. perilous
4. polite
5. positive
6. partial
7. perfect
8. pardon
9. peace
10. pretty
11. pause

4-23 Antonym Chain

| L | E | N | G | T | H | E | N | A | R | R | O | W | O | R | T | H | L | E | S | S | T | R | A | I | G | H | T | R | U | E |

| E | X | P | A | N | D | I | F | F | I | C | U | L | T | R | I | U | M | P | H | U | M | B | L | E | M | P | T | Y | E | S |

| S | H | A | L | L | O | W | I | S | D | O | M | A | N | Y | O | U | T | H | F | U | L | I | G | H | T | E | R | R | O | R |

| R | E | C | E | I | V | E | N | O | R | M | O | U | S | H | A | R | P | R | O | F | I | T | H | I | N | O | T | I | C | E |

| E | N | T | H | U | S | I | A | S | M | A | S | C | U | L | I | N | E | N | O | U | G | H | E | A | V | Y | I | E | L | D | S |

4-24 Homonyms

1. idyll (or idyl)
2. lyre
3. pare
4. bole
5. sow
6. caret
7. vane
8. chord
9. pique
10. scents
11. hue
12. seize
13. site
14. rowed
15. reign

The transferred letters spell these words: YOU ARE JUST TOO TENSE.
Too tense are homonyms for *two tents,* which is just what the man said he kept thinking he was (a wigwam and a tepee).

4-25 Animal Homonyms

1. mewl, mule
2. links, lynx
3. new, gnu
4. hoarse, horse
5. towed, toad
6. dear, deer
7. hair, hare
8. taper, tapir
9. bare, bear
10. weather, wether
11. you, ewe
12. dough, doe
13. mousse, moose
14. bore, boar
15. heart, hart

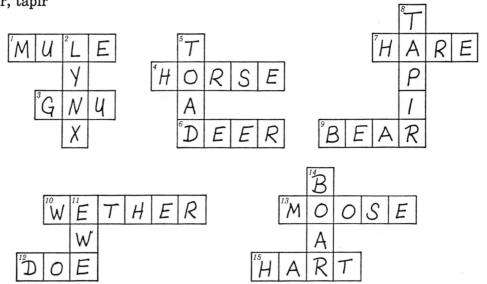

4-26 Heteronyms

1. bass
2. minute
3. wind
4. entrance
5. bow
6. wound
7. tear
8. sake
9. desert
10. invalid
11. lead
12. row
13. does
14. moped

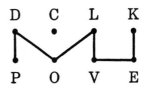

4-27 Anagrams

Part 1
1. yam (may)
2. trap (part)
3. won (now)
4. loot (tool)
5. ten (net)
6. stop (pots)
7. teams (meats)
8. stare (tears)

Part 2
9. realtor
10. editors
11. telegraph
12. despair
13. elephant
14. parallel

4-28 More Anagrams

1. listen
2. silent
3. enlist
4. tinsel
5. inlets
6. tales
7. steal
8. stale
9. least
10. slate
11. staple
12. pastel
13. petals
14. plates
15. pleats
16. stable
17. tables
18. ablest
19. bleats

The circled letters spell PEAS, APES, and APSE.

Bonus

The words that can be made from the letters *I S T R E P* are: *stripe, sprite, ripest, priest,* and *esprit.*

4-29 Palindromes

1. mom, dad, sis
2. eye, peep
3. kayak, sagas
4. shahs, deified
5. tenet, civic
6. repaper, level
7. pop, bib, tot
8. did, refer, radar, noon
9. aha (or wow), rotator
10. pup, gag

4–30 Spelling Demons

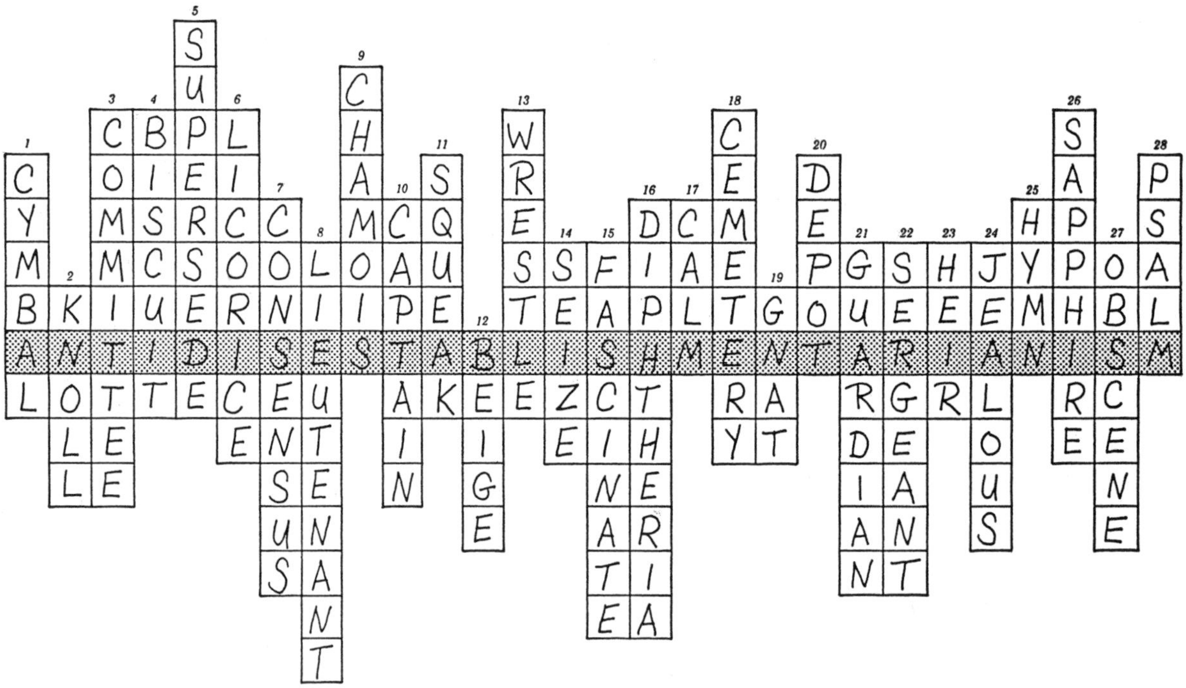

(crossword answer grid; the shaded row across the center reads:)

ANTIDISESTABLISHMENTARIANISM

4–31 Spelling Hexagon

Examples of four-letter words: noun, test, tons, tune, rage, torn, rain, prom, page

Examples of five-letter words: stone, mount, pages, snout, prone, panes, storm, armor, motel, notes, pants, apron, stout, inlet, tents, paint

Examples of longer words: garage, pronoun, stoning, raining, morning, elegant, promote

4–32 Spelling Maze

exaggerate	liquefy	antique	digestible	surgeon	
occasion	dietition	fude	nickle	millionaire	**Exit**
secretary	calander	complection	chaufer	omision	
rebelled	paralel	beggar	solemn	separate	
burglar	schedual	●	judgement	wrestle	
squeak	sincerly	truely	aironautiks	reign	
panicked	inoculate	eligible	sphere	recommend	

Bonus

The line connecting these words forms the letter *G*, which suggests that you might say "Gee!" when you reach the exit.

4–33 Pronunciation

1. probably
2. picture
3. sandwich
4. representative
5. government
6. library
7. Arctic
8. recognize
9. February
10. surprise
11. candidate
12. chimney
13. drowned
14. pronunciation
15. mischievous
16. sherbet
17. athletics
18. perspiration
19. introduce
20. lightning
21. across
22. burglar
23. etcetera

The completed sentence is as follows: Raquel, pack my box with five dozen jugs. This sentence is a *pangram.*

Bonus

A pangram is a sentence that contains every letter of the alphabet.

4–34 Same Spelling but Different Pronunciation

1. been, seen
2. boot, foot
3. lose, dose
4. sew, few
5. good, food
6. worse, horse
7. post, lost
8. never, fever
9. height, weight
10. rush, push
11. done, phone
12. word, cord

4–35 Accent Shift

1. rebel
2. contest
3. increase
4. conduct
5. insult
6. convict
7. permit
8. address
9. refuse

The circled letters spell BORN LITER.

4–36 Enunciation

No answers are needed for this contest.

Section 5 NAMES OF PEOPLE, PLACES, AND THINGS

5–1 Places in the U.S. Named After People

1. Juneau
2. Lincoln
3. Madison
4. Washington
5. Pennsylvania
6. Hudson
7. Columbus
8. Houston
9. Jackson
10. Carson City
11. Pike's Peak
12. Louisiana

5-2 Places in the World Named After People

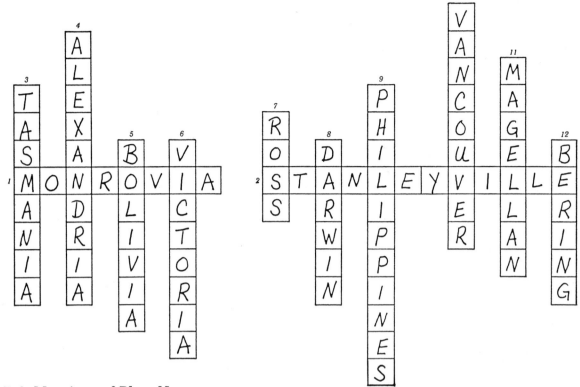

5-3 Meanings of Place Names

1. Alcatraz	6. Ecuador
2. Easter	7. Florida
3. Chicago	8. Bosporus
4. Galapagos	9. Pacific
5. Vermont	10. Bern

The letters in the vertical column spell ASIA (which means "east") and EUROPE (which means "west").

5-4 Places with Colorful Names

First paragraph: white, black, gray

Second paragraph: red, yellow

Third paragraph: green, blue

Fourth paragraph: orange, gold, brown, purple

The circled letters spell the word RAINBOW, which fits into the last sentence.

5–5 Items Named After Places

1. G	7. O
2. N	8. A
3. C	9. J
4. K	10. B
5. E	11. L
6. I	

A	D	C
L	F	N
C	M	I
J	H	K
E	G	B

The shaded area forms the letter U, the jolliest letter because it is always in the middle of FUN!

Bonus

The extra words are as follows: *hamburger* from Hamburg in Germany, *angora* from Ankara in Turkey, *champagne* from a French province, and *Edam,* a cheese from the Netherlands.

5–6 Origins of Surnames

1. towns	9. prefixes
2. York	10. Irish
3. river	11. Iceland
4. Hall	12. family
5. Noble	13. members
6. physical	14. same
7. colors	15. maiden
8. Italian	16. hyphenate

5–7 Surnames Based on Occupations

Part 1

1. Stewart	7. Cartwright
2. Sherman	8. Butler
3. Collier	9. Clark
4. Potter	10. Foster
5. Hatcher	11. Turner
6. Mason	

Part 2

The two names that appear in the vertical column are SMITH (a metal worker) and MILLER (grinder of grain).

5–8 Names Related to Animals

1. lion	7. bee
2. wolf	8. serpent
3. bear	9. gazelle
4. eagle	10. dove
5. boar	11. blackbird
6. dog	12. sheep

The circled letters, when rearranged, spell ANDREW (manly, brave) and ELVERA (courage). ANDREW is from Greek and ELVERA is from Latin.

5–9 Names of Writers

1. Wylie
2. Frost
3. Bunyan
4. Carroll
5. Holmes
6. Harte
7. Bellow
8. Burns
9. Hawthorne
10. Hood
11. Wilde
12. Donne
13. Potter
14. Pound
15. Swift

The circled letters spell these words: A PROFESSIONAL WRITER IS AN AMATEUR WHO DIDN'T QUIT.

5–10 Items Names After People

1. Baby Ruth
2. cardigan
3. leotard
4. poinsettia
5. diesel
6. pasteurization
7. Stroganoff
8. watt
9. Ferris (wheel)
10. Levi's
11. derrick
12. melba
13. Phillips

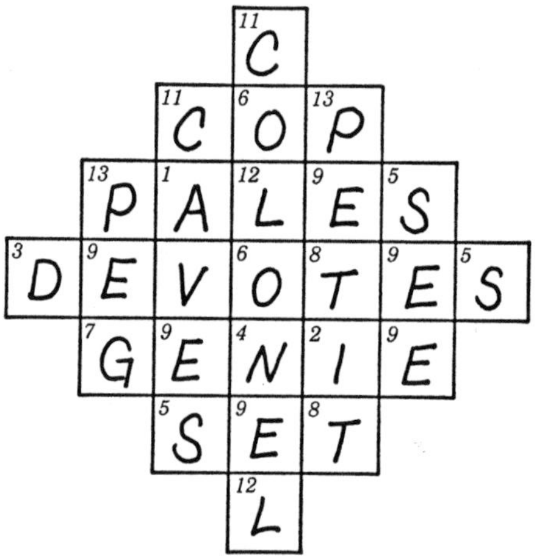

Crossword grid (boxed letters):

```
              C
        C  O  P
     P  A  L  E  S
  D  E  V  O  T  E  S
     G  E  N  I  E
        S  E  T
              L
```

5–11 Words from Mythology

1. uranium
2. Thursday
3. vulcanization
4. martial
5. Herculean
6. titanic
7. amazon
8. cereal
9. odyssey
10. helium
11. January
12. Venus
13. atlas
14. Oedipus
15. siren

The two names spelled out by the boxed and circled letters are PANDORA and ACHILLES. We speak of a "Pandora's box" in reference to numerous troubles. An Achilles' heel is a vulnerable point.

5–12 Origins of Brand Names

1. Dr. Pepper
2. O Henry
3. Ivory
4. Comet
5. Coast
6. Camel
7. Xerox
8. Avon

9. Sanka (from the French, *sans caffeine*)
10. Dixie
11. Greyhound
12. Carnation
13. Arm and Hammer
14. Birdseye
15. Talon
16. Tide

The circled letters spell the name PROCTER AND GAMBLE.

5-13 Names of Cars

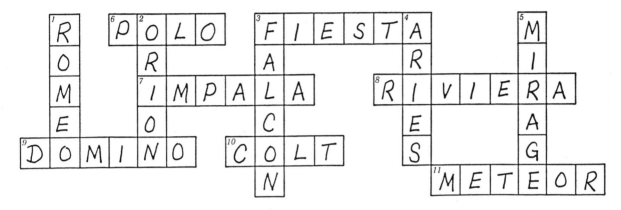

5-14 Names of Birds

1. bunting
2. quail
3. oriole
4. cardinal
5. grouse
6. crow
7. swift
8. crane
9. flicker
10. pigeon
11. swallow
12. turkey
13. hawk
14. eagle
15. lark

The circled letters spell BIRDS OF A FEATHER. The complete expression is: BIRDS OF A FEATHER FLOCK TOGETHER.

5-15 Names of Flowers

1. bachelor's button
2. carnation
3. baby's breath
4. mum (chrysanthemum)
5. poppy
6. forget-me-not
7. phlox
8. iris
9. foxglove
10. sweet pea
11. goldenrod
12. larkspur
13. rose
14. snapdragon
15. bluebell
16. bleeding heart
17. buttercup

The circled letters spell LAVENDER, PINK, and VIOLET.

5-16 Occupational Names

1. Aiken
2. August
3. Booth
4. Brewster
5. Drew
6. Harry

7. Owen	13. Dinah
8. Percy	14. Gail
9. Rod	15. Ginny
10. Betty	16. Milly
11. Bridget	17. Pearl
12. Carol	18. Violet

5–17 *Names of Imaginary People*

1. Jack Pot	14. Bob White (or Bob O'Link)
2. Mike Robe (or Mike Roscope)	15. Bill Board
3. Polly Ester	16. Doug Out
4. Ben Gay	17. Minny Apolis
5. Jerry Atrics	18. Rose Bush
6. Sandy Shore (or Sandy Beach)	19. Dee Tective
7. Nick O'Teen	20. Ginger Ale
8. Tim Burr	21. Clara Net
9. Tom Atoe	22. Rosie Scenario
10. Chris Anthemum	23. Chuck Roast
11. Jan Itor	24. Barbie Cue
12. Al Bum	25. May Flower
13. Sarah Nade	

Section 6 LANGUAGE AS AN ART FORM

6–1 *Techniques in Prose Writing*

1. visualize	7. caricature
2. vivid	8. verbs
3. unsaid	9. active
4. assume	10. roundabout
5. dialogue	11. lightning
6. stereotype	12. lightning

The completed statement is as follows: She couldn't decide whether to marry for butter or verse.

6–2 *Terms Used by Writers*

1. editorial	8. lyric
2. blank	9. epic
3. epilogue	10. allegory
4. tragedy	11. melodrama
5. flashback	12. scene
6. satire	13. soliloquy
7. gothic	14. stanza

The completed quotation is as follows: "A real book is not one that's read but one that reads us."

6–3 *Figures of Speech*

1. personification	3. hyperbole
2. irony	4. apostrophe

5. euphemism
6. simile
7. metaphor

8. metonymy
9. antithesis

6–4 Similes and Metaphors

1. church mouse
2. blind
3. toast
4. pretty
5. right

6. elephant
7. wink
8. molasses
9. easy
10. cool

The circled letters, when transferred, spell AUTHOR-ITIS.

6–5 Euphemisms

1. T (5)
2. F (9)
3. O (11)
4. H (3)
5. S (14)

6. T (2)
7. Y (6)
8. U (7)
9. E (4)
10. R (12)

11. N (10)
12. W (1)
13. A (15)
14. H (8)
15. A (13)

The transferred circled letters form this quotation from the Bible: "A soft answer turneth away wrath."

Bonus

Euphemisms for the terms suggested include:

tyrant: leader, ruler, boss, chief, commander
loud-mouthed: vocal, talkative, verbose
stupid: lacking in judgment, unwise, slow
cowardly: lacking in courage, timid, faint-hearted
skinny: thin, slender, emaciated, lean

6–6 Antithesis

1. what
2. city
3. talking
4. earth
5. say
6. arose
7. money
8. sees

9. one
10. plan
11. fear
12. debate
13. live
14. years
15. dead

The circled letters complete the statement this way: EACH ONE PLAYED WITH SOMEONE ELSE.

6–7 Biblical Allusions

1. Cain
2. David
3. Jezebel
4. Job
5. Joseph

6. Joshua
7. Judas
8. Lazarus
9. Methuselah
10. Moses

11. Noah
12. Salome
13. Samson
14. Solomon
15. Thomas

6–8 *Allusions to Fables, Myths, and Literature*

1. H (5)
2. O (9)
3. R (12)
4. A (3)
5. T (7)
6. I (10)
7. O (8)
8. A (2)
9. L (1)
10. G (6)
11. E (11)
12. R (4)

The letters spell the name of HORATIO ALGER, a writer whose stories all involved persons who rose to success in spite of hardships. Consequently, similar situations are often referred to as "Horatio Alger stories."

6–9 *Symbolism*

1. goal
2. opportunity
3. sadness
4. venture
5. grievances
6. possessions
7. child
8. truth
9. trouble

The numbers formed by the lines are 2 and 1, suggesting the proverb "Two heads are better than one." It might also suggest the following proverb: "One bird in the hand is worth two in the bush."

6–10 *Parallel Proverbs*

1. M (9)
2. O (6)
3. N (3)
4. O (10)
5. G (11)
6. E (2)
7. N (7)
8. E (4)
9. S (5)
10. I (1)
11. S (8)

The circled letters spell MONOGENESIS.

6–11 *Malapropisms*

Across
1. varicose (very close)
2. deterrent (detergent)
3. clambered (clamored)
4. maneuver (remover)
5. unanimous (anonymous)

Down
2. decimal (dismal)
6. phase (phrase)
7. quench (clench)
8. parcel (partial)
9. commandments (amendments)
10. elegy (allergy)
11. syllable (cylinder)

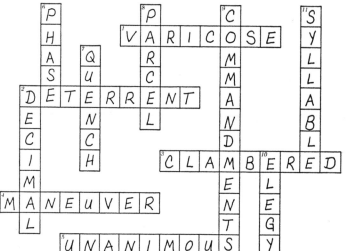

6–12 Oxymorons

1. heavyweight
2. definition
3. sweet
4. familiar
5. appropriate
6. misunderstood
7. glasses
8. burn
9. unfinished
10. war
11. lethal
12. host
13. odds
14. frozen
15. awful
16. dressed
17. ice
18. news
19. phony
20. grief
21. shrimp
22. maybe
23. chocolate
24. opinion
25. sorrow

The circled letters spell these words: HIS FRIEND WAS ON A RESPIRATOR. Therefore, he could not survive a ten-minute electrical outage.

6–13 Connotation

Answers will vary.

6–14 Sound Effects

1. alliteration
2. assonance
3. onomatopoeia
4. consonance

The circled letters spell E. A. POE.

6–15 Tautonymic Expressions

1. boo-boo
2. bonbon
3. tom-tom
4. dodo
5. haha
6. choo-choo
7. twenty-twenty
8. yoyo
9. tsetse
10. hula-hula
11. tutu
12. dumdum
13. cancan
14. Pago Pago
15. so-so
16. pooh-pooh

6–16 Inner Rhyme

1. kiwi
2. nitwit
3. hobnob
4. super-duper
5. hurdy-gurdy
6. razzle-dazzle
7. hi-fi
8. hanky-panky
9. humdrum
10. tepee

Bonus

Other words starting with the letter *H* that contain inner rhyme include: *heyday, hoodoo, hubbub, hoipolloi, hocus-pocus, handy-dandy, hoity-toity, hokeypokey, hurly-burly, helter-skelter, harum-scarum, hugger-mugger, heebie-jeebies,* etc.

6–17 Vowel Change

Part 1
1. singsong
2. wigwag
3. pitter-patter
4. flimflam
5. chitchat
6. wishy-washy
7. mishmash
8. knickknack
9. zigzag
10. fiddle-faddle

Part 2
1. pack, peck, pick, pock, puck
2 last, lest, list, lost, lust
3. ball, bell, bill, boll, bull
4. band, bend, bind, bond, bund
5. pat, pet, pit, pot, put
6. bag, beg, big, bog, bug

6–18 Echoic Words (Onomatopoeia)

1. splash
2. tinkle
3. buzz
4. crack
5. hiss
6. bowwow
7. coo
8. cuckoo
9. sizzle
10. crash
11. clang
12. wheeze
13. squeak
14. whisper
15. rustle
16. snap
17. squish

The three words formed by the circled letters are HICCUP, TWITTER, and CLICK.

Note: In connection with onomatopoeia, the students might enjoy reading aloud Robert Southey's "The Cataract of Lodore" and then trying to write a sound-filled poem, with each person adding one line.

6–19 Rhyme

A. 5 E. 7
B. 2 F. 6
C. 1 G. 3
D. 4

A 5	B 2
C 1	D 4	E 7
F 6	G 3

The total in all directions is 12.

Item 8 is not a rhyme since *night* and *knight* sound exactly the same, although spelled differently. Rhyme is determined strictly by the sound.

6–20 Rhyme Schemes and Stanzas

A. 3   F. 6
B. 7   G. 9
C. 5   H. 1
D. 8   I. 2
E. 4

A + G + D = 20
B + G + E = 20
F + G + C = 20

6–21 Rhythm

1. iambic	8. trimeter
2. trochaic	9. tetrameter
3. anapestic	10. pentameter
4. dactylic	11. hexameter
5. spondaic	12. heptameter
6. monometer	13. octameter
7. dimeter	

The circled letters form these words: "Poetry lies its way to the truth."
Bonus
Shakespeare's lines are written in iambic pentameter.

6–22 Concrete Poems (Calligrams)

There are no answers, since the activity involves the students' creativeness.

Section 7 MISCELLANEOUS WORD GAMES

7–1 October Quiz

1. E	6. F
2. G	7. C
3. I	8. A
4. J	9. B
5. H	10. D

Thought question: It requires 48 zeros to write the number octillion.

Bonus

1. hex pot
2. rendez-boo
3. wash 'n' werewolf
4. blood bank
5. bantam phantom

7–2 Thanksgiving

1. champagne	10. turkey with dressing
2. pea soup	11. ham
3. shrimp cocktail	12. rolls
4. fruit salad on lettuce	13. java (slang for coffee)
5. tomatoes	14. brownies
6. pickles	15. baked Alaska
7. corn	16. apple pie
8. hot potato	17. nuts
9. sweet potato	18. mints

7–3 Yuletide

1. holly
2. wreaths
3. boughs
4. cedar
5. –
6. hymns
7. priest
8. altar
9. aisle
10. pageant
11. –
12. –
13. myrrh
14. pews
15. –
16. manger
17. sumptuous
18. –
19. tinsel
20. baubles
21. mistletoe
22. hearth
23. creche
24. carol
25. candelabra

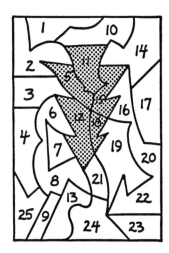

An upside-down Christmas tree appears.

7–4 January Game

1. janitor
2. febrile
3. marsupial
4. apricot
5. mayonnaise
6. juniper
7. julep
8. auger
9. sepulcher
10. octet
11. novice
12. decapitate

The connecting lines form the numbers 3, 6, and 5 (the number of days in a year).

7–5 Be My Valentine

1. Have a heart
2. Cross my heart
3. Broke my heart
4. Did my heart good
5. From the bottom of my heart
6. Have my heart set against it
7. By heart
8. After my own heart
9. Had a change of heart
10. Take to heart
11. To my heart's content
12. Wearing your heart on your sleeve
13. Having a heart-to-heart talk
14. Set your heart on it
15. Give heart to
16. Hard-hearted
17. Downhearted
18. Heartthrob

The circled letters complete the statement this way: He decided to get married, thus putting his heart before the course.

7–6 Presidents' Day

Part 1

1. Taylor
2. Garfield
3. Grant
4. Fillmore
5. Hayes
6. Hoover
7. Truman
8. Ford
9. Carter
10. Pierce
11. Bush
12. Polk
13. Madison

The letters on the vertical line spell ADAMS and HARRISON. Both were related to other presidents by the same name. (John Adams was the father of John Quincy Adams, and William Henry Harrison was the grandfather of Benjamin Harrison.)

Part 2

Roman numeral MDCCLXXVI (1776) is the year of the signing of the Declaration of Independence.

7–7 March Game

Part 1

1. malpractice
2. accomplice
3. sacrifice
4. licorice
5. justice
6. advice
7. spice
8. rice

Part 2

1. Leon
2. lean
3. loan
4. loin
5. lain
6. laid
7. land
8. lane
9. lame

7–8 Easter Eggs

Part 1

1. expensive
2. exist
3. exhausted
4. excellent
5. exterior
6. exorbitant
7. execute
8. examine
9. extinct
10. exclaim
11. example
12. exodus

The marked letters spell ETHER BUNNIES.

Part 2

1. stuffed
2. deviled
3. sunny-side up
4. hard-boiled
5. poached
6. eggs Benedict
7. fried
8. runny
9. three-minute
10. over easy

7–9 Arbor Day

1. ash
2. maple
3. pine
4. spruce
5. beech
6. rubber
7. plum
8. locust
9. cork
10. walnut
11. peanut
12. hazelnut
13. Brazil nut
14. cashew
15. chestnut
16. butternut

Bonus

The peanut is the nut that does not grow on a tree.

7–10 Mother's Day and Father's Day

1. moment
2. impair
3. chrysanthemum
4. poplar
5. daddy longlegs
6. aftermath
7. compass
8. population
9. asparagus
10. mumble
11. drama
12. pamphlet
13. amateur
14. poppycock
15. momentous
16. depart
17. diplomat
18. minimum
19. reprimand
20. impatient
21. crawdad
22. majority
23. papyrus

7–11 Shopping for Rhymes

1. hare snare
2. crime chime
3. fake snake
4. book nook
5. tall stall
6. flag bag
7. trash cache
8. crop cop
9. spare hair
10. Cuba tuba
11. gory story
12. caffeine machine
13. tweeter treater
14. annual manual
15. spreadable edible
16. Havana banana

7–12 Hink Pink People

1. dead Red
2. top cop
3. chief thief
4. French wench
5. late mate
6. sleek Greek
7. slain Dane
8. Ghent gent
9. yellow fellow
10. reader feeder
11. partial marshal
12. wheeler dealer
13. gizzard wizard
14. viper piper
15. winker tinker
16. phony crony
17. Brazilian civilian
18. subterranean Pennsylvanian
19. temperamental Oriental
20. sinister minister

7-13 Tom Twisties

1. chirped	11. crowed
2. pointed	12. noted
3. muttered	13. gushed
4. demanded	14. snapped
5. chuckled	15. railed
6. insisted	16. fumed
7. whined	17. speculated
8. wailed	18. consoled
9. pleaded	19. volunteered
10. pined	20. objected

7-14 Animals in Sayings

1. ape	14. lion
2. beaver	15. loon
3. bull	16. mule
4. canary	17. owl
5. cat	18. pig
6. chicken	19. possum
7. dog	20. rat
8. elephant	21. snail
9. fish	22. squirrel
10. fox	23. tiger
11. frog	24. turkey
12. goose	25. wolf
13. hog	

7-15 Terms Related to Animals

Part 1

1. S	6. T(2)
2. Q	7. D
3. U	8. O
4. I	9. T(1)
5. R	10. Z

The letters spell the names SQUIRT and DOTZ.

Part 2

1. P	5. H	9. E(1)
2. A	6. E(2)	10. N
3. T	7. S	11. D
4. C	8. M	12. Y

The letters spell the names PATCHES and MENDY.

7–16 More Animal Terms

Part 1

1. gander	6. hen
2. bull	7. drake
3. lioness	8. mare
4. ram	9. donkey
5. vixen	10. doe

Part 2

1. L	4. I
2. U	5. N
3. P	6. E

H⁶	E⁷	A¹	R⁴	T
E⁷	M⁸	B²	E⁷	R⁴
A¹	B²	A¹	S³	E⁷
R⁴	E⁷	S³	I⁵	N⁹
T	R⁴	E⁷	N⁹	D¹⁰

These letters spell LUPINE, an adjective referring to wolves.

7–17 Sounds Animals Make

Part 1

1. W	5. O
2. A(1)	6. L
3. G	7. I
4. N	8. A(2)

The letters spell the name WAGNOLIA.

Part 2

1. P	6. Y
2. E	7. G
3. A(2)	8. A(1)
4. R	9. I
5. L	10. T

The letters spell the name PEARLY GAIT.

7–18 Dogs

1. doggone	10. underdog
2. top dog	11. dog collar
3. dog tag	12. raining cats and dogs
4. dogwood	13. a dog's life
5. going to the dogs	14. dog biscuit
6. dog tired	15. in the doghouse
7. dogfight	16. the dog star
8. dog paddle	17. doggerel
9. dogface	

The circled letters complete the man's statement this way: "I'm not allowed on the furniture."

7–19 Colorful Expressions

1. red	4. pink
2. brown	5. purple
3. blue	6. Orange

7. yellow   11. green
8. Gray   12. silver
9. black   13. gold
10. white

The remaining letters in the first set spell ONE and those in the second set spell VERMILLION. He said his girlfriend was "one in vermillion" because red-orange was her favorite color.

Bonus

AZURE is the color to use to form a title that sounds like one of Shakespeare's plays—Azure Like It (*As You Like It*).

7-20 *Expressions Using* Up

1. upbringing
2. updraft
3. upkeep
4. uppity
5. upheaval
6. upgrade
7. upright
8. uproot
9. upset
10. uptight
11. up-to-date
12. face up to it
13. hole up
14. hold up
15. hurry up
16. mixed up
17. makeup
18. bear up under it
19. live it up
20. wind it up
21. up the ante
22. up-and-coming

```
B   E   A   F   H
J   T       C   L
S   R       U   O
M   P       K   Q
W   D       V   Y
X   G   Z   N   I
```

7-21 *Expressions Involving a Series*

1. borrow
2. came
3. barrel
4. always
5. by
6. clothing
7. Tom
8. look
9. arithmetic
10. animal
11. win
12. drink
13. willing
14. women

The circled letters spell BELL, BOOK, and CANDLE—terms that refer to the ceremony of excommunication.

Bonus

Winston Churchill's statement: "I have nothing to offer but blood, toil, tears, and sweat."

7-22 *Expressions Involving Food*

1. cherries
2. crab
3. butter
4. lemon
5. apple
6. pickle (or stew)
7. bananas
8. jam
9. mustard
10. cucumber
11. cake
12. pie
13. cookie
14. noodle (or bean)
15. ginger
16. fat
17. punch
18. egg

19. beans
20. toast
21. clams
22. lettuce (or bread or cabbage)

7-23 Misleading Expressions

1. bowl
2. shop
3. hide
4. stretch
5. fly
6. split
7. date
8. dressing
9. nip
10. ring
11. trot
12. work
13. napping
14. dial
15. shed
16. roll
17. turnover
18. break
19. walk

7-24 Terms Containing Body Parts

1. hair
2. neck
3. arm
4. bust
5. foot
6. lip
7. chest
8. skin
9. rib
10. ear
11. head
12. hand
13. chin
14. hip
15. shin
16. heel
17. leg
18. face
19. eye
20. face
21. back
22. sole
23. toe
24. heart
25. ankle
26. tongue
27. back
28. knuckle
29. hand

7-25 Expressions Involving Body Parts

1. face
2. eye
3. nose
4. neck
5. ear
6. tongue
7. hair
8. arm
9. legs
10. heart
11. liver
12. foot
13. skin
14. hand
15. toe
16. finger
17. tooth
18. shoulder
19. rib
20. chest
21. knee

7-26 Double Meanings

Answers will vary.

7–27 Misinterpretations

1. He is high-strung.
2. The prisoner has broken out.
3. Grandma doesn't use glasses.
4. Beat it.
5. I have better quarters now.
6. I got a car for my wife.
7. He draws women.
8. The door was cracked.
9. I'll give you a ring.
10. She was held up.
11. Cut it out.
12. They are shooting a pilot.
13. He beats his wife up.
14. I have pressing problems.

7–28 Money Terms

1. $100 + $10 + $5 + 25¢ = $115.25
2. $1000 + $1 + 50¢ + 1¢ = $1001.51
3. $20 + 10¢ + 5¢ + 1¢ = $20.16

The boys have only $1136.92 and therefore cannot make the investment.

7–29 Postal Abbreviations

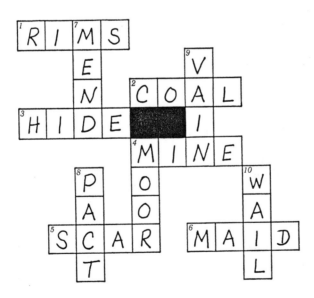

Bonus #1

The three state abbreviations the boy might use are "OH, HI, PA."

Bonus #2

Answers will vary.

7–30 Gobbledygook

1. F
2. N
3. L
4. B
5. H
6. W
7. A
8. O
9. R
10. S
11. D
12. T
13. E

Winston Churchill's statement: "The short words are best, and the old words are best of all."

7–31 Letterspeak

1. UL (yule)
2. NV (envy)
3. IC (icy)
4. MT (empty)
5. NX (annex)
6. ME (Emmy)
7. TP (tepee)
8. SA (essay)
9. YN (wine)
10. IV (ivy)
11. TT (tease)
12. OO (owes)
13. YY (wise)
14. QQ (cues)
15. EE (ease)
16. UU (use)
17. NDN (Indian)
18. NML (animal)
19. BUT (beauty)
20. NME (enemy)
21. PNE (peony)
22. NRG (energy)
23. XTC (ecstasy)
24. XMN (examine)
25. XLNC (excellency)

The circled letters are IMAUMBN (I am a human being).

7–32 Daffy Definitions

1. D
2. C
3. H
4. M
5. P
6. U
7. Y
8. A
9. V
10. L
11. N
12. O
13. E
14. S
15. B

The transferred letters form this sentence: Unemployed teachers have no class.

7–33 Baseball and Football Terms

1. base
2. Homer
3. safe
4. catcher
5. fly
6. liner
7. batter
8. strike
9. down
10. quarter
11. tackle
12. block
13. interference
14. pass
15. receiver

The shape formed by the unshaded portion is a diamond.

7-34 *Words Containing Roman Numerals*

1. arrive
2. vibrate
3. prefix
4. exist
5. axle
6. liver
7. excess
8. recite
9. civet
10. distant
11. divorce
12. Dixie
13. permit
14. mixture
15. summer

7-35 *Numerical Prefixes*

A. 4
B. 6
C. 8
D. 2
E. 7
F. 3
G. 1
H. 10
I. 5
J. 1
K. 2
L. 6
M. 9
N. 3
O. 5
P. 7

When the mathematical process is completed, the answer is zero.

7-36 *The Wicked Witch*

Boys
1. Oscar
2. Keith
3. Edwin
4. Samuel
5. Felix
6. Abner
7. Lester
8. Brian

Girls
1. Linda
2. Carol
3. Wilma
4. Carmen
5. Emily
6. Mary
7. Thelma
8. Olive

Bonus
The circled letters spell CHRYSANTHEMUM.

7-37 *Break-aparts*

1. pantry
2. asphalt
3. sealed
4. malady
5. budget
6. earnest
7. legend
8. massacre
9. implied
10. sinus
11. papal
12. notice
13. beginning
14. finale
15. patriot
16. weevil
17. restore

The circled letters form this sentence: They ended up in a tie.

7–38 Phobias

1. F	9. S	
2. L	10. B	
3. P	11. O	
4. A	12. E	
5. H	13. T	
6. C	14. I	
7. J	15. K	
8. N	16. G	

Fear of the number 13 is known as TRISKAIDEKAPHOBIA.

7–39 Repeated Words

1. M	5. P	9. L
2. O	6. E	10. I
3. S	7. C	11. A
4. T	8. U	12. R

The letters complete the sentence this way: The English language is most peculiar.

7–40 Most Beautiful Words

1. chimes	6. luminous
2. dawn	7. mist
3. golden	8. melody
4. hush	9. murmuring
5. lullaby	10. tranquil

The circled and boxed letters spell CHECK ENCLOSED.

7–41 The End

1. offend	9. portend
2. dividend	10. minuend
3. transcend	11. amend
4. friend	12. extend
5. spend	13. comprehend
6. ascend	14. apprehend
7. recommend	15. suspend
8. pretend	16. stipend

The circled letters spell the Latin phrase *Finis coronat opus.*